Early Pee

JOHN M. GREGG
Part One

Heritage Books, Inc.

Published 1993 By

HERITAGE BOOKS, INC.
1540-E Pointer Ridge Place, Bowie, MD 20716
(301) 390-7709

ISBN 1-55613-912-8

A Complete Catalog Listing Hundreds of Titles
on History, Genealogy, and Americana Available
Free upon Request

This work is dedicated
to the descendants of these Early Pee Dee Settlers.
Most particularly to Mary, Maxcy, Ginny Lynne,
Richard, Christopher, Ryan, Stuart,
and
Garrett.

A CAROLINA SPRING

When you see the dogwood blooming
Underneath a cloud flecked sky;
When you see the yellow jasmine
In the tree tops swinging high;

When you see the peach and apple blossoms
Drifting down like pale pink snow;
When you see the brightest sunshine
That this world will ever know;

When your step begins to quicken
and your heart begins to sing,
And you think – "This must be Heaven" –
You've seen a Carolina Spring.

Genevieve Purvis Gregg

CONTENTS

Maps

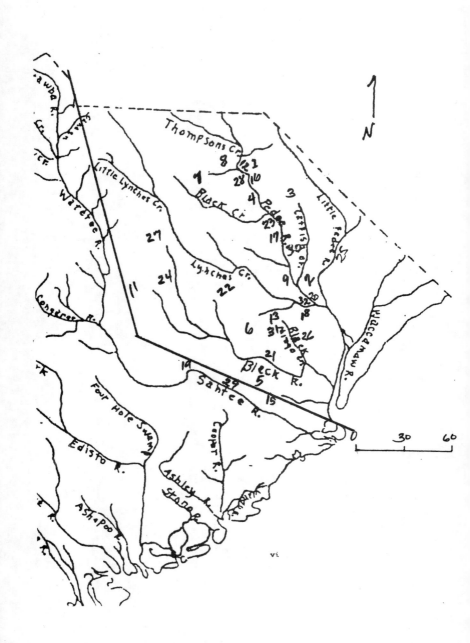

Locations in the Pee Dee

During the Colonial Period

1. Beauty Spot
2. Britton's Neck
3. Buck Swamp
4. Cashaway
5. Cedar Cr. (Williamsburg)
6. Cedar Swamp
7. Cedar Cr. (St. David's)
8. Cheraw
9. Dewitt's Bluff
10. Hayes Swamp
11. High Hills
12. Hunt's Bluff
13. Indiantown
14. Irishtown
15. Lenud's Ferry
16. Long Bluff

17. Mars Bluff
18. Muddy Creek
19. Nelson's Ferry
20. Port's Ferry
21. Potato Ferry
22. Pudden Swamp
23. Red Bluff
24. Salem
25. Sandy Bluff
26. Shepard's Ferry
27. Shiloh
28. Society Hill
29. Whittee Creek
30. Wiggin's Landing
31. Willtown
32. Witherspoon's Ferry

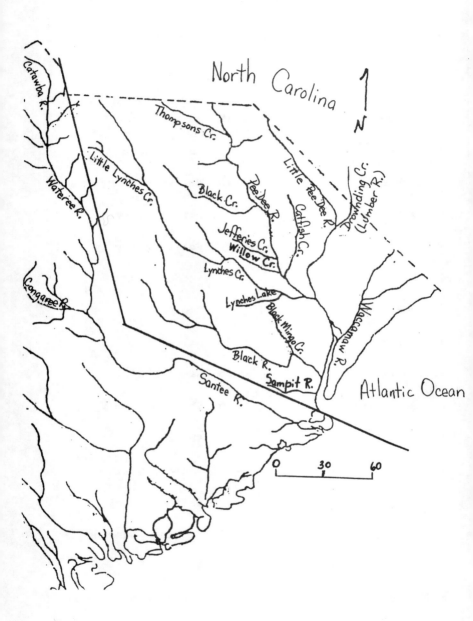

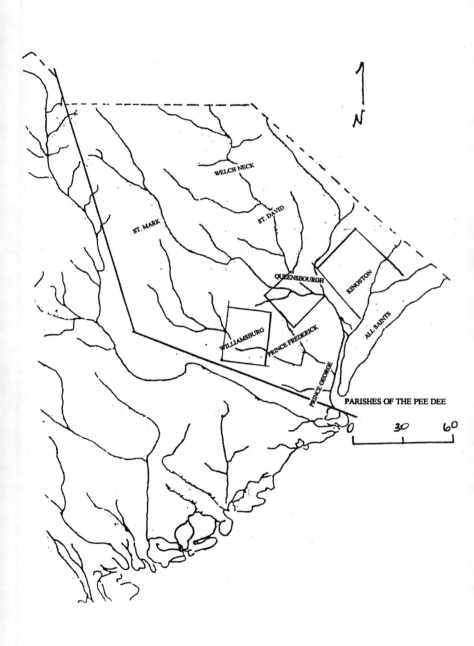

N

WELCH NECK

ST. MARK

ST. DAVID

QUEENSBOURGH

KINGSTON

WILLIAMSBURG

PRINCE FREDERICK

ALL SAINTS

PRINCE GEORGE

PARISHES OF THE PEE DEE

0   30   60

PREFACE

It has been said that I am an ancestor worshipper. I am not, of course, at least, not in the sense of some cultures. I do profess to having a considerable admiration and respect for the stalwart men and women who laid the foundation of this great country, and I am proud to be descended from some of the early settlers of the Pee Dee.

I have been able to identify nearly six thousand individuals who lived in the Pee Dee area of South Carolina before 1790. I chose the year 1790 as a cutoff due to the obvious need for limitation of number and the fact that the first complete census was made shortly afterwards.

The book is divided into two parts. The first part contains the individuals about whom I have been able to find more than just basic information. The second part is a listing of other individuals with their general location who are known to have lived in the Pee Dee.

Spouses are listed separately if their previous name is known. Redundant information may not be listed. Children are listed separately only if additional information is available about them. Otherwise, they are listed only with their families.

A name shown thus, (Smith), indicates another name for that person. Generally, this would be a female married the second time or perhaps a maiden name when that fact is not certain. It is also used to show married names of children.

Mostly, I have spelled names as they were found. In a few instances, I have used the modern or prevalent spelling in order to compare information more easily. It is always advisable to look for various spellings. One family name is spelled six different ways. Even today this particular family spells it two ways among close relatives.

Names can become confusing. The custom appears to have been for brothers to name their offspring for the other. To make matters more confusing, one son would be named for the brother and the other for the father. Junior was often used in both instances. For these and other reasons, I have refrained from guessing at relationships, leaving it to the reader to make his own deductions.

Name duplication is ever a problem. After the revolution, more than twenty applications were received from individuals named John Brown. This is the exception, but in most families there will be several with the same or similar name. I can attest that this is a problem that continues into the present. I have made every effort to eliminate duplication of individuals.

Locations are shown as precisely as space and knowledge permit. However, remember the changing political divisions. A person shown in Prince Frederick Parish may have lived in one of the other parishes after that parish was formed. Occupations are given when known, but it must be remembered that most of these, even with an occupation stated, were planters. There are duplicate place names as well as individuals. For example, there are at least two Cedar Creeks and Cedar Swamps.

Revolutionary War service is stated if found. I show nearly eight hundred men who where willing to give their life and livelihood to freedom and a few dozen Tories. Most of these patriots served in Francis Marion's Brigade. Marion kept no records, so this information comes from a variety of sources. One possible source for this information is a list compiled by W. W. Boddie that contains over two thousand names. I have used this list for verification purposes only. In the Pee Dee, Marion never commanded more than five or six hundred at any given time. Only in the last stages of the war when he assumed over-all command in the state did the numbers approach this total. I, therefore, am reluctant to say that a person lived in the Pee Dee on the strength of this list alone.

I must acknowledge and express appreciation to my wife Mary for the support and for keeping me close to the rules of grammar and spelling. She made a valiant effort, but I must assume responsibility for those remaining. I thank my daughter-in-law Jean for assistance on the maps. Finally, I owe a debt of gratitude to the following for sharing the information contained in

their files: Peggy Cansler, William H. Chandler, Hasel Coyne, Patsy Stewart
Delaroderie, William O. Hatchell, Thomas J. Jenkins, James O. King, Thomas
S. McCaskey, Margaret Ball Miller, Janie Parker Price, Fannie Jordan
Purvis, Jary Palmer Williams, Horace F. Rudisill and his staff at the
Darlington County Historical Commission, and John Andrews Jr., Wally
Turbeville and other members of The Old Darlington District Genealogical
Society.

I envision this as an on going, never finished project. I am hopeful that
the reader can provide additional information and corrections. The data base
is maintained in a computer file. Purchasers of the book can obtain updated or
the entire file for a nominal fee. A telephone call will save time in determining
the proper media for your needs.

4 July 1993
John Maxcy Gregg
1008 Alton Circle
Florence, South Carolina
(803) 662 9500

INTRODUCTION

The Pee Dee Basin covers the eastern part of South Carolina and is drained by that long, muddy river which originates in the mountains of North Carolina and traverses a large portion of both states. The river is currently called The Great Pee Dee in South Carolina and the Yadkin in North Carolina. It provided a natural highway into the interior of the state, enabling settlers to penetrate quickly and deeply. Two other large streams, the Black and the Waccamaw, cross the region, joining the Pee Dee a short distance from the sea. The three converge at Winyah Bay and are the most navigable rivers in the state. Several others contribute to this drainage system and provide navigation to smaller boats for short distances.

The Pee Dee area covers nearly one third of South Carolina. The natural boundaries are the Santee River on the south and the Wateree on the west. To the north and east, it is bounded by North Carolina and the Atlantic Ocean. This description covers more area than is today considered "The Pee Dee" but fits the area opened to settlement by the colonial government in 1700 at which time there was only one known European settler in the area. Before this time, only a few Indian traders had entered the locality.

The native Indians were not extensively ensconced. Only a few small tribes frequented the area regularly. Perhaps they were smarter than the European settlers who suffered greatly from the heat, malaria, and other insect borne disease. In any event, the Indians were not a big problem to the settlers of the Pee Dee.

Settlement was slow at first. George Hunter, Surveyor General, stated on a map compiled in 1730 that there were not more than five families north of the Santee. However, he numbers the militia company of Georgetown at 170. There appears to be fewer than twenty taxpayers in The Pee Dee in 1720, those mostly in or near George Town. Reverend John Fordyce's estimate of population in 1738 is 2600 total, including 400 Anglicans, 800 "dissenters of all sorts", "papists none", "heathens and infidels" about 1400.

Early Pee Dee Settlers
Introduction

The first settlements were mainly around Winyah Bay and gradually spread along the Black, Pee Dee, Sampit, and Waccamaw Rivers until the 1730's, at which time the settlers by-passed most of the region near the coast in favor of the higher ground farther inland.

French Huguenot settlements had earlier been established on the south side of Santee River at Jamestown and St. Stephens. Since only ten miles separate the Black and Santee Rivers, a good portion of the earliest Pee Dee settlers were these who began to spill over to the north bank.

The number of settlers greatly increased as a result of several factors. The colonial legislature, fearful of an uprising by the ever increasing population of slaves, passed the The Township Act which provided for land and supplies to Protestant settlers. Townships were laid out as a buffer to the Indians which were an occasional problem in the western part of the state. Several bounties were offered during the years following, including payment of passage and additional land grants. Free land and other social factors soon prompted a brisk migration.

The events that cause the first influx into the Pee Dee were the requirement in Ireland that everyone pay tithes to the Church of England, a large increase in land rents, the sacramental test for qualification of office holders, and general economic conditions in Ireland. These led to a large number of immigrants from the North of Ireland that slowed only with the restrictions imposed by England a short time before the out break of the rebellion. These are often referred to as Irish in colonial records, but being mainly of Scots descent, they are generally referred to as "Scotch Irish". In 1732, Williamsburg township was established on the upper reaches of Black River for these immigrants.

It is interesting to note that the Black and Santee are only ten to fifteen miles apart in the area designated for the settlement of these immigrants from Ireland. The Huguenots were already settled on the south side of the Santee. I am sure that this proximity contributed greatly to the early mixing of these ethnic groups. In just a few years, they were intermarrying and worshipping together.

Early Pee Dee Settlers
Introduction

About 1735, a large tract, (173,840 acres, later extended to run eight miles each side and parallel to the Pee Dee River, northward to the Rocky River) known as the "Welch Tract" was set aside for a party of Welch (Welsh) settlers who had settled first in Pennsylvania. Finding the religious atmosphere not to their liking, the leaders secured grants in this tract and the group moved to the Pee Dee.

Four townships were designated in the Pee Dee to encourage settlement. The Welch tract as stated above, Williamsburg on the Black River to accommodate the Scotch-Irish, Queensborough below the Welch tract, also to accommodate Scotch-Irish, and Kingston on the Waccamaw River (present town of Conway) was to accommodate English settlers. Queensborough languished and Kingston did not do much better, but the other two flourished.

On October 27, 1732, the ship HAPPY RETURN disembarked eighty-five passengers from Belfast, Ireland. These were the first of many to follow who paid their own passage to take up land in the township of Williamsburg.

The Pee Dee is the area in which that super-patriot Francis Marion operated. Marion kept the British at bay with a handful of Williamsburg men augmented by the descendants of the original Welsh. At no time did Marion have more than six hundred men under his command, usually fewer than one hundred. Although over two thousand have been identified as having served with him at different times, there were crops to plant and families to protect and the call was not always answered. These men served without pay or supplies. They were, indeed, heroes, but for every hero there was a heroine at home caring for the crops and sometimes having to deal with British or Loyalist raiders. During the Revolution, more battles were fought in South Carolina (158) than in any other colony. The majority of these were in the Pee Dee.

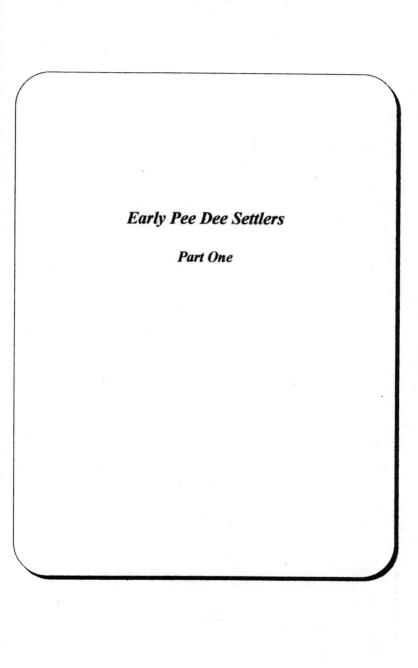

Early Pee Dee Settlers

Part One

ADAIR, ALEXANDER   ID: 4988
Date in Pee Dee: 1780
Location: WILLIAMSBURG
Source(s): BODDIE.
Revolutionary War service: PRIVATE IN MARION'S BRIGADE

ADAIR, BENJAMIN   ID: 4989
Date in Pee Dee: 1780
Location: WILLIAMSBURG
Source(s): BODDIE.
Revolutionary War service: PRIVATE IN MARION'S BRIGADE

ADAIR, JAMES   ID: 4990
Date in Pee Dee: 1780
Location: WILLIAMSBURG
Source(s): BODDIE.
Revolutionary War service: PRIVATE IN MARION'S BRIGADE

ADAIR, JOHN   ID: 4991
Date in Pee Dee: 1780
Location: WILLIAMSBURG
Source(s): BODDIE.
Revolutionary War service: PRIVATE IN MARION'S BRIGADE

ADAMS, CHARLES   ID: 1
Spouse: ESTHER M. IZARD
Date in Pee Dee: 1782
Location: PRINCE GEORGE WINYAH PARISH

Source(s): CLEMENS.
Notes: MARRIED 3 APRIL 1782.

ADAMS, JOSEPH   ID: 5598
Date in Pee Dee: 1759
Location: ST. DAVID'S PARISH
Source(s): MUSTER ROLL.
Notes: SERVED IN FRENCH AND INDIAN WAR AS PRIVATE IN
CAPTAIN JAMES THOMSON'S COMPANY.

ADAMS, WILLIAM   ID: 4260
Date in Pee Dee: 1759   Last Date: 1770
Location: WILLIAMSBURG
Source(s): MOORE V.3.
Notes: SERVED IN FRENCH AND INDIAN WAR AS PRIVATE IN
CAPTAIN JAMES THOMSON'S COMPANY.

ADIER, ANDREW   ID: 4273
Spouse: MARY [--?--]
Children: WILLIAM, JAMES, SAMUEL, ELLY, JEAN.
Date in Pee Dee: 1773   Last Date: 1773 DIED
Location: WILLIAMSBURG
Source(s): MOORE V.3.

ADKINS, WILLIAM   ID: 10
Date in Pee Dee: 1734   Last Date: 1759
Location: PEE DEE BELOW LITTLE PEE DEE
Source(s): COOK, MUSTER ROLL.
Notes: SERVED IN FRENCH AND INDIAN WAR AS PRIVATE IN
MCINTOSH'S COMPANY.

ALISON, HECTOR   ID: 3376
Spouse: RACHEL [--?--]
Children: JAMES, HUGH, MARY, SARAH.
Date in Pee Dee: 1763   Last Date: 1767 DIED
Location: PEE DEE R. NEAR JEFFERIES & CATFISH CRK.
Source(s): MOORE V.3, COOK.
Notes: MINISTER OF FIRST WILLIAMSBURG PRESBYTERIAN
CHURCH.

ALLEIN, MARY   ID: 1743
Spouse: GEORGE DICK
Date in Pee Dee: 1735
Location: PRINCE FREDERICK PARISH
Source(s): RBPPFW.

ALLEN, JEREMIAH   ID: 2
Date in Pee Dee: 1782
Source(s): GREGG P.405.
Revolutionary War service: MILITIA LIEUTENANT.

ALLEN, JOSEPH   ID: 15
Spouse: MARY ANNE TAYLOR
Date in Pee Dee: 1741   Last Date: 1767
Location: PRINCE FREDERICK PARISH
Source(s): COOK, MOORE V.3, SMITH, H., RBPPFW.
Notes: SMITH SPELLS ALLEIN. MARRIED 18 JULY 1747 AT
PRINCE FREDERECK PARISH.

ALLISON, JAMES H.   ID: 4977
Date in Pee Dee: 1780
Location: WILLIAMSBURG
Source(s): BODDIE.
Revolutionary War service: LIEUTENANT IN MARION'S
BRIGADE.

ALLISON, ROBERT   ID: 18
Date in Pee Dee: 1737   Last Date: 1768
Location: CENTRAL ST. DAVID PARISH
Source(s): COOK, JVSDP, BODDIE.
Notes: ORIGINAL BOARD MEMBER OF ST. DAVID'S PARISH.

ALLSTON, ANNE   ID: 3534
Spouse: THOMAS WATIES
Children: WILLIAM, THOMAS, JOHN, ANN.
Date in Pee Dee: 1744
Location: PRINCE GEORGE WINYAW PARISH
Source(s): MOORE V.3.
Notes: DAUGHTER OF WILLIAM #33.

Early Pee Dee Settlers
--A--

ALLSTON, JOHN   ID: 25
Spouse: ESTHER MARION
Children: MARTHA.
Date in Pee Dee: 1711   Last Date: 1751
Location: PEE DEE RIVER WEST BANK
Source(s): COOK, BASS, ROGERS.

ALLSTON, JOSEPH   ID: 2709
Spouse: ELIZABETH ROTHMAHLER
Children: WILLIAM, THOMAS, SAMUEL
Date in Pee Dee: 1733   Last Date: 1734
Location: ALL SAINT'S PARISH
Source(s): ROGERS.
Notes: SON OF WILLIAM SR.

ALLSTON, JOSHAS   ID: 3683
Spouse: ANN PROCTOR
Children: JOHN, WILLIAM, HANNAH, MARTHA, ANNE.
Date in Pee Dee: 1765
Location: PRINCE GEORGE WINYAW PARISH
Source(s): MOORE V.3, COOK.
Notes: FOUR OTHER CHILDREN. SON OF JOHN #2622.

ALLSTON, MARTHA   ID: 622
Spouse: BENJAMIN MARION
Date in Pee Dee: 1749
Location: PRINCE GEORGE WINYAW PARISH
Source(s): MOORE.
Notes: DAUGHTER OF JOHN #2662.

ALLSTON, THOMAS   ID: 30
Spouse: MARY ALLSTON
Date in Pee Dee: 1795
Location: ALL SAINT'S PARISH
Source(s): COOK, CLEMENTS.
Notes: MARRIED IN CHARLESTON 21 JULY 1785.

ALLSTON, WILLIAM   ID: 31
Date in Pee Dee: 1749   Last Date: 1795

Location: ALL SAINT'S PARISH
Source(s): COOK, MOORE.
Notes: REPRESENTATIVE TO POST WAR SC LEGISLATURE. SON OF JOHN #2662.

ALQUIN, ABRAHAM   ID: 34
Date in Pee Dee: 1775
Location: ST. DAVID'S PARISH
Source(s): COOK.
Revolutionary War service: LIDE'S COMPANY.

ALRAN, JOHN   ID: 1851
Date in Pee Dee: 1749   Last Date: 1768
Location: ST. DAVID'S PARISH
Source(s): GREGG, JVSDP, MOORE.
Revolutionary War service: MILITIA

ALRIDGE, MICHAEL   ID: 5638
Date in Pee Dee: 1759
Location: ST. DAVID'S PARISH
Source(s): MUSTER ROLL.
Notes: SERVED IN FRENCH AND INDIAN WAR AS PRIVATE WITH LIDE'S COMPANY.

ALSTON, WILLIAM   ID: 2641
Spouse: MARY ASHE
Children: MARIA, JOSEPH, JOHN ASHE, WILLIAM ALGERNON, CHARLOTTE.
Date in Pee Dee: 1756   Last Date: 1839
Location: "CLIFTON" ON WACCAMAW
Source(s): ROGERS, BODDIE.
Notes: SECOND MARRIED MARY BREWTON MOTTE. HE DROPPED ONE "L" TO DISTINGUISH FROM OTHER WILLIAM ALLSTON.
Revolutionary War service: COLONEL IN MARION'S BRIGADE.

AMMONS, JOHN   ID: 1956
Date in Pee Dee: 1782
Source(s): GREGG P.405.
Revolutionary War service: PRIVATE IN MARION'S BRIGADE.

AMMONS, THOMAS   ID: 2010
Date in Pee Dee: 1782
Source(s): GREGG P.405.
Revolutionary War service: PRIVATE IN MARION'S BRIGADE.

ANDERSON, CHARLES   ID: 3933
Date in Pee Dee: 1766
Location: ST. MARK'S PARISH
Source(s): MOORE V.3.
Notes: STEPSON OF WILLIAM ANDERSON.

ANDERSON, DAVID   ID: 36
Date in Pee Dee: 1755   Last Date: 1768
Location: WILLIAMSBURG (SALEM)
Source(s): COOK, BODDIE, MOORE.
Notes: SERVED AS CAPTAIN DURING FRENCH AND INDIAN WAR.

ANDERSON, JAMES   ID: 37
Date in Pee Dee: 1780
Location: PRINCE FREDERICK PARISH
Source(s): COOK.
Revolutionary War service: LIEUTENANT IN MARION'S
BRIGADE.

ANDERSON, JOHN   ID: 1237
Children: JOHN.
Date in Pee Dee: 1737
Location: GEORGETOWN
Source(s): SMITH, H., BODDIE, MOORE V.3.
Notes: BROTHER OF JOSEPH AND WILLIAM. BODDIE NAMES AS
EARLY WILLIAMSBURG SETTLER.

ANDERSON, JOSEPH   ID: 1240
Spouse: ELIZABETH FITCH
Date in Pee Dee: 1760   Last Date: 1764 DIED
Location: SANTEE RIVER
Source(s): MOORE V.3, CLEMENS.
Notes: AN UNBORN CHILD AT DEATH. BROTHERS JOHN AND
WILLIAM. MARRIED 21 FEBRUARY 1760 AT SANTEE.

ANDERSON, MARY   ID: 3467
Spouse: NATHANIEL MCCORMACK
Children: MARY, JAMES.
Date in Pee Dee: 1760   Last Date: 1760   DIED
Location: PRINCE FREDERICK PARISH
Source(s): MOORE V.3.
Notes: MOTHER WAS ALSO MARY ANDERSON.

ANDERSON, SUSAN   ID: 1593
Spouse: JOHN COOPER
Children: WILLIAM.
Date in Pee Dee: 1770
Location: WILLIAMSBURG
Source(s): WITHERSPOON.

ANDERSON, WILLIAM   ID: 39
Spouse: ANN (BAXTER)
Children: ALEXANDER, ANN, CHARLES ANDERSON (STEPSON).
Date in Pee Dee: 1741   Last Date: 1746 DIED
Location: PRINCE GEORGE PARISH.
Source(s): COOK, BODDIE, MOORE.
Notes: BROTHER OF JOSEPH AND JOHN.

ANDREWS, MARY   ID: 4119
Date in Pee Dee: 1763   Last Date: 1778
Source(s): MOORE V.3, RWNBC.
Notes: MAY HAVE BEEN WIFE OF THOMAS ANDREWS.

ANDREWS, SAMUEL   ID: 40
Date in Pee Dee: 1780
Source(s): COOK.
Notes: HANGED BY BRITISH AT CAMDEN.

ARMSTRONG, ELIZABETH   ID: 1072
Date in Pee Dee: 1750
Location: WILLIAMSBURG
Source(s): MOORE.
Notes: DAUGHTER OF JANET BLAKLEY #445.

ARMSTRONG, JAMES   ID: 41
Spouse: MARY MONTGOMERY
Date in Pee Dee: 1732   Last Date: 1780
Origin: NORTHERN IRELAND
Location: WILLIAMSBURG (SALEM)
Source(s): BODDIE, WITHERSPOON, MOORE, STEPHENSON.
Notes: SON OF JANET BLAKLEY #445. SERVED IN FRENCH AND
INDIAN WAR.
Revolutionary War service: PRIVATE IN MARION'S BRIGADE..

ARMSTRONG, JANE   ID: 1832
Date in Pee Dee: 1750
Location: WILLIAMSBURG
Source(s): MOORE.
Notes: DAUGHTER OF JANET BLAKLEY 445.

ARMSTRONG, JOHN   ID: 1012
Date in Pee Dee: 1750   Last Date: 1780
Location: WILLIAMSBURG
Source(s): MOORE, BODDIE.
Notes: SON OF JANET BLAKLEY 445.
Revolutionary War service: CAPTAIN IN MARION'S BRIGADE.

ARMSTRONG, MARY   ID: 2760
Date in Pee Dee: 1750
Location: WILLIAMSBURG
Source(s): MOORE.
Notes: DAUGHTER OF JANET BLAKLEY 445.

ARMSTRONG, WILLIAM   ID: 4993
Date in Pee Dee: 1780
Location: WILLIAMSBURG
Source(s): BODDIE.
Revolutionary War service: PRIVATE IN MARION'S BRIGADE

ARNAL, ANTHONY   ID: 5606
Date in Pee Dee: 1759
Location: ST. DAVID'S PARISH
Source(s): MUSTER ROLL.

Notes: SERVED IN FRENCH AND INDIAN WAR IN CAPTAIN JAMES
THOMSON'S COMPANY. LISTED AS DESERTER.

ARNETT, JAMES   ID: 4839
Date in Pee Dee: 1777
Location: PRINCE FREDERICK PARISH
Source(s): MOORE V.3, BODDIE.
Notes: SON OF JOHN #4838. HE APPEARS NOT TO HAVE
SURRIVED BEYOND 1780. WIFE SUPPLIED MARION.

ARNETT, JOHN   ID: 4837
Spouse: MARGARET [--?--]
Children: JAMES, JOHN, ALEXANDER, ELIZABETH, MARGARET,
MARY, ANN.
Date in Pee Dee: 1777   Last Date: 1777 DIED
Location: PRINCE FREDERICK PARISH
Source(s): MOORE V.3.

ARRINO, JOHN   ID: 57
Spouse: MARY MCDANIEL
Date in Pee Dee: 1749
Location: PRINCE FREDERICK PARISH
Source(s): RBPPFW.

ASHE, MARY   ID: 2693
Spouse: WILLIAM ALSTON
Date in Pee Dee: 1770
Location: PRINCE GEORGE WINYAW PARISH

ASKEW, JOHN   ID: 1862
Date in Pee Dee: 1759   Last Date: 1782
Location: MARION DISTRICT
Source(s): GREGG P.405, MUSTER ROLL.
Notes: THOMAS REPORTS NAME TO BE HASKEW. PRIVATE IN
KOLB'S COMPANY IN FRENCH AND INDIAN WAR.
Revolutionary War service: PRIVATE IN MARION'S BRIGADE.

ASKIN, WILLIAM   ID: 5200
Spouse: MARY GREGG

Children: SAMUEL, JOHN, ROBERT, WILLIAM.
Date in Pee Dee: 1791
Source(s): GREGG, MCCARTY.

ASKINS, SAMUEL   ID: 1459
Spouse: MARY GREGG
Children: SAMUEL, JOHN, ROBERT, WILSON.
Date in Pee Dee: 1765
Location: CHERAW DISTRICT
Source(s): GREGG, MCCARTY.

ATKINS, EDMUND   ID: 47
Spouse: ANN MCKENZIE
Date in Pee Dee: 1735   Last Date: 1761 DIED
Origin: EXETER, ENGLAND
Location: MARS BLUFF
Source(s): COOK, MOORE V.3.
Notes: MAY NEVER HAVE LIVED ON THIS LAND.

ATKINS, SARAH   ID: 1454
Spouse: JOSEPH GREGG
Children: ALEXANDER, MARY, ROBERT, MARGARET, JOSEPH,
SARAH, JENNET.
Date in Pee Dee: 1760
Location: JEFFERIES CREEK
Source(s): GREGG, MCCARTY, DAR.

ATKINSON, ANTHONY   ID: 50
Spouse: MARY [--?--]
Children: GEORGE, JANE (DIED 1732).
Date in Pee Dee: 1728   Last Date: 1749 DIED
Location: BLACK RIVER
Source(s): MOORE, SMITH, H..
Notes: MARY DIED 1740. HE WAS A VESTRY MAN AT PARISH OF
PRINCE FREDERICK WINYAW FOR NUMBER OF YEARS.

ATKINSON, ELIZABETH   ID: 5406
Spouse: THOMAS MITCHEL
Date in Pee Dee: 1752 DIED

Location: PRINCE FREDERICK PARISH
Source(s): RBPPFW.

ATKINSON, GEORGE   ID: 51
Spouse: MARY STUART
Date in Pee Dee: 1740   Last Date: 1756
Location: PRINCE GEORGE WINYAW PARISH
Source(s): COOK, RBPPFW, MOORE.
Notes: SON OF ANTHONY #50. BROTHER OF MARY (HUGHES) AND
CATHERINE (PYATT).

ATKINSON, MARY   ID: 648
Spouse: [--?--] HUGHES
Children: HENRY.
Date in Pee Dee: 1754   Last Date: 1754 DIED
Location: PRINCE FREDERICK PARISH
Source(s): MOORE.
Notes: SISTER OF GEORGE ATKINSON AND CATHERINE (PYATT).

ATNOR, SARAH   ID: 5438
Spouse: JOHN BRYAN
Date in Pee Dee: 1747
Location: PRINCE FREDERICK PARISH
Source(s): RBPPFW.

ATWOOD, CORNELIUS   ID: 52
Date in Pee Dee: 1775
Location: ST. DAVID'S PARISH
Source(s): COOK.
Revolutionary War service: LIDE'S COMPANY

AUSTIN, FRANCIS   ID: 4994
Date in Pee Dee: 1780
Location: WILLIAMSBURG
Source(s): BODDIE.
Revolutionary War service: PRIVATE IN MARION'S BRIGADE

AUSTIN, JOHN   ID: 4995
Date in Pee Dee: 1780

Location: WILLIAMSBURG
Source(s): BODDIE.
Revolutionary War service: PRIVATE IN MARION'S BRIGADE.

AUSTIN, THOMAS   ID: 4780
Date in Pee Dee: 1777
Source(s): MOORE V.3, BODDIE.
Notes: SON OF WILLIAM #4776.
Revolutionary War service: PRIVATE IN MARION'S BRIGADE.

AUSTIN, WILLIAM   ID: 4776
Spouse: ELIZABETH [--?--]
Children: SAMUEL, BARTHOLOMEW, ELNDE, THOMAS, ELIZABETH.
Date in Pee Dee: 1777   Last Date: 1777 DIED
Source(s): MOORE V.3.

AVANT, BENJAMIN   ID: 54
Spouse: MARY [--?--]
Children: BENJAMIN, HANNAH, ANN.
Date in Pee Dee: 1728   Last Date: 1742
Location: PEE DEE BELOW LITTLE PEE DEE
Source(s): COOK, RBPPFW.
Notes: ANN APPEARS TO BE DAUGHTER OF ANOTHER WIFE, ANN
BRUNSTON.

AVANT, CALEB   ID: 56
Spouse: MARY [--?--]
Date in Pee Dee: 1734
Location: PEE DEE BELOW LITTLE PEE DEE
Source(s): COOK, RBPPFW.
Notes: SUBSCRIBED TO PEW #14 OF PARISH OF PRINCE
FREDERICK WINYAW AT A COST 14 POUNDS.

AVANT, CATHERINE   ID: 16
Spouse: STEPHEN CLYAT
Date in Pee Dee: 1748
Location: PRINCE FREDERICK PARISH
Source(s): RBPPFW.

Early Pee Dee Settlers
--A--

AVANT, FRANCIS   ID: 2889
Spouse: SARAH WIGFALL
Children: ANNA, SARAH WIGFALL.
Date in Pee Dee: 1729   Last Date: 1747
Location: PRINCE FREDERICK PARISH
Source(s): MOORE, COOK, RBPPFW.
Notes: SON OF JOHN #2887. MARRIED 6 JANUARY 1744 AT
PRINCE FREDERECK PARISH. SARAH WAS WIDOW OF [--?--]
THOMPSON.

AVANT, JOHN   ID: 2887
Spouse: HANNAH [--?--]
Children: FRANCIS, JOHN, LYDIA, REBECCA, HANNAH.
Date in Pee Dee: 1724   Last Date: 1747 DIED
Location: PRINCE FREDERICK PARISH
Source(s): MOORE, RBPPFW, BODDIE.
Notes: WIFE DIED IN 1744.

AVANT, LYDIA   ID: 2890
Spouse: WILLIAM GREEN
Children: JOHN.
Date in Pee Dee: 1740   Last Date: 1747
Location: PRINCE FREDERICK PARISH
Source(s): MOORE, RBPPFW.
Notes: DAUGHTER OF JOHN #2887. MARRIED 31 MARCH 1741 AT
PARISH OF PRINCE FREDERICK WINYAW.

AVANT, PERSIS   ID: 5412
Spouse: AMOS SHAW
Date in Pee Dee: 1746
Location: PRINCE FREDERICK PARISH
Source(s): RBPPFW.

AVANT, SARAH   ID: 2894
Date in Pee Dee: 1747
Location: PRINCE FREDERICK PARISH
Source(s): MOORE.
Notes: GRAND-DAUGHTER OF JOHN AVANT #2887.

Early Pee Dee Settlers
--A--

AYER, LEWIS MALONE   ID: 1625
Date in Pee Dee: 1780
Location: HUNT'S BLUFF
Source(s): GREGG.
Notes: SON OF THOMAS #60. MOVED TO BARNWELL.

AYER, THOMAS   ID: 60
Children: THOMAS AYER, LEWIS MALONE, HARTWELL.
Date in Pee Dee: 1758   Last Date: 1779
Origin: NORTHERN IRELAND
Location: HUNT'S BLUFF
Source(s): COOK, RWNBC, GREGG, THOMAS.
Notes: CAME THROUGH VIRGINIA.

AYERS, ANNE PEGGY   ID: 4631
Date in Pee Dee: 1779
Location: ST. DAVID'S PARISH
Source(s): RWNBC.
Notes: MAY HAVE BEEN WIFE OF THOMAS AYER.

BACOT, ELIZABETH   ID: 4145
Spouse: JOHN SMITH
Date in Pee Dee: 1767
Source(s): MOORE V.3, CLEMENTS.
Notes: NIECE OF ELIAS FOISSIN #416. MARRIED 11 FEBRUARY
1768 AT SANTEE.

BACOT, MARY   ID: 4146
Date in Pee Dee: 1767
Source(s): MOORE V.3.
Notes: NIECE OF ELIAS FOISSIN #416.

BACOT, SAMUEL   ID: 1743
Spouse: [--?--] ALLSTON
Children: SAMUEL, CYRUS.
Date in Pee Dee: 1769
Location: ST. DAVID'S PARISH
Source(s): GREGG.
Notes: GRANDFATHER, PIERRE IN CHARLESTOWN 1694.

BAGNAL, CHARLES   ID: 5719
Date in Pee Dee: 1759
Location: ST. DAVID'S PARISH
Source(s): MUSTER ROLL.
Notes: LISTED AS A DESERTER FROM HITCHCOCK'S COMPANY
DURING FRENCH AND INDIAN WAR.

BAKER, ELIZABETH   ID: 5383
Spouse: GEORGE LOGAN

17

Date in Pee Dee: 1743
Location: PRINCE FREDERICK PARISH
Source(s): RBPPFW.
Notes: MARRIED 3 FEBRUARY 1743 AT PARISH OF PRINCE
FREDERICK WINYAW. LOGAN WAS FROM CHRIST CHURCH PARISH.

BAKER, HENRY   ID: 5593
Date in Pee Dee: 1759
Location: ST. DAVID'S PARISH
Source(s): MUSTER ROLL.
Notes: SERVED IN FRENCH AND INDIAN WAR IN CAPTAIN DAVID
EVANS' COMPANY. LISTED AS DESERTER.

BAKER, WILLIAM   ID: 2502
Spouse: [--?--] EVANS
Children: WILLIAM, JOHN.
Date in Pee Dee: 1735   Last Date: 1740
Location: CATFISH CREEK
Source(s): SELLERS, GREGG.
Notes: WIFE WAS DAUGHTER OF NATHAN EVANS.

BALDEE, PAUL   ID: 26
Date in Pee Dee: 1759   Last Date: 1784 DIED
Location: ST. DAVID'S PARISH
Source(s): RWNBC, MUSTER ROLL.
Notes: SERVED IN FRENCH AND INDIAN WAR AS PRIVATE WITH
MCINTOSH'S COMPANY.

BALL, BARTHOLOMEW   ID: 63
Spouse: ELIZABETH [--?--]
Children: BARTHOLOMEW, EDWARD.
Date in Pee Dee: 1732   Last Date: 1759
Location: CASHAWAY FERRY
Source(s): COOK, RBPPFW.
Notes: SERVED IN FRENCH AND INDIAN WAR AS PRIVATE IN
CAPTAIN JAMES THOMSON'S COMPANY.

BALL, ELIAS   ID: 64
Spouse: CATHERINE GAILLARD

Children: BARTHOLOMEW.
Date in Pee Dee: 1730
Location: WHITTEE CREEK
Source(s): COOK, CLEMENS.
Notes: MARRIED AT SANTEE 14 MAY 1765.

BALL, ELIZABETH   ID: 5378
Spouse: ALEXANDER DAVIDSON
Date in Pee Dee: 1742
Location: PRINCE FREDERICK PARISH
Source(s): RBPPFW.

BALL, JOSEPH   ID: 1729
Spouse: [--?--] WISE
Date in Pee Dee: 1770
Source(s): GREGG.
Notes: MARRIED DAUGHTER OF SAMUEL WISE.

BALL, ROBERT   ID: 5225
Spouse: MERCY [--?--]
Children: ELIZABETH.
Date in Pee Dee: 1741
Location: PRINCE FREDERICK PARISH
Source(s): RBPPFW.
Notes: ELIZABETH WAS ABOUT 18 YEARS IN 1741.

BALL, SAMPSON   ID: 2056
Date in Pee Dee: 1754
Location: CRAVEN COUNTY
Source(s): MOORE.
Notes: GRAND-SON OF LEWIS GOURDIN #2266.

BALL, STEPHEN   ID: 5402
Spouse: LYDIA SANDERS
Date in Pee Dee: 1744
Location: PRINCE FREDERICK PARISH
Source(s): RBPPFW.
Notes: MARRIED 1 JANUARY 1745 AT PARISH OF PRINCE
FREDERICK WINYAW.

BALLANTINE, WILLIAM   ID: 5237
Spouse: ELEONER [--?--]
Children: CATHERINE.
Date in Pee Dee: 1742
Location: PRINCE FREDERICK PARISH
Source(s): RBPPFW.

BALLARD, JESSE   ID: 2669
Date in Pee Dee: 1780
Location: PRINCE GEORGE WINYAW PARISH
Source(s): ROGERS.
Notes: PROBABLY A TORY. HE SIGNED LOYALITY OATH.

BARBER, JOHN   ID: 5672
Date in Pee Dee: 1759
Location: ST. DAVID'S PARISH
Source(s): MUSTER ROLL.
Notes: SERVED IN FRENCH AND INDIAN WAR AS PRIVATE WITH
MCINTOSH'S COMPANY.

BARKER, KESIAH   ID: 5536
Date in Pee Dee: 1767 DOB Last Date: 1773
Location: ST. DAVID'S PARISH
Source(s): JVSDP.
Notes: SISTER OF SARAH AND MARY. BOUND TO MARY
HOLLINGSWORTH FOR 12 YEARS BY PARISH.

BARKER, MARY   ID: 5537
Date in Pee Dee: 1763 DOB Last Date: 1773
Location: ST. DAVID'S PARISH
Source(s): JVSDP.
Notes: SISTER OF SARAH AND KESIAH. BOUND TO MARY
HOLLINGSWORTH FOR 8 YEARS BY PARISH.

BARKER, SARAH   ID: 5535
Date in Pee Dee: 1760 DOB Last Date: 1773
Location: ST. DAVID'S PARISH
Source(s): JVSDP.

Notes: SISTER OF KESIAH AND MARY. BOUND TO MARY
HOLLINGSWORTH FOR 5 YEARS BY PARISH.

BARLOW, ELIZABETH   ID: 4799
Spouse: [--?--] BARLOW
Children: RICHARD, ANN (SIMSON).
Date in Pee Dee: 1776
Source(s): MOORE V.3.
Notes: LATER MARRIED ROBERT BYERS.

BARNS, JOHN   ID: 4019
Spouse: MARGARET [--?--]
Date in Pee Dee: 1759   Last Date: 1768 DIED
Location: BLACK MINGO CREEK
Source(s): MOORE V.3.

BARR, JAMES   ID: 71
Date in Pee Dee: 1759   Last Date: 1781
Location: PRINCE FREDERICK'S PARISH
Source(s): COOK, BODDIE, MOORE V.3.
Notes: SON OF WILLIAM. SERVED AS PRIVATE DURING FRENCH
AND INDIAN WAR.

BARR, JOHN   ID: 2907
Spouse: [--?--] DREW
Date in Pee Dee: 1750
Location: WILLIAMSBURG
Source(s): MOORE, BODDIE.
Notes: MARRIED DAUGHTER OF NATHANIEL DREW.

BARR, MARGARET   ID: 3419
Spouse: NATHANIEL DREW
Children: SAMUEL, DAUGHTER (BROCKINGTON), DAUGHTER
(NESMITH).
Date in Pee Dee: 1761   Last Date: 1763 DIED
Location: WILLIAMSBURG
Source(s): MOORE V.3.

BARR, WILLIAM   ID: 3549

Spouse: ESTHER [--?--]
Children: JAMES, NATHAN, ISAAC, CALEB, JACOB, SILAS,
JOHN, WILLIAM, MARGARET, RACHEL, ESTHER.
Date in Pee Dee: 1764   Last Date: 1764 DIED
Location: LONG CANE
Source(s): MOORE V.3, BODDIE.

BARTON, HANNAH   ID: 2573
Spouse: ANTHONY JR. WHITE
Date in Pee Dee: 1760   Last Date: 1770
Location: LOWER BLACK RIVER
Source(s): STRAWN, CLEMENS, MOORE V.3.
Notes: SISTER OF MARY ANN. DAUGHTER OF WILLIAM SR.
#4012. MARRIED 30 AUGUST 1770 AT SANTEE.

BARTON, HESTER   ID: 4014
Spouse: [--?--] MOORE
Date in Pee Dee: 1768
Location: PRINCE FREDRICK PARISH
Source(s): MOORE V.3.
Notes: DAUGHTER OF WILLIAM SR. #4012.

BARTON, JOHN   ID: 5242
Spouse: HONORA BONNELL
Children: HONORA.
Date in Pee Dee: 1736   Last Date: 1742
Location: PRINCE FREDERICK PARISH
Source(s): RBPPFW.
Notes: MARRIED 4 JUNE 1741 AT PARISH OF PRINCE FREDERICK
WINYAW. CHURCH WARDEN OF PARISH OF PRINCE FREDERICK
WINYAW IN 1736.

BARTON, MARY ANN   ID: 2577
Spouse: ANTHONY SR. WHITE
Children: ANTHONY, MARY, HANNAH.
Date in Pee Dee: 1730   Last Date: 1768
Location: LOWER BLACK RIVER
Source(s): STRAWN, MOORE V.3.
Notes: SISTER OF HANNAH. DAUGHTER OF WILLIAM SR. #4012.

BARTON, SARAH   ID: 4015
Spouse: STEPHEN FORD
Date in Pee Dee: 1761   Last Date: 1768
Location: PRINCE FREDRICK PARISH
Source(s): MOORE V.3, CLEMENS.
Notes: DAUGHTER OF WILLIAM SR. #4012. MARRIED 25 JANUARY
1761 AT SANTEE.

BARTON, WILLIAM JR.   ID: 4013
Spouse: JANE THOMPSON
Date in Pee Dee: 1768
Location: PRINCE FREDRICK PARISH
Source(s): MOORE V.3, CLEMENS.
Notes: SON OF WILLIAM SR. #4012. MARRIED 24 SEPTEMBER
1773 AT SANTEE.

BASSET, NATHAN   ID: 75
Date in Pee Dee: 1733
Source(s): COOK.
Notes: PASTOR OF CIRCULAR CHURCH.

BASSNETT, JOHN   ID: 727
Date in Pee Dee: 1737   Last Date: 1743
Location: PRINCE FREDERICK PARISH
Source(s): RBPPFW, BODDIE.
Notes: PARISH OF PRINCE FREDERICK WINYAW CHURCH WARDEN
IN 1743. PROBABLY THE SAME AS BASSETT.

BAUSUR, MARIAN   ID: 1109
Date in Pee Dee: 1754
Location: CRAVEN COUNTY
Source(s): MOORE.
Notes: GRAND-DAUGHTER OF LEWIS GOURDIN #2266.

BAXTER, ISRAEL   ID: 4996
Date in Pee Dee: 1780
Location: WILLIAMSBURG
Source(s): BODDIE.
Revolutionary War service: PRIVATE IN MARION'S BRIGADE.

Early Pee Dee Settlers
--B--

BAXTER, JOHN   ID: 2771
Spouse: [--?--] LYNCH
Children: JOHN
Date in Pee Dee: 1727   Last date: 1789 DIED
Origin: NORTHERN IRELAND
Location: PRINCE FREDERICK'S PARISH
Source(s): COOK, MOORE, BODDIE, ROGERS, MCCARTY.
Notes: A MERCHANT ON BLACK RIVER AT THIS TIME. MINISTER
OF THE FIRST PRESBYTERIAN CHURCH IN SC OUTSIDE OF
CHARLESTON, LOCATED NORTH OF BLACK RIVER BELOW BLACK
MINGO CREEK. HE APPEARS TO HAVE BEEN INSTRUMENTAL IN THE
IMMIGRATION OF MANY FROM NORTHERN IRELAND, PERHAPS EVEN
THE FIRST WILLIAMSBURG SETTLERS.

BAXTER, JOHN   ID: 81
Spouse: SARAH [--?--]
Date in Pee Dee: 1733
Location: PRINCE FREDERICK'S PARISH
Source(s): COOK, MOORE, BODDIE, ROGERS, MCCARTY.
Notes: REPRESENTATIVE TO POST WAR SC LEGISLATURE ALSO
PRINCE GEORGE WINYAW PARISH.
Revolutionary War service: COLONEL IN MARION'S BRIGADE.

BEALE, OTHNEIL   ID: 84
Date in Pee Dee: 1730   Last Date: 1731
Occupation: SEA CAPTAIN   Origin: NEW ENGLAND
Location: PEE DEE NEAR LYNCH'S CREEK.
Source(s): COOK, SMITH, H..
Notes: FIRST LAND GRANTED ON UPPER PEE DEE. HE MAY NOT
HAVE OCCUPIED.

BEARMIN, MARY (WIDOW)   ID: 4157
Children: (GRAND) PHILIP, MARTHA, DANIEL WILLIAMS,
(GRAND) MARY, WIFE OF WILLIAM NEWMAN.
Date in Pee Dee: 1770   Last Date: 1770 DIED
Location: PRINCE GEORGE WINYAW PARISH
Source(s): MOORE V.3.
Notes: COUSIN OF PHILIP COURTURIER.

BEASLEY, DANIEL   ID: 2001
Date in Pee Dee: 1782
Source(s): GREGG P.405.
Revolutionary War service: PRIVATE IN BENTON'S REGIMENT.

BEASLEY, WILLIAM   ID: 2015
Date in Pee Dee: 1782
Source(s): GREGG P.405.
Revolutionary War service: PRIVATE IN BENTON'S REGIMENT.

BEDINGFIELD, CHARLES   ID: 88
Spouse: MARY [--?--]
Children: JOHN, BETTY.
Date in Pee Dee: 1762   Last Date: 1773 DIED
Location: UPPER ST. DAVID'S PARISH
Source(s): COOK, JVSDP, MOORE V.3.
Notes: ORIGINAL COMMISSIONER OF ST. DAVID'S PARISH.

BEDON, STEPHEN   ID: 90
Spouse: RUTH NICHOLLS
Date in Pee Dee: 1735
Location: BLACK MINGO CREEK
Source(s): COOK, CLEMENS.
Notes: MARRIED 11 AUGUST 1743 AT CHARLESTON.

BEECH, JOSEPH   ID: 163
Spouse: MARY [--?--]
Children: MARY.
Date in Pee Dee: 1729
Location: PRINCE FREDERICK PARISH
Source(s): RBPPFW.

BELIN, ALLARD   ID: 3088
Children: THOMAS, PETER, SARAH, ALLARD.
Date in Pee Dee: 1749
Location: PRINCE GEORGE WINYAW PARISH
Source(s): MOORE, BODDIE.

BELIN, JAMES   ID: 2824

Spouse: SARAH [--?--]
Children: WILLIAM, ALLARD, JAMES, MARY, ELIZABETH.
Date in Pee Dee: 1744   Last Date: 1744 DIED
Location: PRINCE FREDERICK PARISH
Source(s): MOORE.
Notes: GRAND-SONS WERE BARTHOLOMEW AND JAMES GAILLARD.

BELIN, MARY   ID: 3092
Children: JOHN.
Date in Pee Dee: 1756
Location: PRINCE GEORGE WINYAW PARISH
Source(s): MOORE.
Notes: PROBABLY WIFE OF ALLARD BELIN.

BELL, JAMES   ID: 3469
Spouse: JEAN ANDERSON
Date in Pee Dee: 1760
Location: PRINCE FREDERICK PARISH
Source(s): MOORE V.3, CLEMENS.
Notes: MARRIED 14 FEBRUARY 1764 AT SANTEE. APPEARS TO
HAVE MARRIED ESTHER CHOVIN IN 1768.

BELL, JOHN JR   ID: 91
Spouse: MARTHA [--?--]
Date in Pee Dee: 1704   Last Date: 1730 DIED
Location: NORTH OF SANTEE
Source(s): COOK, RBPPFW, ROGERS.

BELL, MARMADUKE   ID: 5416
Spouse: MARY GEURIN
Date in Pee Dee: 1746
Location: PRINCE FREDERICK PARISH
Source(s): RBPPFW.
Notes: MARRIED 21 MAY 1746 AT PARISH OF PRINCE FREDERICK
WINYAW.

BELL, WILLIAM   ID: 4296
Spouse: ELIZABETH ANDERSON
Children: WILLIAM, MARY.

Date in Pee Dee: 1765   Last Date: 1773 DIED
Location: PRINCE GEORGE WINYAW PARISH
Source(s): MOORE V.3, CLEMENS.
Notes: MARRIED 8 MAY 1765 AT SANTEE.

BENISON, WILLIAM   ID: 95
Date in Pee Dee: 1775   Last Date: 1782
Location: PRINCE GEORGE WINYAW PARISH
Source(s): COOK, MOORE V.3.
Notes: REPRESENTATIVE TO POST WAR SC LEGISLATURE.

BENJAMIN, TIMEO   ID: 5706
Date in Pee Dee: 1759
Location: ST. DAVID'S PARISH
Source(s): MUSTER ROLL.
Notes: SERVED IN HITCHCOCK'S COMPANY DURING FRENCH AND
INDIAN WAR.

BENNET, MARY   ID: 5385
Spouse: JOSEPH GRAVES
Date in Pee Dee: 1743
Location: PRINCE FREDERICK PARISH
Source(s): RBPPFW.

BENNET, SARAH   ID: 5343
Spouse: WILLIAM SMITH
Date in Pee Dee: 1738
Location: PRINCE FREDERICK PARISH
Source(s): RBPPFW.
Notes: MARRIED 22 MARCH 1738 AT PARISH OF PRINCE
FREDERICK WINYAW.

BENNET, THOMAS   ID: 3887
Date in Pee Dee: 1744   Last Date: 1762 DIED
Location: PRINCE FREDERICK PARISH
Source(s): MOORE V.3, RBPPFW.
Notes: SON OF HENRY. DOB 11 JULY 1743.

BENNETT, HENRY   ID: 3180

Spouse: REBECCA [--?--]
Date in Pee Dee: 1736
Location: PRINCE FREDERICK PARISH
Source(s): BODDIE.

BENNETT, SAMUEL   ID: 4272
Date in Pee Dee: 1771   Last Date: 1780
Location: LOWER MARK'S PARISH (WILLIAMSBURG)
Source(s): MOORE V.3, BODDIE.
Notes: SUPPLIED MARION.
Revolutionary War service: PRIVATE IN MARION'S BRIGADE.

BENOIST, CHARLES   ID: 2634
Spouse: MARY ANN [--?--]
Children: MARY ANN, MAGDALENE.
Date in Pee Dee: 1737   Last Date: 1744 DIED
Location: PRINCE GEORGE WINYAW PARISH
Source(s): MOORE.

BENOIST, PETER   ID: 3045
Spouse: ELIZABETH [--?--]
Children: DANIEL.
Date in Pee Dee: 1732   Last Date: 1754 DIED
Location: CASHAWAY FERRY
Source(s): MOORE.
Notes: AN UNBORN CHILD AT DEATH.

BENOIST, SAMUEL   ID: 79
Spouse: JANE [--?--]
Date in Pee Dee: 1732   Last Date: 1732   DIED
Location: CASHAWAY
Source(s): MOORE V.1.
Notes: AN UNBORN CHILD AT TIME OF DEATH.

BENTLY, EDMUND   ID: 5363
Spouse: MARY WELLS
Date in Pee Dee: 1741
Location: PRINCE FREDERICK PARISH
Source(s): RBPPFW.

Notes: **MARRIED 15 SEPTEMBER 1741 AT PARISH OF PRINCE FREDERICK WINYAW.**

BENTON, AARON   ID: 97
Date in Pee Dee: 1775
Location: ST. DAVID'S PARISH
Source(s): COOK.
Revolutionary War service: LIDE'S COMPANY

BENTON, CHARLOTTE   ID: 1716
Spouse: LAURENCE PRINCE
Date in Pee Dee: 1770
Location: CHERAW DISTRICT
Source(s): GREGG.
Notes: DAUGHTER OF LEMUEL #98.

BENTON, CLARISSA   ID: 1715
Spouse: WILLIAM L. THOMAS
Children: WILLIAM LITTLE, ALEXANDER.
Date in Pee Dee: 1770
Location: CHERAW DISTRICT
Source(s): GREGG.
Notes: DAUGHTER OF LEMUEL #98.

BENTON, ELIZABETH   ID: 1718
Spouse: GEORGE BRUCE
Date in Pee Dee: 1770
Location: CHERAW DISTRICT
Source(s): GREGG.
Notes: DAUGHTER OF LEMUEL #98.

BENTON, GILLY   ID: 1717
Spouse: ISAIAH DUBOSE
Date in Pee Dee: 1770
Location: CHERAW DISTRICT
Source(s): GREGG.
Notes: DAUGHTER OF LEMUEL #98.

BENTON, LEMUEL   ID: 98

Spouse: [--?--] KIMBROUGH
Children: JOHN, CLARISSA, LEMUEL, CHARLOTTE, BUCKLEY,
GILLY, ALFRED, ELIZABETH.
Date in Pee Dee: 1760   Last Date: 1782
Origin: GRANVILLE COUNTY NC
Location: ST. DAVID'S PARISH (N. OF CASHAWAY)
Source(s): COOK, GREGG.
Notes: REPRESENTATIVE TO POST WAR SC LEGISLATURE.

BENTON, PENELOPE   ID: 1492
Spouse: WILLIAM BROCKINGTON
Date in Pee Dee: 1765
Location: CHERAWS DISTRICT
Source(s): GREGG.

BENTON, SAMUEL   ID: 2051
Date in Pee Dee: 1775
Location: ST. DAVID'S PARISH
Source(s): GREGG.
Revolutionary War service: MILITIA

BERNARD, ELISHA   ID: 4307
Date in Pee Dee: 1774
Location: PRINCE FREDERICK PARISH
Source(s): MOORE V.3.
Notes: SON OF JAMES #4302. NEPHEW OF ELISHA JAUDON.

BERNARD, ESTHER   ID: 4308
Spouse: WILLIAM LEIGH
Date in Pee Dee: 1775
Location: PRINCE FREDERICK PARISH
Source(s): MOORE V.3, CLEMENS.
Notes: DAUGHTER OF JAMES #4302. MARRIED 27 AUGUST 1778
AT SANTEE.

BERNARD, JAMES   ID: 4302
Spouse: ESTHER JAUDON
Children: PAUL, JAMES, WILLIAM, SAMUEL, ELISHA, ESTHER.
Date in Pee Dee: 1775   Last Date: 1775 DIED

Early Pee Dee Settlers
--B--

Location: PRINCE FREDERICK PARISH
Source(s): MOORE V.3.

BERRY, ANDREW   ID: 2479
Spouse: [--?--] HAYS
Children: HENRY, STEPHEN, JOHN, ANDREW, SAMUEL.
Date in Pee Dee: 1735
Location: SANDY BLUFF
Source(s): SELLERS.

BERRY, HENRY   ID: 2480
Spouse: [--?--] HAYS
Children: DENNIS, SLAUGHTER.
Date in Pee Dee: 1750
Location: MARION COUNTY
Source(s): SELLERS.

BERRY, WILLIAM   ID: 2096
Date in Pee Dee: 1782
Source(s): GREGG P.405.
Revolutionary War service: SERGEANT IN MARION'S BRIGADE.

BERTHIER,   ID: 2500
Date in Pee Dee:
Source(s): .
Notes: SEE BETHEA.

BERWICK, JAMES   ID: 3130
Date in Pee Dee: 1755   Last Date: 1764
Location: WILLIAMSBURG
Source(s): MOORE, BODDIE.
Notes: SERVED IN FRENCH AND INDIAN WAR.

BEST, ABSALOM   ID: 5702
Date in Pee Dee: 1759
Location: ST. DAVID'S PARISH
Source(s): MUSTER ROLL.

Notes: LISTED AS DESERTER FROM KOLB'S COMPANY DURING
FRENCH AND INDIAN WAR.

BETHEA, JOHN   ID: 2501
Spouse: ABSALA PARKER
Children: PARKER, WILLIAM, JAMES, PHILLIP, ELISHA,
SALLIE, PATTIE, MOLLIE, ABSALA.
Date in Pee Dee: 1750
Location: BUCK SWAMP MARION COUNTY
Source(s): SELLERS.
Notes: BORN IN CAPE FEAR NC AREA, HIS FATHER JOHN,
GRANDFATHER JOHN FROM VA. BROTHER OF WILLIAM #1468.

BEVIL, JAMES   ID: 74
Date in Pee Dee: 1779
Location: ST. DAVID'S PARISH
Source(s): ANDREWS.
Notes: HANGED AS A TORY.

BIGHAM, JAMES   ID: 78
Spouse: JANNET GREGG
Children: WILLIAM.
Date in Pee Dee: 1770
Location: WILLIAMSBURG
Source(s): MCCARTY.

BIGHAM, WILLIAM   ID: 4785
Spouse: MARGARET GREGG
Children: EUNICE, ELIZA, JOHN H., AMBROSE, ELIZABETH.
Date in Pee Dee: 1770
Location: WILLIAMSBURG
Source(s): MCCARTY.

BILLING, ZENOBIA   ID: 4317
Date in Pee Dee: 1772   Last Date: 1772 DIED
Location: GEORGETOWN
Source(s): MOORE V.3.
Notes: A SPINSTER, NIECE OF MARY DICK.

Early Pee Dee Settlers
--B--

BINGHAM, THOMAS   ID: 100
Date in Pee Dee: 1759   Last Date: 1780
Location: ST. DAVID'S PARISH
Source(s): COOK, JVSDP, GREGG.
Notes: CHURCH WARDEN ST. DAVID'S. SERVED AS PRIVATE IN
LIDE'S COMPANY DURING FRENCH AND INDIAN WAR.

BIRD, WILLIAM   ID: 2067
Date in Pee Dee: 1782
Source(s): GREGG P.405.
Revolutionary War service: PRIVATE IN MARION'S BRIGADE.

BISHOP, WILLIAM   ID: 5186
Spouse: ELIZABETH [--?--]
Date in Pee Dee: 1790   Last Date: 1796 DIED
Location: CHERAW DISTRICT
Source(s): CHERAW DISTRICT REC., BODDIE.
Revolutionary War service: PRIVATE MARION'S BRIGADE

BLACK, DAVID   ID: 5602
Date in Pee Dee: 1759
Location: ST. DAVID'S PARISH
Source(s): MUSTER ROLL.
Notes: SERVED IN FRENCH AND INDIAN WAR AS PRIVATE IN
CAPTAIN JAMES THOMSON'S COMPANY.

BLACKWELL, THOMAS   ID: 3224
Spouse: MARY JOHNSON
Children: HONOURE.
Date in Pee Dee: 1731
Location: CRAVEN COUNTY
Source(s): MOORE V.1.

BLACKWOOD, ABRAM   ID: 1872
Date in Pee Dee: 1782
Source(s): GREGG P.405.
Revolutionary War service: PRIVATE IN MARION'S BRIGADE.

BLAIR, WADE   ID: 3373

Date in Pee Dee: 1763   Last Date: 1763 DIED
Location: PRINCE FREDERICK PARISH
Source(s): MOORE V.3.
Notes: FATHER AND MOTHER WERE REV. WILLIAM AND LUCY
BLAIR OF INVERNESS, SCOTLAND.

BLAKE, JOHN   ID: 5210
Spouse: ANN [--?--]
Children: JOHN, ELIZABETH.
Date in Pee Dee: 1738   Last Date: 1742
Location: PRINCE FREDERICK PARISH
Source(s): RBPPFW.
Notes: MAY HAVE HAD AN EARLIER SON JOHN.

BLAKE, RICHARD   ID: 5223
Spouse: ELIZABETH STAPLES
Children: ANN, RICHARD.
Date in Pee Dee: 1739   Last Date: 1741
Location: PRINCE FREDERICK PARISH
Source(s): RBPPFW.
Notes: MARRIED 25 DECEMBER 1739 AT PARISH OF PRINCE
FREDERICK WINYAW.

BLAKELY, JAMES   ID: 103
Spouse: ELIZABETH MCMULLIN
Children: JANNET (BLAKELY).
Date in Pee Dee: 1732   Last Date: 1766
Origin: NORTHERN IRELAND
Location: WILLIAMSBURG
Source(s): COOK, BODDIE, MOORE.
Notes: BROTHER OF JOHN #105.

BLAKELY, JOHN   ID: 105
Spouse: ELIZABETH FLEMING
Date in Pee Dee: 1732   Last Date: 1744 DIED
Origin: NORTHERN IRELAND
Location: WILLIAMSBURG
Source(s): COOK, BODDIE, MOORE.
Notes: FOUR CHILDREN. BROTHER OF JAMES.

Early Pee Dee Settlers
--B--

BLAKENEY, JOHN   ID: 1684
Children: JOHN, WILLIAM.
Date in Pee Dee: 1770   Last Date: 1832 DIED
Origin: IRELAND
Location: LYNCHES (UPPER)
Source(s): GREGG, JVSDP.
Notes: DOB 1732

BLAKENEY, MARY   ID: 4
Spouse: CHARLES EVANS
Date in Pee Dee: 1776
Location: LYNCHES CREEK (UPPER)
Source(s): GREGG.

BLAKENEY, ROBERT   ID: 2042
Date in Pee Dee: 1782
Source(s): GREGG P.405.
Revolutionary War service: PRIVATE IN MARION'S BRIGADE.

BLAKENEY, THOMAS   ID: 2014
Date in Pee Dee: 1782
Source(s): GREGG P.405.
Revolutionary War service: PRIVATE IN MARION'S BRIGADE.

BLAKENEY, WILLIAM   ID: 1686
Children: J.W..
Date in Pee Dee: 1770
Location: LYNCHES (UPPER)
Source(s): GREGG.
Notes: SON OF WILLIAM #1684.
Revolutionary War service: MILITIA

BLAKLEY, JANET   ID: 445
Spouse: [--?--] ARMSTRONG
Children: JOHN, JAMES, ELIZABETH, MARY, JANE.
Date in Pee Dee: 1750   Last Date: 1750 DIED
Location: WILLIAMSBURG
Source(s): MOORE.
Notes: ALSO SPELLED BLEAKLEY.

Early Pee Dee Settlers
--B--

BLAKNEY, JOHN   ID: 107
Date in Pee Dee: 1781
Location: CHERAWS DISTRICT
Source(s): COOK.
Revolutionary War service: MILITIA SC & VA.

BLANSHARD, JOSIAH   ID: 4319
Spouse: MARY [--?--]
Children: ABSOLOM.
Date in Pee Dee: 1773
Location: ST. MARK'S PARISH
Source(s): MOORE V.3.

BLASSINGHAM, THOMAS   ID: 5630
Date in Pee Dee: 1759
Location: ST. DAVID'S PARISH
Source(s): MUSTER ROLL.
Notes: SERVED IN FRENCH AND INDIAN WAR AS PRIVATE IN
CAPTAIN GEORGE HICK'S COMPANY.

BLISS, JOHN   ID: 4252
Spouse: MARY SPRY
Date in Pee Dee: 1737   Last Date: 1771
Location: ST. MARK'S PARISH (WILLIAMSBURG)
Source(s): MOORE V.3, BODDIE.

BLUSET, DANIEL   ID: 4969
Date in Pee Dee: 1737   Last Date: 1759
Location: WILLIAMSBURG
Source(s): BODDIE.
Notes: SERVED IN FRENCH AND INDIAN WAR.

BLYTHE, THOMAS   ID: 109
Date in Pee Dee: 1730   Last Date: 1757
Location: BETWEEN PEE DEE AND WACCAMAW (KINGSTON)
Source(s): COOK, ROGERS, SMITH, H..
Notes: LIEUTENANT IN GEORGETOWN MILITIA.

BOAREE, STEPHEN   ID: 5340

Spouse: ELIZABETH HEADWIT
Date in Pee Dee: 1738
Location: PRINCE FREDERICK PARISH
Source(s): RBPPFW.
Notes: MARRIED 27 FEBRUARY 1738.

BOATWRIGHT, DANIEL   ID: 660
Date in Pee Dee: 1759
Location: ST. DAVID'S PARISH
Source(s): MUSTER ROLL.
Notes: SERVED IN FRENCH AND INDIAN WAR AS LIEUTENANT
WITH MCINTOSH'S COMPANY.

BOISSEAU, MARIAN   ID: 4419
Date in Pee Dee: 1773
Source(s): MOORE V.3.
Notes: NIECE OF THEODORE GOURDINE.

BOND, ABRAHAM   ID: 114
Spouse: ABIGAIL [--?--]
Children: MARY.
Date in Pee Dee: 1730   Last Date: 1741
Location: BLACK RIVER
Source(s): COOK, MOORE V.1, SMITH, H., RBPPFW.

BONNELL, HONORA   ID: 5360
Spouse: JOHN BARTON
Date in Pee Dee: 1741
Location: PRINCE FREDERICK PARISH
Source(s): RBPPFW.

BONNELL, JOHN   ID: 4276
Spouse: HONORA [--?--]
Children: HANNAH, ELIZABETH, ANTHONY, SARAH.
Date in Pee Dee: 1730   Last Date: 1744
Location: PRINCE FREDERICK PARISH
Source(s): RBPPFW.

BONNELL, MARY   ID: 2783

Date in Pee Dee: 1766
Location: PRINCE FREDERICK PARISH
Source(s): ROGERS.
Notes: INSANE, SUPPORTED BY THE CHURCH.

BOODY, JOHN   ID: 5365
Spouse: SARAH EVANS
Date in Pee Dee: 1741
Location: PRINCE FREDERICK PARISH
Source(s): RBPPFW.
Notes: POSSIBLY SAME AS BODDIE. MARRIED 22 NOVEMBER 1741
AT PARISH OF PRINCE FREDERICK WINYAW.

BOONE, CAPERS   ID: 119
Spouse: MARY SMITH
Date in Pee Dee: 1767   Last Date: 1781
Location: PRINCE FREDERICK'S PARISH
Source(s): COOK, CLEMENS.
Notes: MARRIED 16 JULY 1767 AT SANTEE.

BOONE, JOHN   ID: 4304
Spouse: ELIZABETH JORDAN
Date in Pee Dee: 1759   Last Date: 1762
Location: WILLIAMSBURG
Source(s): BODDIE, MUSTER ROLL.
Notes: MARRIED 19 JANUARY 1762 AT SANTEE. SERVED AS
PRIVATE IN LIDE'S COMPANY DURING FRENCH AND INDIAN.

BOONE, THOMAS JR.   ID: 4478
Spouse: HANNAH ATKINSON
Date in Pee Dee: 1774
Location: PRINCE FREDERICK PARISH
Source(s): MOORE V.3, CLEMENS.
Notes: MARRIED 14 SEPTEMBER 1769 AT SANTEE.

BOOTH, CHARLES   ID: 3541
Date in Pee Dee: 1759   Last Date: 1761
Location: PRINCE FREDERICK PARISH (WELCH TRACT)
Source(s): MOORE V.3, MUSTER ROLL.

Notes: SON OF JOHN #3540. SERVED IN FRENCH AND AND
INDIAN WAR AS PRIVATE IN LIDE'S COMPANY.

BOOTH, JOHN   ID: 121
Date in Pee Dee: 1759   Last Date: 1775
Location: CHERAW DISTRICT
Source(s): COOK, MOORE V.3.
Notes: SON OF JOHN #3540 BY ANOTHER WIFE. PRIVATE IN
LIDE'S COMPANY DURING FRENCH AND INDIAN WAR.
Revolutionary War service: WISE'S COMPANY OF INFANTRY.

BOOTH, JOHN   ID: 3540
Spouse: SARAH ROGERS
Children: CHARLES, JOSEPH, BENJAMIN, MARY, SARAH, JOHN
(BY FORMER WIFE).
Date in Pee Dee: 1761   Last Date: 1765 DIED
Location: PRINCE FREDERICK PARISH
Source(s): MOORE V.3, RWNBC.
Notes: ONE OF THE GIRLS MARRIED JOHN GRAHAM.

BOOTH, JOHN   ID: 5222
Spouse: MARGARET [--?--]
Children: ABIGAIL, JOHN.
Date in Pee Dee: 1740
Location: PRINCE FREDERICK PARISH
Source(s): RBPPFW.
Notes: THIS SEEMS TO BE SAME AS #3540 WITH FIRST WIFE.

BOOTH, SARAH   ID: 122
Spouse: [--?--] WILDS
Date in Pee Dee: 1755   Last Date: 1761
Location: WELCH NECK
Source(s): COOK, RWNBC, GREGG, MOORE.
Notes: DAUGHTER OF JOHN #3540.

BORLAND, JOHN   ID: 4037
Date in Pee Dee: 1768   Last Date: 1780
Location: WILLIAMSBURG
Source(s): MOORE V.3, BODDIE.

Revolutionary War service: PRIVATE MARION'S BRIGADE

BORLAND, WILLIAM   ID: 2705
Spouse: MARY [--?--]
Children: WILLIAM, ARCHIBALD, MARY, JEAN, ELIZABETH.
Date in Pee Dee: 1741   Last Date: 1741 DIED
Location: PRINCE GEORGE WINYAW PARISH
Source(s): MOORE, BODDIE.

BOSHER, JOHN   ID: 5394
Spouse: MARY WHITTON
Date in Pee Dee: 1744
Location: PRINCE FREDERICK PARISH
Source(s): RBPPFW.
Notes: MARRIED 22 JULY 1744 AT PARISH OF PRINCE
FREDERICK WINYAW.

BOSSARD, ANN JUDITH   ID: 4241
Spouse: [--?--] CUTTINO
Date in Pee Dee: 1771
Location: PRINCE GEORGE WINYAW PARISH
Source(s): MOORE V.3.
Notes: DAUGHTER OF HENRY #125.

BOSSARD, HENRY   ID: 125
Spouse: CLARY WOLF
Children: HENRY, ELIZABETH, ANN JUDITH (CUTTINO), SARAH
(HENNING).
Date in Pee Dee: 1730   Last Date: 1770 DIED
Location: SAMPIT RIVER
Source(s): COOK, RBPPFW, MOORE V.3.
Notes: LIVING IN PRINCE FREDERICK PARISH AT DEATH.
MARRIED AT PARISH OF PRINCE FREDERICK WINYAW 8 MAY 1760.

BOSSARD, SARAH   ID: 4243
Spouse: [--?--] HENNING
Date in Pee Dee: 1771
Location: PRINCE GEORGE WINYAW PARISH
Source(s): MOORE V.3.

Notes: DAUGHTER OF HENRY #125.

BOTSFORD, EDMUND   ID: 126
Date in Pee Dee: 1779   Last Date: 1784
Location: WELCH NECK
Source(s): COOK, ROGERS, RUDISILL.
Notes: CHAPLIN FOR WILLIANSON'S REGIMENT. CAME AS AN
INDENTURED CARPENTER.

BOUTWELL, BURTONHEAD   ID: 128
Spouse: PATIENCE [--?--]
Children: SAMUEL.
Date in Pee Dee: 1735   Last Date: 1766
Location: BLACK MINGO CREEK
Source(s): COOK, MOORE V.3.
Notes: SECOND WIFE WAS PROBABLY ELIZABETH COMMANDER.

BOWEN, MATTHEW   ID: 5690
Date in Pee Dee: 1759
Location: ST. DAVID'S PARISH
Source(s): MUSTER ROLL.
Notes: SERVED IN FRENCH AND INDIAN WAR AS PRIVATE IN
PLEDGER'S COMPANY.

BOWERS, GILES   ID: 5257
Spouse: MARTHA [--?--]
Children: ARTHUR, JOHN.
Date in Pee Dee: 1743   Last Date: 1745
Location: PRINCE FREDERICK PARISH
Source(s): RBPPFW.

BOWLS, JOHN   ID: 5408
Spouse: SUSANNAH SAUNDERS
Date in Pee Dee: 1745
Location: PRINCE FREDERICK PARISH
Source(s): RBPPFW.
Notes: MARRIED 9 DECEMBER 1745 AT PARISH OF PRINCE
FREDERICK WINYAW.

Early Pee Dee Settlers
--B--

BOWMAN, JOHN   ID: 2653
Spouse: SABRINA (LYNCH) CATTELL
Date in Pee Dee: 1780
Location: GEORGETOWN
Source(s): ROGERS.
Notes: HER SECOND MARRIAGE.

BOWRY, MARTHA   ID: 3640
Spouse: ALEXANDER MCDOWELL
Children: JOHN THOMAS.
Date in Pee Dee: 1765
Location: PRINCE GEORGE WINYAW PARISH
Source(s): MOORE V.3.

BOYAKIN, FRANCIS   ID: 2075
Date in Pee Dee: 1776
Location: ST. DAVID'S PARISH
Source(s): GREGG.
Revolutionary War service: LIEUTENANT IN MARION'S
BRIGADE.

BOYD, JAMES   ID: 131
Spouse: MEHITABEL CLEGG (WIDOW)
Date in Pee Dee: 1737   Last Date: 1742
Location: PRINCE FREDERICK PARISH
Source(s): COOK, RBPPFW, MOORE, BODDIE.
Notes: MARRIED 7 NOVEMBER 1737 AT PARISH OF PRINCE
FREDERICK WINYAW.

BOYD, JOHN   ID: 5490
Spouse: SUSANNAH RICHARDSON
Children: WILLIAM.
Date in Pee Dee: 1770   Last Date: 1780
Location: WILLIAMSBURG
Source(s): BURGESS, COOK, BODDIE.
Revolutionary War service: PRIVATE MARION'S BRIGADE

BOYD, MARTHA (WIDOW)   ID: 5189
Date in Pee Dee: 1780

Location: WILLIAMSBURG
Source(s): BODDIE.
Notes: SUPPLIED MARION.

BOZEMAN, JOHN   ID: 2079
Date in Pee Dee: 1782
Source(s): GREGG P.405.
Revolutionary War service: PRIVATE IN MARION'S BRIGADE.

BOZEMAN, PETER   ID: 2091
Date in Pee Dee: 1781
Location: CHERAWS DISTRICT
Source(s): GREGG.
Revolutionary War service: MILITIA

BRADFORD, JOHN   ID: 4999
Date in Pee Dee: 1780
Location: WILLIAMSBURG
Source(s): BODDIE.
Revolutionary War service: PRIVATE IN MARION'S BRIGADE.

BRADLEY, ELIZABETH (WIDOW)   ID: 5192
Date in Pee Dee: 1780
Location: WILLIAMSBURG
Source(s): BODDIE.
Notes: SUPPLIED MARION.

BRADLEY, JAMES   ID: 134
Date in Pee Dee: 1742   Last Date: 1782
Origin: NORTHERN IRELAND
Location: WILLIAMSBURG
Source(s): COOK, MOORE, BODDIE.
Notes: SON OF JOHN #2968.
Revolutionary War service: PRIVATE MARION'S BRIGADE

BRADLEY, JAMES   ID: 1599
Date in Pee Dee: 1734   Last Date: 1775 DIED
Origin: NORTHERN IRELAND
Location: WILLIAMSBURG

Source(s): WITHERSPOON, MOORE, BODDIE.
Notes: HIS MOTHER JANE MARRIED WILLIAM BURROWS AS A
WIDOW. HIS SISTER MARY MARRIED ROBERT MCCONNELL.

BRADLEY, JOHN   ID: 1243
Date in Pee Dee: 1750   Last Date: 1775 DIED
Location: WILLIAMSBURG
Source(s): MOORE.
Notes: SON OF JOHN #2968. STEP BROTHER OF GEORGE AND
SAMUEL BURROWS.
Notes: SERVED IN FRENCH AND INDIAN WAR.

BRADLEY, JOHN   ID: 2968
Spouse: JEAN [--?--]
Children: JOHN, JAMES, MARY.
Date in Pee Dee: 1750   Last Date: 1750 DIED
Location: WILLIAMSBURG
Source(s): MOORE.
Notes: BROTHER OF SAMUEL BRADLEY, BROTHER-IN-LAW OF
ROBERT WILSON.

BRADLEY, JOSEPH   ID: 2967
Spouse: [--?--] PORTER
Date in Pee Dee: 1750
Location: WILLIAMSBURG
Source(s): MOORE.
Notes: BROTHER-IN-LAW OF JOHN PORTER.

BRADLEY, MARY   ID: 4325
Spouse: ROBERT MCCONNEL
Date in Pee Dee: 1775
Location: PRINCE FREDERICK PARISH
Source(s): MOORE V.3.
Notes: DAUGHTER OF JAMES #2968.

BRADLEY, SAMUEL   ID: 135
Children: JAMES.
Date in Pee Dee: 1742   Last Date: 1761
Location: WILLIAMSBURG (SALEM)

Source(s): COOK, BODDIE, MOORE.
Notes: UNCLE OF JAMES BRADLEY #1599.

BRANFORD, ANN   ID: 2518
Spouse: THOMAS HORRY
Children: ELIAS HORRY (III).
Date in Pee Dee: 1760
Location: PRINCE GEORGE WINYAW PARISH
Source(s): ROGERS.
Notes: DAUGHTER OF WILLIAM BRANFORD.

BRANFORD, ELIZABETH   ID: 575
Spouse: ELIAS HORRY
Children: MARGARET.
Date in Pee Dee: 1750
Location: NORTH SIDE OF SANTEE
Source(s): SMITH, H, CLEMENS.
Notes: DAUGHTER OF WILLIAM BRANFORD OF CHARLESTON AREA.

BRANFORD, WILLIAM   ID: 2849
Spouse: SAVAGE ELIZABETH
Date in Pee Dee: 1749
Location: PRINCE GEORGE WINYAW PARISH
Source(s): MOORE, CLEMENS.
Notes: MARRIED 24 APRIL 1751 AT CHARLESTON.

BRAVEBOY, JOSHUA   ID: 5001
Date in Pee Dee: 1780
Location: WILLIAMSBURG
Source(s): BODDIE.
Revolutionary War service: PRIVATE MARION'S BRIGADE

BRAWLER, JACOB   ID: 3
Date in Pee Dee: 1776
Location: CATFISH CREEK
Source(s): GREGG.
Notes: HE AND 22 SONS DIED IN REVOLUTION.

BRETTEN, HANNAH   ID: 2371

Spouse: [--?--] RAY
Date in Pee Dee: 1729
Location: PRINCE GEORGE WINYAW PARISH
Source(s): MOORE V.1.
Notes: SISTER OF JOHN, FRANCIS, AND TIMOTHY.

BRETTEN, JOHN   ID: 232
Spouse: RACHEL [--?--]
Date in Pee Dee: 1729   Last Date: 1729 DIED
Location: PRINCE GEORGE WINYAW PARISH
Source(s): MOORE V.1.
Notes: BROTHER OF FRANCIS #145 AND TIMOTHY #149.

BRETTEN, MARY   ID: 2385
Spouse: [--?--] BALOUGH
Date in Pee Dee: 1729
Location: PRINCE GEORGE WINYAW PARISH
Source(s): MOORE V.1.
Notes: SISTER OF JOHN, FRANCIS, AND TIMOTHY.

BRETTON, MARTHA   ID: 5330
Spouse: JOHN SINKLER
Date in Pee Dee: 1738
Location: PRINCE FREDERICK PARISH
Source(s): RBPPFW.
Notes: MARRIED 15 MAY 1738 AT PARISH OF PRINCE FREDERICK
WINYAW. MAY BE BRITTON.

BRITT, MARY   ID: 5380
Spouse: GEORGE GREEN
Date in Pee Dee: 1742
Location: PRINCE FREDERICK PARISH
Source(s): RBPPFW.

BRITT, WILLIAM   ID: 1699
Spouse: MARY (POLLY) MCDOWELL
Children: WILLIAM.
Date in Pee Dee: 1770
Location: WELCH NECK

Early Pee Dee Settlers
--B--

Source(s): GREGG, MCCARTY.
Revolutionary War service: MILITIA

BRITTON, DANIEL   ID: 142
Spouse: ELIZABETH HYRNE
Date in Pee Dee: 1735   Last Date: 1748 DIED
Location: BRITTON'S NECK
Source(s): COOK, RBPPFW, BODDIE.
Notes: MARRIED AT PARISH OF PRINCE FREDERICK WINYAW 26
JANUARY 1747.

BRITTON, DANIEL LAINE   ID: 143
Date in Pee Dee: 1776   Last Date: 1780
Location: PRESENT MARION COUNTY
Source(s): COOK, MOORE, GREGG, BODDIE.
Notes: SON OF MOSES #147.
Revolutionary War service: FIRST LIEUTENANT WITH
MARION'S BRIGADE.

BRITTON, ELIZABETH   ID: 144
Spouse: SAMUEL JENKINS
Children: JAMES, JOHN, SAMUEL.
Date in Pee Dee: 1735   Last Date: 1773
Location: BRITTON'S NECK
Source(s): COOK, MOORE V.3.
Notes: POSSIBLY DAUGHTER OF JOSEPH #2853.

BRITTON, FRANCIS   ID: 141
Children: FRANCIS, TIMOTHY, DANIEL, PHILLIP, MOSES, AND
JOSEPH.
Date in Pee Dee: 1729
Location: NORTH SIDE OF SAMPIT RIVER.
Source(s): COOK, SCDAH

BRITTON, FRANCIS   ID: 145
Spouse: ANN [--?--]
Children: MOSES, FRANCIS, HENRY, MARY.
Date in Pee Dee: 1729   Last Date: 1766 DIED
Location: BRITTON'S NECK

Source(s): COOK, BODDIE, MOORE.
Notes: BROTHERS JOSEPH, MOSES, JOHN, TIMOTHY, AND PHILLIP.

BRITTON, HENRY   ID: 2066
Date in Pee Dee: 1766   Last Date: 1775
Location: ST. DAVID'S PARISH
Source(s): GREGG, MOORE V.3.
Notes: SON OF FRANCIS #145.
Revolutionary War service: LIEUTENANT IN MARION'S BRIGADE.

BRITTON, JOSEPH   ID: 2853
Spouse: ANN [--?--]
Children: ELIZABETH, THOMAS, MOSES, JOSEPH, JOHN, MARY, MARTIN, MARTHA, PHILLIP.
Date in Pee Dee: 1749   Last Date: 1773 DIED
Location: PRINCE FREDERICK PARISH
Source(s): MOORE, ODDIE.
Notes: BROTHER OF MOSES, FRANCIS, PHILLIP, AND TIMOTHY.

BRITTON, MOSES   ID: 147
Spouse: HESTER JOLLY
Children: DANIEL LAINE, BENJAMIN, ANN, REBECCA.
Date in Pee Dee: 1735   Last Date: 1773 DIED
Location: BRITTON'S NECK
Source(s): COOK, BODDIE, MOORE, RBPPFW.
Notes: BROTHERS JOSEPH, PHILLIP, JOHN, AND TIMOTHY.
MARRIED 23 APRIL 1741. SECOND MARRIED ANN.

BRITTON, PHILLIP   ID: 148
Spouse: JANE [--?--]
Date in Pee Dee: 1735   Last Date: 1749 DIED
Location: BRITTON'S NECK
Source(s): COOK, BODDIE, MOORE.
Notes: BROTHERS JOSEPH, MOSES, FRANCIS, AND TIMOTHY.
NEPHEW JOHN RAE.

BRITTON, SARAH   ID: 5450

Spouse: MICHAEL MIXAN
Date in Pee Dee: 1747
Location: PRINCE FREDERICK PARISH
Source(s): RBPPFW.

BRITTON, TIMOTHY   ID: 149
Spouse: MARY [--?--]
Date in Pee Dee: 1729   Last Date: 1749 DIED
Location: BRITTON'S NECK
Source(s): COOK, BODDIE, MOORE.
Notes: BROTHERS JOSEPH, MOSES, JOHN, FRANCIS, AND
PHILLIP.

BROCKINGTON, ELIZABETH   ID: 1749
Spouse: HARRIS DEWITT
Date in Pee Dee: 1770
Location: CHERAWS DISTRICT
Notes: DAUGHTER OF RICHARD.

BROCKINGTON, REBECCA   ID: 1491
Spouse: JAMES PAWLEY
Date in Pee Dee: 1765
Location: CHERAWS DISTRICT
Source(s): GREGG.
Notes: DAUGHTER OF RICHARD #1488.

BROCKINGTON, RICHARD   ID: 1489
Spouse: MARY HART
Children: ELIZABETH.
Date in Pee Dee: 1765   Last Date: 1784
Location: CHERAWS DISTRICT
Source(s): GREGG, COOK.
Notes: SON OF RICHARD #1488.

BROCKINGTON, WILLIAM   ID: 1490
Spouse: PENELOPE BENTON
Date in Pee Dee: 1765
Location: CHERAWS DIDTRICT
Source(s): GREGG.

Notes: SON OF RICHARD #1488.

BROCKINTON, ELIZABETH   ID: 1048
Spouse: JAMES HEPBURN
Date in Pee Dee: 1759
Location: WILLIAMSBURG
Source(s): MOORE V.3.
Notes: DAUGHTER OF WILLIAM #4887.

BROCKINTON, HANNAH   ID: 3274
Spouse: JAMES HOOLE
Date in Pee Dee: 1759
Location: WILLIAMSBURG
Source(s): MOORE V.3, BODDIE.
Notes: DAUGHTER OF WILLIAM #4887. MOORE STATES MARRIED
HOOKE.

BROCKINTON, JOHN   ID: 150
Spouse: [--?--] DREW
Date in Pee Dee: 1759   Last Date: 1780
Location: WILLIAMSBURG
Source(s): COOK, MOORE V.3, ROGERS, BODDIE.
Notes: MARRIED DAUGHTER OF NATHANIEL DREW. SON OF
WILLIAM #4887.
Revolutionary War service: TORY CAPTAIN

BROCKINTON, MARY   ID: 3272
Spouse: JOSHUA JOLLY
Date in Pee Dee: 1759
Location: WILLIAMSBURG
Source(s): MOORE V.3, BODDIE.
Notes: DAUGHTER OF WILLIAM #4887.

BROCKINTON, RICHARD   ID: 1488
Children: WILLIAM, RICHARD, REBECCA.
Date in Pee Dee: 1756
Location: CHERAWS DISTRICT
Source(s): GREGG, BODDIE, MOORE V.3.
Notes: SON OF WILLIAM #4887.

BROCKINTON, SARAH JANE　　　　　　　ID: 3273
Spouse: [--?--] LANE
Date in Pee Dee: 1759
Location: WILLIAMSBURG
Source(s): MOORE V.3, BODDIE.
Notes: DAUGHTER OF WILLIAM #4887.

BROCKINTON, WILLIAM　　　　　　　　ID: 4887
Spouse: SARAH [--?--]
Children: WILLIAM, JOHN, RICHARD, ELIZABETH (HEPBURN),
MARY (JOLLY), HANNAH (HOOLE), SARAH JANE.
Date in Pee Dee: 1736　　　Last Date: 1741 DIED
Location: SOUTH SIDE OF BLACK MINGO CREEK
Source(s): BODDIE.

BROCKINTON, WILLIAM JR.　　　　　　ID: 152
Spouse: RACHEL COMMANDER
Children: JOSEPH (?).
Date in Pee Dee: 1722　　　Last Date: 1744 DIED
Location: BLACK RIVER
Source(s): COOK, BODDIE, MOORE.
Notes: SON OF WILLIAM #4887.

BROMLY, ELIZABETH　　　　　　　　ID: 487
Spouse: DR. REES
Date in Pee Dee: 1784
Location: GEORGETOWN
Source(s): CLEMENS.
Notes: MARRIED DECEMBER 1784 AT GEORGETOWN.

BROOKS, RICHARD　　　　　　　　　ID: 2580
Date in Pee Dee: 1775　　　Last Date: 1780
Location: PRINCE GEORGE WINYAW PARISH
Source(s): ROGERS, MOORE V.3.
Notes: PROBABLY A TORY. SIGNED LOYALITY OATH.

BROWN, ABRAHAM　　　　　　　　　ID: 155
Spouse: SARAH [--?--]
Children: ALPHEUS, ZACCHEUS.

Date in Pee Dee: 1761   Last Date: 1775
Location: ST. DAVID'S PARISH
Source(s): COOK, RBPPFW.
Notes: ONE OTHER SON.
Revolutionary War service: LIDE'S COMPANY

BROWN, ALEXANDER   ID: 2620
Spouse: MARY [--?--]
Children: MARY, SARAH.
Date in Pee Dee: 1740   Last Date: 1749
Location: PRINCE FREDERICK PARISH
Source(s): MOORE, RBPPFW, COOK.
Notes: BROTHER OF WILLIAM #167. WIFE DIED 19 MAY 1746.
HE DIED Ca. 1750.

BROWN, ELIZABETH   ID: 5355
Spouse: JAMES MCPHERSON
Date in Pee Dee: 1740
Location: PRINCE FREDERICK PARISH
Source(s): RBPPFW.

BROWN, FRANCES   ID: 5397
Spouse: JAMES JENNER
Date in Pee Dee: 1744
Location: PRINCE FREDERICK PARISH
Source(s): RBPPFW.

BROWN, GEOFRY   ID: 5273
Spouse: RACHEL BURKITT
Children: REBECCA, MESSER, CATHERINE.
Date in Pee Dee: 1745
Location: PRINCE FREDERICK PARISH
Source(s): RBPPFW.
Notes: MARRIED AT PRINCE FREDERICK PARISH ON 20 FEBRUARY
1745 OR 46.

BROWN, GEORGE   ID: 158
Spouse: MARY [--?--]

Children: FRANCIS, WILLIAM, GEORGE, MARGARET, JUDITH, SARAH, MARY ANN (REMBERT).
Date in Pee Dee: 1730   Last Date: 1756 DIED
Location: WHITTEE CREEK
Source(s): COOK, MOORE.
Notes: WIFE BELIEVED TO BE MARY HARRIS #3308.

BROWN, GEORGE   ID: 3067
Spouse: ANN LIEBERT
Date in Pee Dee: 1756   Last Date: 1797
Location: IRISHTOWN
Source(s): MOORE, CLEMENS.
Notes: SON OF GEORGE #158. MARRIED 5 AUGUST 1797 AT
CHARLESTON.

BROWN, JAMES   ID: 2303
Date in Pee Dee: 1780
Location: WILLIAMSBURG
Source(s): GREGG, BODDIE.
Revolutionary War service: PRIVATE MARION'S BRIGADE.

BROWN, JAMES   ID: 2747
Spouse: HANNAH [--?--]
Children: HANNAH.
Date in Pee Dee: 1726   Last Date: 1729 DIED
Location: GEORGETOWN
Source(s): ROGERS, RBPPFW, COOK.
Notes: HE DIED 30 AUGUST 1729. HIS WIDOW MARRIED WILLIAM
SWINTON.

BROWN, JOHN   ID: 162
Spouse: SARAH [--?--]
Date in Pee Dee: 1750   Last Date: 1759
Location: WELCH NECK
Source(s): COOK, GREGG.
Notes: BORN IN NEW JERSEY. PASTOR OF WELCH NECK BAPTIST
CHURCH 1753.

BROWN, JOHN   ID: 1852

Date in Pee Dee: 1768   Last Date: 1780
Location: ST. DAVID'S PARISH
Source(s): GREGG, COOK, BODDIE.
Revolutionary War service: PRIVATE MARION'S BRIGADE.

BROWN, JONATHAN   ID: 814
Spouse: MARGARET [--?--]
Children: JONATHAN.
Date in Pee Dee: 1729   Last Date: 1731
Location: PRINCE FREDERICK PARISH
Source(s): RBPPFW.
Notes: BUILT TWO CHIMNEYS, PLASTERED AND WHITE WASHED
PARISH OF PRINCE FREDERICK WINYAW CHURCH FOR 23 PDS
MONEY, 200 POUNDS OF MEAT, AND 1 GALLON OF RUM.

BROWN, JONATHAN   ID: 5275
Spouse: MARY SHAW
Date in Pee Dee: 1731   Last Date: 1747
Location: PRINCE FREDERICK PARISH
Source(s): RBPPFW.
Notes: MARRIED AT PRINCE FREDERICK PARISH ON 7 SEPTEMBER
1747. SON OF JONATHAN #814.

BROWN, MARY ANN   ID: 3071
Spouse: [--?--] REMBERT
Date in Pee Dee: 1756
Location: IRISHTOWN
Source(s): MOORE.
Notes: DAUGHTER OF GEORGE #158.

BROWN, MORGAN   ID: 164
Date in Pee Dee: 1780   Last Date: 1785
Location: CHERAWS DISTRICT
Source(s): COOK, GREGG.
Revolutionary War service: MILITIA

BROWN, MOSES   ID: 5276
Date in Pee Dee: 1768   Last Date: 1772

Location: PRINCE FREDERICK PARISH
Source(s): RBPPFW.
Notes: OVERSEER PRINCE FREDERICK PARISH. GRANT MIDWAY
PRESENT LAKE CITY AND JOHNSONVILLE.

BROWN, REBECCA   ID: 5376
Spouse: THOMAS MOONEYS
Date in Pee Dee: 1742
Location: PRINCE FREDERICK PARISH
Source(s): RBPPFW.

BROWN, ROBERT   ID: 165
Spouse: JUDITH HULL
Date in Pee Dee: 1732   Last Date: 1741
Location: NORTH SIDE OF SANTEE RIVER
Source(s): COOK, ROGERS.

BROWN, SAMUEL   ID: 5272
Spouse: SARAH [--?--]
Children: JAMES.
Date in Pee Dee: 1746
Location: PRINCE FREDERICK PARISH
Source(s): RBPPFW.

BROWN, STEPHEN   ID: 5522
Date in Pee Dee: 1770
Location: ST. DAVID'S PARISH
Source(s): JVSDP.
Notes: APPEARS TO HAVE DIED AND HIS 3 CHILDREN WERE TO
JOHN HUSBAND.

BROWN, THOMAS   ID: 166
Children: THOMAS.
Date in Pee Dee: 1730
Location: BETWEEN PEE DEE AND WACCAMAW (KINGSTON)
Source(s): COOK, BODDIE, REMBERT.
Notes: HIS SON APPEARS TO BE IN THE WELCH NECK IN 1748.
MAY HAVE MARRIED ELIZABETH DUBOSE.

Early Pee Dee Settlers
--B--

BROWN, WILLIAM   ID: 167
Spouse: HESTER [--?--]
Children: JEAN, HESTER, HANNAH, JANE.
Date in Pee Dee: 1736   Last Date: 1749 DIED
Location: PRINCE FREDERICK PARISH
Source(s): COOK, RBPPFW, MOORE, BODDIE.

BRUCE, ANN   ID: 5359
Spouse: JOHN MYERS
Date in Pee Dee: 1741
Location: PRINCE FREDERICK PARISH
Source(s): RBPPFW.
Notes: MARRIED 15 MAY 1741 AT PARISH OF PRINCE FREDERICK
WINYAW.

BRUCE, GEORGE   ID: 1721
Spouse: ELIZABETH BENTON
Date in Pee Dee: 1746   Last Date: 1770
Location: CHERAW DISTRICT
Source(s): GREGG, MOORE.

BRUNSON, DANIEL   ID: 3669
Spouse: SARAH MELLET
Date in Pee Dee: 1763   Last Date: 1770
Location: WILLIAMSBURG
Source(s): MOORE V.3.
Notes: SON OF ISAAC SR. #2770.

BRUNSON, ELIZABETH   ID: 3805
Date in Pee Dee: 1755
Location: WILLIAMSBURG
Source(s): MOORE V.3.
Notes: GRAND CHILD OF SARAH COOPER #3505.

BRUNSON, ISAAC   ID: 2770
Spouse: MARY [--?--]
Children: DANIEL, DAVID, JOSIAH, MATTHEW, MOSES,
SUSANNA, MARY (MELLET).
Date in Pee Dee: 1737   Last Date: 1770 DIED

Location: PRINCE FREDERICK PARISH (LOWER BLK R.)
Source(s): ROGERS, BODDIE, MOORE V.3.
Notes: CAPTAIN BLACK RIVER CHURCH COMPANY. LIVING IN ST.
MARK'S PARISH AT DEATH.

BRUNSON, JAMES SR.   ID: 4188
Date in Pee Dee: 1770   Last Date: 1780
Location: WILLIAMSBURG
Source(s): MOORE V.3, BODDIE.
Revolutionary War service: PRIVATE MARION'S BRIGADE

BRUNSON, JOHN   ID: 5477
Spouse: ANNE [--?--]
Date in Pee Dee: 1730
Location: PRINCE FREDERICK PARISH
Source(s): RBPPFW.
Notes: ANNE DIED IN 1730.

BRUNSON, MARY   ID: 2607
Spouse: PETER MELLET
Date in Pee Dee: 1742   Last Date: 1770
Location: PRINCE FREDERICK PARISH
Source(s): MOORE.
Notes: DAUGHTER OF ISAAC SR. #2770.

BRUNSON, WILLIAM   ID: 5002
Date in Pee Dee: 1780
Location: WILLIAMSBURG
Source(s): BODDIE.
Revolutionary War service: PRIVATE MARION'S BRIGADE

BRUNSTON, ABIGAIL   ID: 5415
Spouse: STEPHEN PEAK
Date in Pee Dee: 1746
Location: PRINCE FREDERICK PARISH
Source(s): RBPPFW.

BRUNSTON, JOHN   ID: 175
Spouse: SUSANNA ROBINSON (WID)

Date in Pee Dee: 1730   Last Date: 1743
Location: SANTEE RIVER NORTH SIDE
Source(s): COOK, RBPPFW.
Notes: THIS IS PROBABLY BRUNSON. FIRST WIFE ANNE DIED IN 1730. MARRIED SUSANNA 13 AUGUST 1743.

BRUNSTONE, JOHN JR.   ID: 5308
Spouse: MARY [--?--]
Children: BENJAMIN.
Date in Pee Dee: 1747
Location: PRINCE FREDERICK PARISH
Source(s): RBPPFW.

BRYAN, JOHN   ID: 5437
Spouse: SARAH ATNOR
Date in Pee Dee: 1747
Location: PRINCE FREDERICK PARISH
Source(s): RBPPFW.
Notes: MARRIED 26 OCTOBER 1747 AT PARISH OF PRINCE FREDERICK WINYAW.

BRYAN, JOHN   ID: 5447
Spouse: SARAH MARGARETA FINLAY
Date in Pee Dee: 1747
Location: PRINCE FREDERICK PARISH
Source(s): RBPPFW.
Notes: MARRIED AT PARISH OF PRINCE FREDERICK WINYAW 9 APRIL 1747.

BRYAN, RICHARD   ID: 5665
Date in Pee Dee: 1759
Location: ST. DAVID'S PARISH
Source(s): MUSTER ROLL.
Notes: SERVED IN FRENCH AND INDIAN WAR AS PRIVATE WITH MCINTOSH'S COMPANY.

BRYANT, GRAY   ID: 2073
Date in Pee Dee: 1781
Source(s): GREGG P.405.

Revolutionary War service: PRIVATE IN BENTON'S REGIMENT.

BRYANT, HARDY   ID: 1977
Date in Pee Dee: 1781
Source(s): GREGG P.405.
Revolutionary War service: PRIVATE IN BENTON'S REGIMENT.

BRYANT, JESSE   ID: 2483
Spouse: [--?--] TURBEVILLE
Children: WILLIAM, STEPHEN, JESSE.
Date in Pee Dee: 1735
Origin: ENGLAND
Location: SANDY BLUFF
Source(s): SELLERS.
Notes: WIFE WAS SISTER OF WILLIAM TURBEVILLE.

BRYANT, WILLIAM   ID: 2484
Spouse: REBECCA MILLER
Children: JOHN, ELI, SOLOMON, DAVID, PINCKNEY, HUGH.
Date in Pee Dee: 1750
Origin: ENGLAND
Location: SANDY BLUFF
Source(s): SELLERS.

BUCHANAN, MARY ANNE   ID: 3054
Spouse: [--?--] WITHERS
Date in Pee Dee: 1756
Location: NORTH SIDE OF SANTEE RIVER
Source(s): MOORE.
Notes: DAUGHTER OF WILLIAM #2757.

BUCKELLS, MARY   ID: 5424
Spouse: JOHN DEXTER
Date in Pee Dee: 1747
Location: PRINCE FREDERICK PARISH
Source(s): RBPPFW.

BUCKHOLDT, ABRAHAM   ID: 1419
Date in Pee Dee: 1740

Origin: PRUSSIA
Location: WELCH TRACT
Source(s): GREGG, THOMAS.
Notes: BROTHER OF PETER AND JACOB. LEFT AREA EARLY.
JUSTICE OF PEACE IN 1756.

BUCKHOLDT, JACOB   ID: 177
Date in Pee Dee: 1740   Last Date: 1759
Origin: PRUSSIA
Location: CHERAW DISTRICT (PIDGEON CREEK (BUCKHOLDT'S))
Source(s): COOK, GREGG.
Notes: BROTHER OF ABRAHAM AND PETER. ALL LEFT PEE DEE
EARLY. SERVED IN FRENCH AND INDIAN WAR.

BUCKHOLDT, PETER   ID: 1418
Date in Pee Dee: 1740
Origin: PRUSSIA
Location: WELCH TRACT
Source(s): GREGG.
Notes: BROTHER OF ABRAHAM AND JACOB. LEFT AREA.

BUCKHOLTS, ELIZABETH   ID: 5315
Spouse: JONATHAN CRATCHLEY
Date in Pee Dee: 1736
Location: PRINCE FREDERICK PARISH
Source(s): RBPPFW.
Notes: MARRIED 2 AUGUST 1737 AT PARISH OF PRINCE
FREDERICK WINYAW.

BUCKHOLTS, HENRY   ID: 5596
Date in Pee Dee: 1759
Location: ST. DAVID'S PARISH
Source(s): MUSTER ROLL.
Notes: SERVED IN FRENCH AND INDIAN WAR AS CLERK IN
CAPTAIN JAMES THOMSON'S COMPANY.

BUFORD, WILLIAM   ID: 4421
Date in Pee Dee: 1773
Location: PRINCE FREDERICK PARISH

Source(s): MOORE V.3, BODDIE.
Revolutionary War service: MAJOR IN MARION'S BRIGADE.

BULLANE, ELIZABETH   ID: 3057
Spouse: [--?--] BROWN
Date in Pee Dee: 1750   Last Date: 1750 DIED
Location: PRINCE GEORGE WINYAW PARISH
Source(s): MOORE.
Notes: SISTER OF MICHAEL, WILLIAM, SOONANER, AND MARY
BULLANE.

BULLANE, MARY   ID: 3059
Date in Pee Dee: 1750
Location: PRINCE GEORGE WINYAW PARISH
Source(s): MOORE.
Notes: SISTER OF MICHAEL, WILLIAM, ELIZABETH, AND
SOONANER BULLANE.

BULLANE, MICHAEL   ID: 3060
Date in Pee Dee: 1750
Location: PRINCE GEORGE WINYAW PARISH
Source(s): MOORE.
Notes: BROTHER OF MARY, WILLIAM, ELIZABETH AND SOONANER
BULLANE.

BULLANE, SOONANER   ID: 3058
Date in Pee Dee: 1750
Location: PRINCE GEORGE WINYAW PARISH
Source(s): MOORE.
Notes: SISTER OF MICHAEL, WILLIAM, ELIZABETH, AND MARY
BULLANE.

BULLANE, WILLIAM   ID: 3061
Date in Pee Dee: 1750
Location: PRINCE GEORGE WINYAW PARISH
Source(s): MOORE.
Notes: BROTHER OF MARY, MICHAEL, ELIZABETH AND SOONANER
BULLANE.

Early Pee Dee Settlers
--B--

BURCH, EDWARD   ID: 1709
Spouse: MARY WILSON
Date in Pee Dee: 1770
Location: WELCH NECK
Source(s): GREGG.

BURDELL, JOHN   ID: 5398
Spouse: MARY LIEUBRAY
Date in Pee Dee: 1744
Location: PRINCE FREDERICK PARISH
Source(s): RBPPFW.
Notes: MARRIED 23 AUGUST 1744 AT PARISH OF PRINCE
FREDERICK WINYAW.

BURDELL, THOMAS   ID: 5270
Spouse: MARY [--?--]
Children: SARAH, THOMAS.
Date in Pee Dee: 1744   Last Date: 1747
Location: PRINCE FREDERICK PARISH
Source(s): RBPPFW.

BURDELL, THOMAS JR.   ID: 3891
Spouse: MARGARET WRIGHT
Date in Pee Dee: 1742   Last Date: 1766
Location: PRINCE FREDRICK PARISH
Source(s): MOORE V.3, RBPPFW.
Notes: MARRIED 16 JANUARY 1742 AT PARISH OF PRINCE
FREDERICK WINYAW.

BURGESS, JOSEPH   ID: 5003
Date in Pee Dee: 1780
Location: WILLIAMSBURG
Source(s): BODDIE.
Revolutionary War service: PRIVATE MARION'S BRIGADE.

BURGESS, WILLIAM   ID: 5004
Date in Pee Dee: 1775   Last Date: 1780
Location: WILLIAMSBURG
Source(s): BODDIE.

Revolutionary War service: PRIVATE MARION'S BRIGADE.

BURKETT, MARY   ID: 5464
Spouse: JOHN COPE
Date in Pee Dee: 1748
Location: PRINCE FREDERICK PARISH
Source(s): RBPPFW.

BURKETT, RACHEL   ID: 5411
Spouse: GODFREY BROWN
Date in Pee Dee: 1746
Location: PRINCE FREDERICK PARISH
Source(s): RBPPFW.

BURKITT, SAMUEL   ID: 1889
Date in Pee Dee: 1781
Source(s): GREGG P.405.
Notes: ALSO SPELLED BURQUETT.
Revolutionary War service: PRIVATE IN BENTON'S REGIMENT.

BURNET, EDWARD   ID: 3277
Spouse: MARGERY [--?--]
Date in Pee Dee: 1734   Last Date: 1734 DIED
Location: PRINCE GEORGE WINYAW PARISH
Source(s): MOORE V.1.

BURNHAM, THOMAS   ID: 2663
Date in Pee Dee: 1780
Location: PRINCE GEORGE WINYAW PARISH
Source(s): ROGERS.
Notes: HE WAS PROBABLY A TORY SINCE HE SIGNED LOYALITY
OATH.

BURNS, JOHN   ID: 182
Children: JOHN, WILLIAM.
Date in Pee Dee: 1760   Last Date: 1780
Location: PRINCE GEORGE WINYAW PARISH
Source(s): COOK, BODDIE, MOORE V.3.
Revolutionary War service: PRIVATE MARION'S BRIGADE.

BURNS, JOHN   ID: 3536
Children: SARAH, HANNAH.
Date in Pee Dee: 1760   Last Date: 1774 DIED
Location: SANTEE RIVER
Source(s): MOORE V.3.
Notes: SON OF JOHN #182.

BURQUETT, EPHRIAM   ID: 183
Date in Pee Dee: 1782
Source(s): COOK.
Notes: MAY BE BURKET
Revolutionary War service: 75 DAYS IN MILITIA.

BURROWS, GEORGE   ID: 4323
Date in Pee Dee: 1737   Last Date: 1775
Location: PRINCE FREDERICK PARISH
Source(s): MOORE V.3, BODDIE.
Notes: BROTHER OF SAMUEL.

BURROWS, SAMUEL   ID: 4324
Date in Pee Dee: 1775
Location: PRINCE FREDERICK PARISH
Source(s): MOORE V.3.
Notes: BROTHER OF GEORGE.

BURROWS, WILLIAM   ID: 5005
Date in Pee Dee: 1780
Location: WILLIAMSBURG
Source(s): BODDIE.
Revolutionary War service: PRIVATE MARION'S BRIGADE.

BURTIN, SARAH   ID: 3077
Spouse: THOMAS POTTS
Date in Pee Dee: 1756
Location: CRAVEN COUNTY
Source(s): MOORE.
Notes: DAUGHTER OF THOMAS #3075.

BURTIN, THOMAS   ID: 3075

Children: THOMAS, SARAH.
Date in Pee Dee: 1756
Location: BRITTON'S NECK
Source(s): MOORE, COOK.

BURTLEY, RICHARD   ID: 5207
Spouse: SARAH [--?--]
Children: SARAH, MARGARET.
Date in Pee Dee: 1737
Location: PRINCE FREDERICK PARISH
Source(s): RBPPFW.

BUTLER, CHRISTOPHER   ID: 102
Spouse: ABIGAIL [--?--]
Children: CHRISTOPHER.
Date in Pee Dee: 1723
Location: PRINCE FREDERICK PARISH
Source(s): RBPPFW.

BUTLER, DANIEL   ID: 4965
Date in Pee Dee: 1740   Last Date: 1759
Location: WILLIAMSBURG
Source(s): BODDIE.
Notes: SERVED IN THE FRENCH AND INDIAN WAR.

BUTLER, EDWARD   ID: 161
Spouse: MARY SKIPPER
Children: BARTHOLOMEW.
Date in Pee Dee: 1724
Location: PRINCE FREDERICK PARISH
Source(s): RBPPFW.
Notes: MARRIED 13 APRIL 1742 AT PARISH OF PRINCE
FREDERICK WINYAW.

BUTLER, JAMES   ID: 4813
Date in Pee Dee: 1776   Last Date: 1776 DIED
Location: ST. DAVID'S PARISH
Source(s): MOORE V.3.

Notes: **MENTIONS BROTHERS SON JAMES AND SISTER SARAH WIFE OF ISAAC HAIGGS.**

BUTLER, JOHN   ID: 2078
Date in Pee Dee: 1781
Location: KINGSTON
Source(s): GREGG P.405, MOORE.
Revolutionary War service: CAPTAIN IN BENTON'S REGIMENT.

BYERS, MARY   ID: 4798
Spouse: JOHN ALLISON
Date in Pee Dee: 1776
Source(s): MOORE V.3.
Notes: DAUGHTER OF ROBERT $4797.

BYERS, ROBERT   ID: 4797
Spouse: ELIZABETH (BARLOW)
Children: ROBERT, MARGARET, MARY (ALLISON).
Date in Pee Dee: 1776   Last Date: 1776 DIED
Location: NELSON'S FERRY ON SANTEE RIVER
Source(s): MOORE V.3.
Notes: BROTHER OF WILLIAM.

CAHUSAC, JOHN   ID: 3393
Spouse: ANN [--?--]
Children: DANIEL, THOMAS, SUSANNAH, ELIZABETH, SARAH,
ANN, MARY.
Date in Pee Dee: 1761   Last Date: 1761 DIED
Source(s): MOORE V.3.

CAHUSAC, ROBERT   ID: 3813
Spouse: ELIZABETH GREENLAND
Date in Pee Dee: 1755   Last Date: 1777
Location: WILLIAMSBURG
Source(s): MOORE V.3.

CAIN, JOHN   ID: 2904
Spouse: ANN POWER
Children: JOHN, SARAH, HANNAH.
Date in Pee Dee: 1738   Last Date: 1747
Location: PRINCE FREDERICK PARISH
Source(s): MOORE, RBPPFW.
Notes: MARRIED 15 APRIL 1737 AT PARISH OF PRINCE
FREDERICK WINYAW.

CAISEE, PEIRRE   ID: 4944
Date in Pee Dee: 1756
Origin: NOVA SCOTIA
Location: WILLIAMSBURG
Source(s): BODDIE.
Notes: HE, WIFE AND CHILDREN WERE ACADIANS TRANSPORTED
FROM NOVA SCOTIA.

CALHOUN, JAMES   ID: 4472
Spouse: MARTHA HULL
Date in Pee Dee: 1773
Location: PRINCE GEORGE WINYAH PARISH
Source(s): MOORE V.3.
Notes: MAY HAVE ALSO BEEN MARRIED TO MARTHA MONK.

CAMPBELL, ALEXANDER   ID: 188
Spouse: PRISCILLA [--?--]
Date in Pee Dee: 1730
Location: BETWEEN PEE DEE AND WACCAMAW
Source(s): COOK, BODDIE.

CAMPBELL, DAVID   ID: 5006
Date in Pee Dee: 1780
Location: WILLIAMSBURG
Source(s): BODDIE.
Revolutionary War service: PRIVATE IN MARION'S BRIGADE.

CAMPBELL, DUNCAN   ID: 5007
Date in Pee Dee: 1780
Location: WILLIAMSBURG
Source(s): BODDIE.
Revolutionary War service: PRIVATE IN MARION'S BRIGADE.

CAMPBELL, GEORGE   ID: 5008
Date in Pee Dee: 1780
Location: WILLIAMSBURG
Source(s): BODDIE.
Revolutionary War service: PRIVATE IN MARION'S BRIGADE.

CAMPBELL, JAMES   ID: 2497
Spouse: JUDITH DWYER
Children: JOHN, THEOPHILUS, JAMES JR, JERE, GADI, NANCY
ANN, MARY.
Date in Pee Dee: 1745   Last Date: 1760
Origin: VIRGINIA
Location: PRESENT MARION COUNTY

Source(s): SELLERS, BODDIE, MOORE.
Notes: MARRIED AT PARISH OF PRINCE FREDERICK WINYAW 3 SEPTEMBER 1749.

CAMPBELL, JAMES JR   ID: 2498
Spouse: MARY (MOLSEY) BARNES
Children: EBBY, JAMES.
Date in Pee Dee: 1770   Last Date: 1780
Location: PRESENT MARION COUNTY
Source(s): SELLERS, GREGG, BODDIE.
Notes: SON OF JAMES #2497.
Revolutionary War service: PRIVATE IN MARION'S BRIGADE.

CAMPBELL, JOHN   ID: 2499
Date in Pee Dee: 1770
Location: MARION COUNTY
Source(s): SELLERS, BODDIE.
Revolutionary War service: PRIVATE IN MARION'S BRIGADE.

CAMPBELL, THOMAS   ID: 5009
Date in Pee Dee: 1780
Location: WILLIAMSBURG
Source(s): BODDIE.
Revolutionary War service: PRIVATE IN MARION'S BRIGADE.

CAMPBELL, WILLIAM   ID: 5010
Date in Pee Dee: 1780
Location: WILLIAMSBURG
Source(s): BODDIE.
Revolutionary War service: PRIVATE IN MARION'S BRIGADE.

CANNON, AGNES   ID: 3385
Spouse: GEORGE SMITH
Date in Pee Dee: 1762
Source(s): MOORE V.3.
Notes: DAUGHTER OF JOHN #3378.

CANNON, JOHN   ID: 3378

Children: SAMUEL, EPHRAIM, JAMES, MARGATE, REBECCA, AGNES (SMITH), MARY (PENNINGTON).
Date in Pee Dee: 1762   Last Date: 1763 DIED
Location: MEADOW BRANCH
Source(s): MOORE V.3.

CANNON, MARY   ID: 3384
Spouse: JACOB PENNINGTON
Date in Pee Dee: 1762
Source(s): MOORE V.3.
Notes: DAUGHTER OF JOHN #3378.

CANTEY, CHARLES   ID: 3401
Date in Pee Dee: 1758   Last Date: 1780
Location: WILLIAMSBURG
Source(s): MOORE V.3, BODDIE.
Notes: SUPPLIED MARION.

CANTEY, CORNFORT   ID: 4345
Spouse: [--?--] GREEN
Date in Pee Dee: 1773
Location: ST. MARK'S PARISH
Source(s): MOORE V.3.
Notes: DAUGHTER OF JOSIAH #4343.

CANTEY, ELIZABETH   ID: 4347
Spouse: [--?--] BRUNSON
Date in Pee Dee: 1773
Location: ST. MARK'S PARISH
Source(s): MOORE V.3.
Notes: DAUGHTER OF JOSIAH #4343.

CANTEY, JOHN   ID: 5017
Date in Pee Dee: 1780
Location: WILLIAMSBURG
Source(s): BODDIE.
Revolutionary War service: PRIVATE IN MARION'S BRIGADE.

CANTEY, JOSEPH   ID: 192

Children: SAMUEL.
Date in Pee Dee: 1730　　Last Date: 1740
Location: MT. HOPE NEAR WILLIAMSBURG LINE AND SANTEE R.
Source(s): COOK, BURGESS, ROGERS.

CANTEY, JOSEPH　　　　　　　　　　　　　　ID: 4343
Spouse: MARY [--?--]
Children: WILLIAM, CORNFORT (BRUNSON), MARTHA
(RICHBURG), SUSANNA (DENNIS), ELIZABETH (BRUNSON),
REBECCA (GALE).
Date in Pee Dee: 1735 DOB Last Date: 1773 DIED
Location: ST. MARK'S PARISH
Source(s): MOORE V.3, RBPPFW, BURGESS.
Notes: APPEARS AS JOSIAH IN MOORE. SON OF SAMUEL #2771.

CANTEY, MARTHA　　　　　　　　　　　　　　ID: 4348
Spouse: [--?--] RICHBURG
Date in Pee Dee: 1742 DOB Last Date: 1773
Location: ST. MARK'S PARISH
Source(s): MOORE V.3, RBPPFW.
Notes: DAUGHTER OF JOSEPH #4343.

CANTEY, MARY　　　　　　　　　　　　　　　ID: 2762
Spouse: RICHARD RICHARDSON
Date in Pee Dee: 1740
Location: PRINCE FREDERICK PARISH
Source(s): ROGERS.

CANTEY, REBECCA　　　　　　　　　　　　　ID: 4349
Spouse: [--?--] GALE
Date in Pee Dee: 1773
Location: ST. MARK'S PARISH
Source(s): MOORE V.3.
Notes: DAUGHTER OF JOSIAH #4343.

CANTEY, SAMUEL　　　　　　　　　　　　　　ID: 2771
Spouse: ANN [--?--]

Children: WILLIAM, JOSEPH, JANE (BY ANN). BY MARTHA BROWN, JOSEPH AND CHRISTIANA. SON SAMUEL JOHN BY AN EARLIER WIFE.
Date in Pee Dee: 1731   Last Date: 1776 DIED
Location: PRINCE FREDERICK PARISH (LATER ST. MARK'S)
Source(s): ROGERS, RBPPFW, MOORE.
Notes: ENSIGN BLACK RIVER HEAD COMPANY MILITIA. ANOTHER WIFE WAS MARTHA BROWN. THOMAS AND MARY SUMTER WERE NEPHEW AND NIECE.

CANTEY, SUSANNA   ID: 4346
Spouse: [--?--] DENNIS
Date in Pee Dee: 1773
Location: ST. MARK'S PARISH
Source(s): MOORE V.3.
Notes: DAUGHTER OF JOSIAH #4343.

CANTLEY, CHARLES   ID: 5018
Date in Pee Dee: 1775   Last Date: 1780
Location: WILLIAMSBURG
Source(s): BODDIE.
Revolutionary War service: PRIVATE IN MARION'S BRIGADE.

CANTY, CHRISTIANA   ID: 5493
Spouse: FRANCIS LESESNE
Children: MARY ANN.
Date in Pee Dee: 1760
Location: ST. MARK'S PARISH
Source(s): BURGESS.
Notes: DAUGHTER OF SAMUEL

CANTY, ELIZABETH   ID: 5332
Spouse: ANTHONY WILLIAMS
Date in Pee Dee: 1738
Location: PRINCE FREDERICK PARISH
Source(s): RBPPFW.
Notes: MARRIED 24 JULY 1738 AT PARISH OF PRINCE FREDERICK WINYAW.

CAREY, MICHAEL   ID: 2781
Date in Pee Dee: 1757   Last Date: 1579
Location: PRINCE FREDERICK PARISH
Source(s): ROGERS.
Notes: BLIND, SUPPORTED BY THE CHURCH.

CARGILL, MAGNUS   ID: 4588
Spouse: SARAH [--?--]
Date in Pee Dee: 1768   Last Date: 1778
Location: ST. DAVID'S PARISH
Source(s): RWNBC, JVSDP.

CARR, HESTER   ID: 4848
Spouse: JOSEPH TAMPLET
Children: STEPHEN, CHARLES.
Date in Pee Dee: 1778
Location: PRINCE FREDERICK PARISH
Source(s): MOORE V.3.
Notes: DAUGHTER OF ISAAC #193.

CARR, ISAAC   ID: 193
Children: STEPHEN, CHARLES, EDMOND, HESTER (TAMPLET),
ABIGAIL.
Date in Pee Dee: 1773   Last Date: 1778
Location: PRINCE FREDERICK PARISH
Source(s): COOK, MOORE V.3.

CARTER, JOHN   ID: 1354
Spouse: MARTHA SARTEN
Children: HESTER.
Date in Pee Dee: 1741   Last Date: 1743
Location: QUEENSBOROUGH TOWNSHIP
Source(s): GREGG, RBPPFW.
Notes: MARRIED 26 MARCH 1742 AT PARISH OF PRINCE
FREDERICK WINYAW.

CARTLIDGE, EDMUND   ID: 5300
Spouse: ELIZABETH KEBLE
Children: JOHN, EDMUND.

Date in Pee Dee: 1743   Last Date: 1747
Location: PRINCE FREDERICK PARISH
Source(s): RBPPFW.
Notes: MARRIED 9 DECEMBER 1743 AT PARISH OF PRINCE
FREDERICK WINYAW.

CASSELS, JAMES   ID: 714
Date in Pee Dee: 1758   Last Date: 1782
Origin: SCOTLAND
Location: WACCAMAW RIVER
Source(s): LAMBERT.
Notes: LEFT FOR EAST FLORIDA AFTER WAR.
Revolutionary War service: TORY COLONEL.

CASSELS, LYDIA   ID: 1632
Spouse: ELIAS DUBOSE
Children: JESSE, ISIAH, JOHN.
Date in Pee Dee: 1760
Location: LYNCHES CREEK
Source(s): GREGG.

CASSITY, ZACHARIAH   ID: 2017
Date in Pee Dee: 1782
Source(s): GREGG P.405.
Revolutionary War service: PRIVATE IN BENTON'S REGIMENT.

CATHRIDGE, EDMUND   ID: 5280
Spouse: ELIZABETH [--?--]
Children: JOHN.
Date in Pee Dee: 1744
Location: PRINCE FREDERICK PARISH
Source(s): RBPPFW.

CATTELL, JOHN   ID: 199
Spouse: SARAH HALL
Date in Pee Dee: 1728   Last Date: 1740
Location: CHERAW DISTRICT
Source(s): COOK, CLEMENS.
Notes: MARRIED AT BERKLEY 24 APRIL 1728.

CATTELL, WILLIAM   ID: 2562
Spouse: SABRINA LYNCH
Date in Pee Dee: 1770
Location: PRINCE GEORGE WINYAW PARISH
Source(s): ROGERS, CLEMENS.
Notes: MARRIED 8 MARCH 1767 AT CHARLESTON.

CHAMBERS, EDWARD   ID: 5241
Children: ELIZABETH (ALIAS MINEALLY).
Date in Pee Dee: 1742
Location: PRINCE FREDERICK PARISH
Source(s): RBPPFW.
Notes: ELIZABETH WAS NATURAL DAUGHTER OF MARY MINEALLY.

CHANDLER, GEORGE   ID: 3913
Date in Pee Dee: 1767   Last Date: 1780
Location: WILLIAMSBURG
Source(s): MOORE V.3, BODDIE.
Revolutionary War service: PRIVATE IN MARION'S BRIGADE.

CHANDLER, ISAAC   ID: 204
Spouse: SALLEY WHITE
Date in Pee Dee: 1740   Last Date: 1780
Location: CHERAW DISTRICT (PIDGEON CREEK (BUCKHOLDT'S))
Source(s): COOK, BODDIE, MOORE.
Notes: COOK SPELLS CHANLER. SON OF ISAAC #4894. MARRIED
9 APRIL 1771 AT CHARLESTON.
Revolutionary War service: PRIVATE IN MARION'S BRIGADE.

CHANDLER, ISAAC   ID: 4894
Spouse: ELIZABETH [--?--]
Children: SAMUEL, ISAAC, ANN.
Date in Pee Dee: 1710   Last Date: 1748 DIED
Occupation: MINISTER   Origin: KITTERY, MAINE
Location: PRINCE FREDERICK PARISH
Source(s): BODDIE.
Notes: CAME WITH AND TRAINED UNDER WILLIAM SCREVEN.

CHANDLER, JAMES   ID: 203

Date in Pee Dee: 1775
Location: ST. DAVID'S PARISH
Source(s): COOK.
Revolutionary War service: LIDE'S COMPANY.

CHANDLER, JESSE   ID: 5012
Date in Pee Dee: 1780
Location: WILLIAMSBURG
Source(s): BODDIE.
Revolutionary War service: PRIVATE IN MARION'S BRIGADE.

CHANDLER, JOSEPH   ID: 4958
Date in Pee Dee: 1737   Last Date: 1759
Location: LOWER BLACK RIVER
Source(s): BODDIE.
Notes: SERVED IN FRENCH AND INDIAN WAR.

CHANDLER, PHILLIP   ID: 2827
Date in Pee Dee: 1743   Last Date: 1743 DIED
Location: GEORGETOWN
Source(s): MOORE.
Notes: WILLED PROPERTY TO NATHANIEL TREGAGLE.

CHAPMAN, ALLEN   ID: 1697
Spouse: RACHEL POWE
Date in Pee Dee: 1770
Location: WELCH NECK
Source(s): GREGG.

CHEAVES, JAMES   ID: 4354
Date in Pee Dee: 1774
Location: GEORGETOWN
Source(s): MOORE V.3.
Notes: BROTHER OF WILLIAM AND THOMAS.

CHEAVES, THOMAS   ID: 4355
Date in Pee Dee: 1774
Location: SAMPIT RIVER
Source(s): MOORE V.3.

Notes: BROTHER OF WILLIAM AND JAMES.

CHEAVES, WILLIAM   ID: 4353
Date in Pee Dee: 1774   Last Date: 1774 DIED
Location: GEORGETOWN
Source(s): MOORE V.3.
Notes: BROTHER OF JAMES AND THOMAS.

CHEESEBOROUGH, JOHN   ID: 1798
Date in Pee Dee: 1757   Last Date: 1768
Location: ST. DAVID'S PARISH
Source(s): GREGG, JVSDP, ROGERS.
Notes: CAPTAIN OF LOWER PEE DEE MILITIA. SON OF JOHN.

CHEESEBOROUGH, JOHN   ID: 3414
Spouse: ELIZABETH [--?--]
Children: EDMOND COUSINS, WILLIAM RIED, JOHN, ELIZABETH.
Date in Pee Dee: 1750   Last Date: 1760
Location: PRINCE GEORGE WINYAW PARISH
Source(s): MOORE V.3.
Notes: DIED BEFORE 1761, SHE IN 1761.

CHEKIN, WILLIAM   ID: 5252
Spouse: ELIZABETH [--?--]
Children: GEORGE.
Date in Pee Dee: 1743
Location: PRINCE FREDERICK PARISH
Source(s): RBPPFW.
Notes: THIS PROBABLY IS SAME NAME AS CHICKEN.

CHERRY, WILLIAM   ID: 209
Spouse: SARAH PEARSON
Date in Pee Dee: 1757   Last Date: 1784
Location: CASHAWAY
Source(s): COOK, RWNBC, MOORE.

CHEVES, THOMAS   ID: 5717
Date in Pee Dee: 1759
Location: ST. DAVID'S PARISH

Source(s): MUSTER ROLL.
Notes: LISTED AS A DESERTER FROM HITCHCOCK'S COMPANY DURING FRENCH AND INDIAN WAR.

CHICKEN, WILLIAM   ID: 3078
Spouse: ELIZABETH CHOVIN
Date in Pee Dee: 1736   Last Date: 1761
Location: PRINCE FREDERICK PARISH
Source(s): BODDIE, CLEMENS.
Notes: MARRIED AT SANTEE 14 MAY 1761.

CHINA, JOHN   ID: 5011
Date in Pee Dee: 1780
Location: WILLIAMSBURG
Source(s): BODDIE.
Revolutionary War service: PRIVATE IN MARION'S BRIGADE.

CHINNERS, ABRAHAM   ID: 3091
Children: JOHN SANDIFORD.
Date in Pee Dee: 1759   Last Date: 1759   DIED
Location: CRAVEN COUNTY
Source(s): MOORE.

CHINNERS, ISAAC   ID: 3859
Spouse: WINEFORD [--?--]
Children: EZEKIEL, THOMAS, ISAAC, WINEFORD, REBECCA, ANN, SARAH, MARY.
Date in Pee Dee: 1737   Last Date: 1765 DIED
Location: BRITTON'S NECK
Source(s): MOORE V.3, RBPPFW.

CHOSEWOOD, ALEXANDER   ID: 4970
Date in Pee Dee: 1759
Location: WILLIAMSBURG
Source(s): BODDIE.
Revolutionary War service: FRENCH AND INDIAN WAR

CHOVINE, ALEXANDER   ID: 4316
Spouse: POLLY TART

Date in Pee Dee: 1772
Location: PRINCE FREDERICK PARISH
Source(s): MOORE V.3, CLEMENS.
Notes: MARRIED NOVEMBER 1772 AT CHARLESTON.

CHRISTIE, ALEXANDER   ID: 2826
Date in Pee Dee: 1744   Last Date: 1756 DIED
Location: PRINCE GEORGE WINYAW PARISH
Source(s): MOORE.
Notes: APPEARS TO HAVE HAD NO DESCENDENTS.

CHRISTMAS, JONATHAN   ID: 5277
Spouse: HESTER MORTON
Children: JOHN.
Date in Pee Dee: 1741   Last Date: 1744
Location: PRINCE FREDERICK PARISH
Source(s): RBPPFW, BODDIE.
Notes: MARRIED 19 JUNE 1741 AT PARISH OF PRINCE
FREDERICK WINYAW.

CLAIG, SAMUEL   ID: 3226
Spouse: MIHITTABELL JOHNSON
Date in Pee Dee: 1731
Location: CRAVEN COUNTY
Source(s): MOORE V.1.
Notes: DAUGHTER OF PETER #3220.

CLAPP, GIBSON   ID: 214
Spouse: SARAH LYNCH
Children: ELIZABETH, MARY (MICHIE).
Date in Pee Dee: 1742
Location: WILLIAMSBURG
Source(s): COOK, BODDIE.
Notes: APPEARS TO HAVE MARRIED A DAUGHTER OF THOMAS
LYNCH. PROBABLY DIED BEFORE 1751.

CLARK, HARMAN   ID: 2046
Date in Pee Dee: 1782
Source(s): GREGG P.406.

Revolutionary War service: PRIVATE IN MARION'S BRIGADE.

CLARK, THOMAS   ID: 5016
Date in Pee Dee: 1780
Location: WILLIAMSBURG
Source(s): BODDIE.
Revolutionary War service: PRIVATE IN MARION'S BRIGADE.

CLARK, WILLIAM   ID: 1752
Spouse: MARY SUMMERS
Date in Pee Dee: 1742
Location: PRINCE FREDERICK PARISH
Source(s): MOORE.

CLARKE, SAMUEL   ID: 4738
Spouse: ANN [--?--]
Date in Pee Dee: 1774   Last Date: 1774 DIED
Location: ST. MARK'S PARISH
Source(s): MOORE V.3.
Notes: SIBLINGS JAMES, DAVID, ABIGAIL JOHNSON, AND SARY
FISH.

CLARY, JOHN   ID: 218
Date in Pee Dee: 1781
Location: WILLIAMSBURG
Source(s): COOK.
Revolutionary War service: MARION'S BRIGADE.

CLARY, ROBERT   ID: 1783
Date in Pee Dee: 1759   Last Date: 1769
Location: ST. DAVID'S PARISH
Source(s): GREGG, JVSDP, MOORE V.3.
Notes: SIGNED NAME WITH MARK. SERVED IN FRENCH AND
INDIAN WAR AS LIEUTENANT WITH LIDE'S COMPANY.

CLAYBURN, FRANCES (WIDOW)   ID: 3544
Children: JOHN, WILLIAM, MARYAN, CERONEY.
Date in Pee Dee: 1765
Location: WELCH NECK

Source(s): MOORE V.3.
Notes: CHILDREN WERE BORN TO PREVIOUS HUSBAND, WETHERS, AND LIVED IN VIRGINIA.

CLAYTON, LAWERENCE   ID: 2026
Date in Pee Dee: 1782
Source(s): GREGG P.406.
Revolutionary War service: PRIVATE MARION'S BRIGADE.

CLEGG, SAMUEL   ID: 886
Spouse: MEHITTOBEL [--?--]
Children: LYDIA.
Date in Pee Dee: 1731
Location: PRINCE FREDERICK PARISH
Source(s): RBPPFW.
Notes: SHE LATER MARRIED BOYD JAMES.

CLEGG, SAMUEL   ID: 2799
Spouse: ELIZABETH [--?--]
Date in Pee Dee: 1767
Location: UPPER BLACK RIVER
Source(s): ROGERS, MOORE V.3, COOK.
Notes: COUSIN OF JOSEPH JOHNSON.

CLELAND, JOHN   ID: 223
Spouse: MARY ESTHER PERRY
Children: ANNE.
Date in Pee Dee: 1735   Last Date: 1760 DIED
Location: PRINCE GEORGE PARISH.
Source(s): COOK, ROGERS, SMITH, H..

CLEMENT, JOSIAH   ID: 224
Date in Pee Dee: 1775
Location: ST. DAVID'S PARISH
Source(s): COOK.
Revolutionary War service: LIDE'S COMPANY.

CLEMENTS, JOSEPH   ID: 2061
Date in Pee Dee: 1782

Source(s): GREGG P.406.
Revolutionary War service: PRIVATE MARION'S BRIGADE.

CLERK, JOSEPH   ID: 5316
Spouse: ANN [--?--]
Date in Pee Dee: 1730
Location: PRINCE FREDERICK PARISH
Source(s): RBPPFW.
Notes: ANN DIED 1730.

CLERK, JOSEPH   ID: 5614
Date in Pee Dee: 1759
Location: ST. DAVID'S PARISH
Source(s): MUSTER ROLL.
Notes: SERVED IN FRENCH AND INDIAN WAR AS SERGEANT IN
CAPTAIN ROBERT WEAVER'S COMPANY.

CLOYD, JOHN   ID: 3278
Spouse: SARAH [--?--]
Date in Pee Dee: 1733   Last Date: 1733 DIED
Location: WACCAMAW
Source(s): MOORE V.1.
Notes: BROTHER OF THOMAS, HALF BROTHER OF HUGH, DAVID,
RICHARD, AND EDWARD CLOYD.

CLYATT, HANNAH   ID: 5345
Spouse: DAVID SWINTON
Date in Pee Dee: 1739
Location: PRINCE FREDERICK PARISH
Source(s): RBPPFW.

CLYATT, STEPHEN   ID: 5462
Spouse: CATHERINE AVANT
Date in Pee Dee: 1748
Location: PRINCE FREDERICK PARISH
Source(s): RBPPFW.
Notes: MARRIED AT PARISH OF PRINCE FREDERICK WINYAW 30
JULY 1748.

COACHMAN, JAMES ID: 3239
Spouse: HANNAH POOLE
Children: WILLIAM.
Date in Pee Dee: 1758   Last Date: 1765
Location: GEORGETOWN
Source(s): MOORE.

COBB, BENJAMIN ID: 5707
Date in Pee Dee: 1759
Location: ST. DAVID'S PARISH
Source(s): MUSTER ROLL.
Notes: SERVED IN HITCHCOCK'S COMPANY DURING FRENCH AND
INDIAN WAR.

COCHRAN, MICHAEL ID: 3478
Spouse: REBECCA SULLIVAN
Date in Pee Dee: 1760
Location: PRINCE FREDERICK PARISH
Source(s): MOORE V.3, CLEMENS.
Notes: MARRIED 11 JANUARY 1759 AT SANTEE.

COCHRAN, THOMAS ID: 225
Date in Pee Dee: 1775
Location: CHERAW DISTRICT
Source(s): COOK.
Revolutionary War service: WISE'S COMPANY OF INFANTRY.

COCKFIELD, WILLIAM ID: 4532
Date in Pee Dee: 1759
Location: WILLIAMSBURG
Source(s): BODDIE, MUSTER ROLL.
Notes: SERVED IN FRENCH AND INDIAN WAR AS SERGEANT IN
CAPTAIN JAMES THOMSON'S COMPANY.

COCKS, EMANUEL ID: 5694
Date in Pee Dee: 1759
Location: ST. DAVID'S PARISH
Source(s): MUSTER ROLL.

Notes: SERVED IN FRENCH AND INDIAN WAR AS SERGEANT WITH KOLB'S COMPANY.

COGDELL, CHARLES   ID: 4583
Spouse: JANE [--?--]
Date in Pee Dee: 1776   Last Date: 1776 DIED
Location: PRINCE GEORGE WINYAH PARISH
Source(s): MOORE V.3.
Notes: MARY BURNET IN NC AND MARY AGERTON WERE SISTERS.

COGDELL, GEORGE   ID: 226
Spouse: [--?--] STEVENS
Date in Pee Dee: 1778   Last Date: 1782
Source(s): COOK, CLEMENS, GREGG.

COHEN, ABRAHAM   ID: 2660
Date in Pee Dee: 1780
Location: PRINCE GEORGE WINYAW PARISH
Source(s): ROGERS.
Notes: PROBABLY A TORY. SIGNED LOYALITY OATH.

COHEN, SOLOMON   ID: 2668
Date in Pee Dee: 1780
Location: PRINCE GEORGE WINYAW PARISH
Source(s): ROGERS.
Notes: PROBABLY A TORY. SIGNED LOYALITY OATH.

COKER, BENJAMIN   ID: 1857
Date in Pee Dee: 1782
Location: WILLIAMSBURG
Source(s): GREGG, BODDIE.
Revolutionary War service: PRIVATE IN MARION'S BRIGADE.

COKER, NATHAN   ID: 2040
Date in Pee Dee: 1782
Location: WILLIAMSBURG
Source(s): GREGG, BODDIE.
Revolutionary War service: PRIVATE IN MARION'S BRIGADE.

COKER, THOMAS   ID: 229
Date in Pee Dee: 1767   Last Date: 1781
Location: CASHAWAY
Source(s): COOK, BODDIE.
Revolutionary War service: PRIVATE IN MARION'S BRIGADE.

COLDIN, JOHN   ID: 5703
Date in Pee Dee: 1759
Location: ST. DAVID'S PARISH
Source(s): MUSTER ROLL.
Notes: LISTED AS DESERTER FROM KOLB'S COMPANY DURING
FRENCH AND INDIAN WAR.

COLE, JAMES   ID: 2069
Date in Pee Dee: 1759   Last Date: 1782
Source(s): GREGG P.406, MOORE V.3.
Notes: SON OF WILLIAM.
Revolutionary War service: SERGEANT IN MARION'S BRIGADE.

COLE, WILLIAM   ID: 3405
Spouse: RACHEL [--?--]
Children: ALEXANDER, WILLIAM, JAMES, THOMAS, ISAAC,
LETES, ANN, ELIZABETH.
Date in Pee Dee: 1745   Last Date: 1761 DIED
Location: ST. DAVID'S PARISH
Source(s): MOORE V.3, RBPPFW.

COLEMAN, JACOB   ID: 5013
Date in Pee Dee: 1780
Location: WILLIAMSBURG
Source(s): BODDIE.
Revolutionary War service: PRIVATE IN MARION'S BRIGADE.

COLEMAN, JAMES   ID: 2058
Date in Pee Dee: 1782
Source(s): GREGG P.406.
Revolutionary War service: PRIVATE IN MARION'S BRIGADE.

COLEMAN, JOHN   ID: 1808

Date in Pee Dee: 1782
Source(s): GREGG P.406, MOORE V.3.
Notes: SIGNED WITH MARK.
Revolutionary War service: PRIVATE IN MARION'S BRIGADE.

COLEMAN, JOSEPH   ID: 230
Date in Pee Dee: 1775
Location: ST. DAVID'S PARISH
Source(s): COOK.
Revolutionary War service: LIDE'S COMPANY.

COLLIER, JOHN   ID: 2048
Date in Pee Dee: 1782
Source(s): GREGG P.406.
Revolutionary War service: PRIVATE IN MARION'S BRIGADE.

COLLINS, ANDREW   ID: 5220
Spouse: SARAH [--?--]
Children: SARAH, ANDREW.
Date in Pee Dee: 1729   Last Date: 1740
Location: PRINCE FREDERICK PARISH
Source(s): RBPPFW.
Notes: FIRST WIFE MARY DIED 1729. HE SERVED AS VESTRY
MAN OF PARISH OF PRINCE FREDERICK WINYAW DURING 1729-31.

COLLINS, ELIZABETH   ID: 4338
Spouse: THOMAS BROWN
Children: ELIZABETH ANN.
Date in Pee Dee: 1751
Location: PRINCE GEORGE WINYAH PARISH
Source(s): MOORE V.3.
Notes: DAUGHTER OF TONER COLLINS #4339.

COLLINS, WILLIAM   ID: 5306
Spouse: ELIZABETH SMITH (WIDOW)
Children: ANNE.
Date in Pee Dee: 1744   Last Date: 1746
Location: PRINCE FREDERICK PARISH
Source(s): RBPPFW.

Notes: MARRIED 28 JUNE 1744 AT PARISH OF PRINCE
FREDERICK WINYAW.

COLLSON, MARTHA   ID: 5445
Spouse: THOMAS JAMES SIMPSON
Date in Pee Dee: 1747
Location: PRINCE FREDERICK PARISH
Source(s): RBPPFW.

COLT, WILLIAM   ID: 233
Spouse: REBECCA ANNE [--?--]
Children: SARAH, WILLIAM SAXBY.
Date in Pee Dee: 1735   Last Date: 1741
Location: PRINCE GEORGE PARISH. N. SIDE SAMPIT R.
Source(s): COOK, MOORE V.1, SMITH, H., RBPPFW.

COMBESS, JOHANNA   ID: 5572
Date in Pee Dee: 1784
Location: ST. DAVID'S PARISH
Source(s): JVSDP.
Notes: AT AGE SEVEN BOUND BY PARISH TO ROBERT BIGGARD
WITH CONSENT OF MOTHER.

COMBESS, JOHN   ID: 5556
Date in Pee Dee: 1773 DOB Last Date: 1782
Location: ST. DAVID'S PARISH
Source(s): JVSDP.
Notes: AT AGE OF NINE BOUND BY PARISH TO ROBERT BIGGART
UNTIL AGE 21.

COMBESS, WINNEY   ID: 5576
Date in Pee Dee: 1785
Location: ST. DAVID'S PARISH
Source(s): JVSDP.
Notes: BOUND BY PARISH TO JOSEPH BOOTH.

COMMANDER, ABIGAIL   ID: 3152
Spouse: JOHN SMITH

Children: ELIZABETH (SHAW) (PUNCH), SAMUEL, MARY, HANNAH.
Date in Pee Dee: 1733   Last Date: 1772
Location: PRINCE GEORGE WINYAW PARISH
Source(s): MOORE, RBPPFW.
Notes: DAUGHTER OF SAMUEL #2547. MARRIED 4 OCTOBER 1737 AT PARISH OF PRINCE FREDERICK WINYAW.

COMMANDER, ELIZABETH   ID: 3249
Spouse: [--?--] BOUTWELL
Date in Pee Dee: 1733
Location: PRINCE GEORGE WINYAW PARISH
Source(s): MOORE V.1.
Notes: DAUGHTER OF SAMUEL #2547.

COMMANDER, FRANCES   ID: 1472
Spouse: EBENEZER DUNNAM
Date in Pee Dee: 1733   Last Date: 1746
Location: PRINCE GEORGE WINYAW PARISH
Source(s): MOORE V.1, RBPPFW.
Notes: DAUGHTER OF SAMUEL #2547.

COMMANDER, HANNAH   ID: 2548
Spouse: ELIAS SCREVEN
Date in Pee Dee: 1734
Location: PRINCE FREDERICK PARISH
Source(s): ROGERS, MOORE V.1.
Notes: DAUGHTER OF SAMUEL SR. #2547.

COMMANDER, JOSEPH   ID: 2437
Spouse: ELIZABETH NELSON
Children: ROBERT L..
Date in Pee Dee: 1737   Last Date: 1772 DIED
Location: PRINCE FREDERICK PARISH
Source(s): SMITH, H., MOORE V.3, REMBERT, BODDIE.
Notes: THREE OTHER CHILDREN. SON OF SAMUEL #2547.

COMMANDER, RACHEL   ID: 2569
Spouse: [--?--] MCCANTS

Children: ELIZABETH (DUNNAM).
Date in Pee Dee: 1733
Location: PRINCE GEORGE WINYAW PARISH
Source(s): MOORE V.1, REMBERT.
Notes: DAUGHTER OF SAMUEL #2547. SHE DIED BEFORE 1772.

COMMANDER, SAMUEL   ID: 2547
Spouse: ELIZABETH [--?--]
Children: HANNAH, JOHN, SAMUEL, SAMUEL, JOSEPH,
ELIZABETH, RACHEL, DOROTHY, FRANCES, ABIGAIL.
Date in Pee Dee: 1732   Last Date: 1733 DIED
Origin: NORTHERN IRELAND
Location: PRINCE FREDERICK PARISH (BLACK RIVER)
Source(s): ROGERS, MOORE V.1, REMBERT, BODDIE.
Notes: PROBABLY HERE MUCH EARLIER.

COMMANDER, SAMUEL JR.   ID: 1505
Spouse: MARY [--?--]
Children: JAMES, THOMAS, SAMUEL, JOSEPH, JESSE, MARTHA.
Date in Pee Dee: 1783   Last Date: 1783 DIED
Origin: NORTHERN IRELAND
Location: WILLIAMSBURG
Source(s): WITHERSPOON, COOK, REMBERT.
Notes: AT POTATO FERRY ON BLACK RIVER. MARY WAS SECOND
WIFE. SON OF SAMUEL #2547.

COMMANDER, THOMAS   ID: 4964
Date in Pee Dee: 1740   Last Date: 1759
Location: WILLIAMSBURG
Source(s): BODDIE.
Notes: SON OF SAMUEL JR. #1535.
Notes: SERVED IN FRENCH AND INDIAN WAR.

CONE, JOHN   ID: 5701
Date in Pee Dee: 1759
Location: ST. DAVID'S PARISH
Source(s): MUSTER ROLL.

Notes: LISTED AS DESERTER FROM KOLB'S COMPANY DURING
FRENCH AND INDIAN WAR.

CONE, MATTHEW   ID: 1887
Date in Pee Dee: 1782
Source(s): GREGG P.406.
Revolutionary War service: PRIVATE IN MARION'S BRIGADE.

CONE, WILLIAM   ID: 5704
Date in Pee Dee: 1759
Location: ST. DAVID'S PARISH
Source(s): MUSTER ROLL.
Notes: LISTED AS DESERTER FROM KOLB'S COMPANY DURING
FRENCH AND INDIAN WAR.

CONN, THOMAS   ID: 236
Spouse: MARY [--?--]
Children: GEORGE, THOMAS, ANN.
Date in Pee Dee: 1734   Last Date: 1767 DIED
Location: PEE DEE BELOW LITTLE PEE DEE
Source(s): COOK, MOORE V.3.

CONNELL, SIMON   ID: 1688
Date in Pee Dee: 1770
Location: LYNCHES (UPPER)
Source(s): GREGG.
Notes: KILLED BY TORIES.

CONNER, HANNAH   ID: 4829
Spouse: JOHN CANTEY
Children: JOHN JAMES.
Date in Pee Dee: 1776
Location: PRINCE FREDERICK PARISH
Source(s): MOORE V.3.
Notes: DAUGHTER OF JOHN.

CONNER, ISAAC SR.   ID: 5492
Spouse: CHRISTIANA (Nee CANTY) LESESNE
Children: ISAAC.

Date in Pee Dee: 1760
Location: ST. MARK'S PARISH
Source(s): BURGESS.
Notes: SHE WAS WIDOW OF FRANCIS LESESNE.

CONNER, JAMES   ID: 2003
Date in Pee Dee: 1770   Last Date: 1782
Source(s): GREGG P.406, MOORE V.3.
Revolutionary War service: PRIVATE IN MARION'S BRIGADE.

CONNER, JOHN   ID: 237
Spouse: ANN MCDANIEL
Children: ARCHIBALD, ADAM, ANN, MARY (YOUNG), HANNAH
(CANTEY), JOHN.
Date in Pee Dee: 1737   Last Date: 1776 DIED
Location: PRINCE FREDERICK PARISH
Source(s): COOK, RBPPFW, MOORE, BODDIE.
Notes: MARRIED 4 AUGUST 1737 AT PARISH OF PRINCE
FREDERICK WINYAW. SECOND MARRIED MARY [--?--].

CONNER, JOSEPH   ID: 5551
Date in Pee Dee: 1776
Location: ST. DAVID'S PARISH
Source(s): JVSDP.
Notes: A FREE MULATTO BOUND BY PARISH TO JOHN STEPHENS.

CONNER, LEWIS   ID: 238
Date in Pee Dee: 1775
Location: CHERAW DISTRICT
Source(s): COOK.
Revolutionary War service: WISE COMPANY INFANTRY.

CONNER, MARY   ID: 4828
Spouse: WILLIAM YOUNG
Date in Pee Dee: 1776
Location: PRINCE FREDERICK PARISH
Source(s): MOORE V.3.
Notes: DAUGHTER OF JOHN.

CONNER, THOMAS   ID: 239
Date in Pee Dee: 1768   Last Date: 1775
Location: CHERAW DISTRICT
Source(s): COOK, JVSDP, GREGG.
Revolutionary War service: WISE COMPANY INFANTRY.

CONNORE, BRYAN   ID: 5453
Spouse: ANNE CAMPBELL (WIDOW)
Date in Pee Dee: 1747
Location: PRINCE FREDERICK PARISH
Source(s): RBPPFW.
Notes: MARRIED AT PARISH OF PRINCE FREDERICK WINYAW 21
DECEMBER 1747.

CONYERS, DANIEL   ID: 240
Spouse: MARY WITHERSPOON
Date in Pee Dee: 1781
Location: WILLIAMSBURG
Source(s): COOK, BODDIE.
Revolutionary War service: CAPTAIN IN MARION'S BRIGADE.

CONYERS, JAMES   ID: 2364
Spouse: MARY MCINTOSH
Date in Pee Dee: 1744   Last Date: 1782 DIED
Location: ST. DAVID'S PARISH
Source(s): RUDISILL, BODDIE.
Notes: ALSO SERVED UNDER HAMPTON, SUMTER, AND GREEN. KIA
AT ROUND O. M. 18 DECEMBER 1744 AT PARISH OF PRINCE
FREDERICK WINYAW.
Revolutionary War service: MAJOR IN MARION'S BRIGADE.

CONYERS, JOHN   ID: 5299
Spouse: ANNE [--?--]
Children: MARY.
Date in Pee Dee: 1736
Location: PRINCE FREDERICK PARISH
Source(s): RBPPFW, BODDIE.

COOK, WEST   ID: 5014

Date in Pee Dee: 1780
Location: WILLIAMSBURG
Source(s): BODDIE.
Revolutionary War service: PRIVATE IN MARION'S BRIGADE.

COOK, WILLIAM   ID: 2012
Date in Pee Dee: 1780
Location: WILLIAMSBURG
Source(s): GREGG, BODDIE.
Revolutionary War service: CONTINENTAL SERGEANT.

COOPER, GEORGE   ID: 1595
Date in Pee Dee: 1780
Location: WILLIAMSBURG
Source(s): WITHERSPOON.
Revolutionary War service: CAPTAIN MARION'S BRIGADE.

COOPER, GEORGE   ID: 3969
Spouse: JANE THOMPSON
Date in Pee Dee: 1763   Last Date: BEFORE 1763
Location: PRINCE FREDRICK PARISH
Source(s): MOORE V.3.
Notes: HER SECOND MARRIAGE.

COOPER, JAMES   ID: 3499
Spouse: MARTHA STRAIN
Children: JAMES, JOSEPH, ADAM, WILLIAM, JANET, ANN,
MARGARET.
Date in Pee Dee: 1761   Last Date: 1771 DIED
Location: WILLIAMSBURG
Source(s): MOORE V.3.
Notes: SON-IN-LAW OF ADAM STRAIN. BROTHER OF SAMUEL
COOPER.

COOPER, JOHN   ID: 1592
Spouse: SUSAN ANDERSON
Children: WILLIAM.
Date in Pee Dee: 1770
Location: WILLIAMSBURG

Source(s): WITHERSPOON.
Notes: SON OF WILLIAM #1590.

COOPER, JOHN   ID: 2190
Spouse: JANE GREGG
Children: ELEANOR MCKNIGHT, JANE, SAMUEL, ROBERT
DRAYTON, JOHN MILTON, FRANK, AMELIA, SUSANNAH ELIZA.
Date in Pee Dee: 1768   Last Date: 1790
Location: MARS BLUFF
Source(s): MCCARTY, JVSDP, GREGG.
Notes: PROBABLY BORN IN WILLIAMSBURG.

COOPER, SAMUEL   ID: 4367
Spouse: JANE [--?--]
Children: SAMUEL, ROBERT, MARY, JANE, JANET.
Date in Pee Dee: 1769   Last Date: 1769 DIED
Location: PRINCE FREDERICK PARISH (MINGO)
Source(s): MOORE V.3.
Notes: BROTHER OF WILLIAM AND JAMES. MAY HAVE MARRIED
JANE GREENLAND.

COOPER, SARAH   ID: 3505
Children: THOMAS, SAMUEL.
Date in Pee Dee: 1755   Last Date: 1767 DIED
Source(s): MOORE V.3.
Notes: APPEARS TO HAVE HAD AT LEAST TWO DAUGHTERS.
PROBABLY WIFE OF THOMAS.

COOPER, SILVANUS   ID: 242
Date in Pee Dee: 1775   Last Date: 1778
Location: CHERAW DISTRICT
Source(s): COOK, RUDISILL.
Revolutionary War service: WISE'S COMPANY OF INFANTRY.

COOPER, THOMAS   ID: 3402
Spouse: SARAH [--?--]
Children: EDWARD, MARY, SARAH, ELIZABETH, REBECCA.
Date in Pee Dee: 1761
Location: PRINCE FREDRICK PARISH

Source(s): MOORE V.3.

COOPER, WILLIAM   ID: 1590
Spouse: JANE JAMES
Children: JOHN, GEORGE.
Date in Pee Dee: 1737   Last Date: 1760
Location: WILLIAMSBURG
Source(s): WITHERSPOON, COOK, BODDIE.

COPE, JOHN   ID: 5463
Spouse: MARY BURKETT
Date in Pee Dee: 1748
Location: PRINCE FREDERICK PARISH
Source(s): RBPPFW.
Notes: MARRIED AT PARISH OF PRINCE FREDERICK WINYAW 7
JUNE 1748.

CORBETT, BRINKLEY   ID: 4350
Spouse: DOROTHY [--?--]
Date in Pee Dee: 1773
Location: ST. MARK'S PARISH
Source(s): MOORE V.3.

CORDES, SAMUEL   ID: 3751
Date in Pee Dee: 1766   Last Date: 1780
Location: NORTH OF SANTEE RIVER
Source(s): MOORE V.3, BODDIE.
Revolutionary War service: PRIVATE MARION'S BRIGADE.

COSGRIEVE, JAMES   ID: 246
Date in Pee Dee: 1766
Location: PRINCE FREDERICK PARISH
Source(s): COOK, RBPPFW.

COSHET, SUSANNAH   ID: 5327
Spouse: WILLIAM SLOPER
Date in Pee Dee: 1739
Location: PRINCE FREDERICK PARISH
Source(s): RBPPFW.

COTTINGHAM, DANIEL   ID: 4978
Date in Pee Dee: 1780
Location: WILLIAMSBURG
Source(s): BODDIE.
Revolutionary War service: LIEUTENANT IN MARION'S
BRIGADE.

COTTINGHAM, DILL   ID: 5015
Date in Pee Dee: 1780
Location: WILLIAMSBURG
Source(s): BODDIE.
Revolutionary War service: PRIVATE IN MARION'S BRIGADE.

COUNCIL, WILLIAM   ID: 1992
Date in Pee Dee: 1782
Source(s): GREGG P.406.
Revolutionary War service: PRIVATE IN MARION'S BRIGADE.

COUNCILL, HARDY   ID: 5293
Spouse: BEATRIX [--?--]
Children: JAMES, SARAH.
Date in Pee Dee: 1745
Location: PRINCE FREDERICK PARISH
Source(s): RBPPFW.

COUNSELL, ROBERT   ID: 1942
Spouse: ELIZABETH [--?--]
Children: JESSE, SARA, TABITHA (JAMES).
Date in Pee Dee: 1764   Last Date: 1764 DIED
Location: ST. DAVID'S PARISH
Source(s): GREGG, JVSDP, MOORE V.3.
Notes: ELIZABETH VOTED IN 1769.

COUNSELL, TABITHA   ID: 4029
Spouse: [--?--] JAMES
Date in Pee Dee: 1764
Location: ST. DAVID'S PARISH
Source(s): MOORE V.3, RWNBC.

Notes: DAUGHTER OF ROBERT #1942.

COURTIS, HENRY ID: 5310
Spouse: MARGARET [--?--]
Children: MARY.
Date in Pee Dee: 1746
Location: PRINCE FREDERICK PARISH
Source(s): RBPPFW.

COURTNEY, JAMES JR ID: 250
Date in Pee Dee: 1775
Location: ST. DAVID'S PARISH
Source(s): COOK.
Revolutionary War service: LIDE'S COMPANY.

COURTNEY, JOHN ID: 1787
Date in Pee Dee: 1759   Last Date: 1768
Location: ST. DAVID'S PARISH
Source(s): GREGG, MUSTER ROLL, JVSDP.
Notes: SERVED IN FRENCH AND INDIAN WAR AS PRIVATE IN
CAPTAIN ROBERT WEAVER'S COMPANY.

COURTNEY, JOHN JR ID: 251
Date in Pee Dee: 1775
Location: ST. DAVID'S PARISH
Source(s): COOK.
Revolutionary War service: LIDE'S COMPANY

COURTNEY, ROBERT JR ID: 252
Date in Pee Dee: 1775
Location: ST. DAVID'S PARISH
Source(s): COOK.
Revolutionary War service: LIDE'S COMPANY

COURTNEY, ROBERT SR ID: 253
Date in Pee Dee: 1775
Location: ST. DAVID'S PARISH
Source(s): COOK.
Revolutionary War service: LIDE'S COMPANY.

COURTNEY, SAMUEL   ID: 254
Date in Pee Dee: 1775
Location: ST. DAVID'S PARISH
Source(s): COOK.
Revolutionary War service: LIDE'S COMPANY.

COURTNEY, STEPHEN   ID: 2086
Date in Pee Dee: 1782
Source(s): GREGG P.406.
Revolutionary War service: PRIVATE IN MARION'S BRIGADE.

COUSAR, JOHN   ID: 5019
Date in Pee Dee: 1780
Location: WILLIAMSBURG
Source(s): BODDIE.
Revolutionary War service: PRIVATE IN MARION'S BRIGADE.

COUTURIER, MARTHA   ID: 3235
Children: SAMUEL.
Date in Pee Dee: 1756
Location: CRAVEN COUNTY
Source(s): MOORE.

COVINGTON, WILLIAM   ID: 255
Date in Pee Dee: 1775
Location: CHERAW DISTRICT
Source(s): COOK.
Revolutionary War service: WISE'S COMPANY OF INFANTRY.

COWARD, WILLIAM   ID: 2032
Date in Pee Dee: 1780
Source(s): GREGG P.406.
Revolutionary War service: MILITIA

COX, JAMES   ID: 2064
Date in Pee Dee: 1782
Source(s): GREGG P.406.
Revolutionary War service: IN MARION'S BRIGADE.

Early Pee Dee Settlers
--C--

COX, JOB   ID: 5325
Spouse: MARY WILDEN
Date in Pee Dee: 1737
Location: PRINCE FREDERICK PARISH
Source(s): RBPPFW.
Notes: MARRIED 7 NOVEMBER 1737 AT PARISH OF PRINCE FREDERICK WINYAW.

COX, JOHN   ID: 2006
Date in Pee Dee: 1782
Source(s): GREGG P.406.
Revolutionary War service: BENTON'S REGIMENT.

COX, JOSIAH   ID: 2065
Date in Pee Dee: 1782
Source(s): GREGG P.406.
Revolutionary War service: PEARSON'S COMPANY PRIVATE.

COX, MANUEL   ID: 258
Date in Pee Dee: 1767   Last Date: 1775
Location: ST. DAVID'S PARISH (CASHAWAY)
Source(s): COOK.
Notes: PROBABLY WELCH LIKELY THE SAME AS EMANUEL.
Revolutionary War service: LIDE'S COMPANY.

COX, SAMUEL   ID: 2036
Spouse: ELIZABETH BROWN
Date in Pee Dee: 1782
Location: CHERAW DISTRICT
Source(s): GREGG, CLEMENS.
Notes: MARRIED 14 FEBRUARY 1782.
Revolutionary War service: PEARSON'S COMPANY PRIVATE.

COX, WILLIAM   ID: 591
Date in Pee Dee: 1782
Source(s): GREGG P.406.
Revolutionary War service: PEARSON'S COMPANY PRIVATE.

CRAIG, ALEXANDER   ID: 2315
Date in Pee Dee: 1772   Last Date: 1788
Origin: ST. DAVID'S PARISH
Location: CHERAWS DISTRICT
Source(s): GREGG, RUDISIL, STEPHENSON, MOORE V3.
Notes: ONE OF THE FEW IN THE 1772 SCOTCH-IRISH
IMMIGRATION TO RECEIVE LAND GRANTS IN THE PEE DEE.

CRATCHLEY, JONATHAN   ID: 5314
Spouse: ELIZABETH BUCKHOLTS
Date in Pee Dee: 1737
Location: PRINCE FREDERICK PARISH
Source(s): RBPPFW.

CRAWFORD, DANIEL   ID: 259
Spouse: POLLY HOLLAND
Date in Pee Dee: 1730   Last Date: 1748
Location: SAMPIT RIVER
Source(s): COOK, CLEMENS, SMITH, H..
Notes: MARRIED FEBRUARY 1748.

CRAWFORD, GEORGE   ID: 4952
Date in Pee Dee: 1759
Location: WILLIAMSBURG
Source(s): BODDIE.
Notes: SERVED AS PRIVATE IN FRENCH AND INDIAN WAR.

CRAWFORD, JAMES   ID: 1392
Date in Pee Dee: 1750
Location: ST. DAVID'S PARISH
Source(s): GREGG.
Notes: SON OF JOHN#1390
Revolutionary War service: CAPTAIN

CRAWFORD, JAMES   ID: 3724
Children: JAMES, HAPPIBETH, PATIENCE, HARDY.
Date in Pee Dee: 1760
Location: WELCH TRACT
Source(s): MOORE V.3.

Notes: HE DIED BEFORE 1765.

CRAWFORD, JAMES   ID: 5249
Spouse: CASSIA (KAZIAH) SAUNDERS
Children: CHARITY, MERCY.
Date in Pee Dee: 1737   Last Date: 1745
Location: PRINCE FREDERICK PARISH
Source(s): RBPPFW, BODDIE.
Notes: MARRIED 15 SEPTEMBER 1739 AT PARISH OF PRINCE
FREDERICK WINYAW.

CRAWFORD, JOHN   ID: 3286
Spouse: [--?--] MARY
Children: JOHN, THOMAS, MICHAEL.
Date in Pee Dee: 1761   Last Date: 1761 DIED
Location: ST. DAVID'S PARISH
Source(s): MOORE V.3.
Notes: SHE APPEARS TO HAVE MARRIED JAMES LAURENS AUGUST
1761.

CRAWFORD, JOHN II   ID: 1735
Children: JAMES, JOHN, HARDY.
Date in Pee Dee: 1761   Last Date: 1769
Location: ST. DAVID'S PARISH (SANDY BLUFF)
Source(s): GREGG, JVSDP, COOK, MOORE.
Notes: SON OF JOHN #3286.

CRAWFORD, THOMAS   ID: 261
Spouse: MARY EVANS
Date in Pee Dee: 1753   Last Date: 1770
Location: LOWER ST. DAVID'S PARISH
Source(s): RBPPFW, JVSDP.
Notes: MARRIED AT PARISH OF PRINCE FREDERICK WINYAW 11
DECEMBER 1753. ORIGINAL COMMISSIONER OF ST. DAVID'S
PARISH. LEFT PROVINCE.

CRIBB, JOHN   ID: 2888
Spouse: ELIZABETH [--?--]
Date in Pee Dee: 1736

Location: PRINCE FREDERICK PARISH
Source(s): BODDIE.

CRIBB, THOMAS   ID: 944
Spouse: ELIZABETH [--?--]
Children: THOMAS, ELIZABETH.
Date in Pee Dee: 1731   Last Date: 1746
Location: PRINCE FREDERICK PARISH
Source(s): RBPPFW.

CROCKATT, JAMES   ID: 2763
Date in Pee Dee: 1740
Location: GEORGETOWN
Source(s): ROGERS.
Notes: A TORY.

CROCKER, JAMES   ID: 2082
Date in Pee Dee: 1778   Last Date: 1782
Location: WELCH NECK
Source(s): GREGG P.406, RWNBC.
Revolutionary War service: IN MARION'S BRIGADE.

CROFT, CHILDERMAS   ID: 4309
Spouse: MARY SIMMONS
Date in Pee Dee: 1767   Last Date: 1775
Location: PRINCE FREDERICK PARISH
Source(s): MOORE V.3, CLEMENS.
Notes: MARRIED 28 MAY 1767 AT SANTEE.

CROFT, GEORGE   ID: 2560
Spouse: ELIZABETH LEGER
Date in Pee Dee: 1775
Location: GEORGETOWN
Source(s): ROGERS, CLEMENS.
Notes: MARRIED 28 JANUARY 1765 AT CHARLESTON.

CROFT, ROBERT   ID: 4314
Spouse: ANN JENKINS
Children: EDWARD, ROBERT.

Date in Pee Dee: 1774   Last Date: 1774 DIED
Location: PRINCE GEORGE WINYAH PARISH
Source(s): MOORE V.3, CLEMENS.
Notes: MARRIED 24 MARCH 1763 AT SANTEE.

CROMBY, JOHN   ID: 1209
Spouse: MARY TOMPKINS
Date in Pee Dee: 1744
Location: PRINCE FREDERICK PARISH
Source(s): RBPPFW.
Notes: MARRIED 19 APRIL 1744 AT PARISH OF PRINCE
FREDERICK WINYAW.

CROMWELL, THOMAS IRETON   ID: 5243
Spouse: MARY [--?--]
Children: OLIVER IRETON, JOHN ALEXANDER, JEMIMA.
Date in Pee Dee: 1742   Last Date: 1747
Location: PRINCE FREDERICK PARISH
Source(s): RBPPFW.

CROSBY, MOSES   ID: 265
Date in Pee Dee: 1736   Last Date: 1767
Location: HURRICANE CREEK (N. OF CASHAWAY)
Source(s): COOK, MOORE V.3.
Notes: SIGNED WITH MARK. ALSO CROSSBE. SERVED IN FRENCH
AND INDIAN WAR WITH THOMSON.

CROSSLAND, EDWARD   ID: 266
Spouse: ANN SNEED
Children: JOHN, DAVID, TEMPERANCE, SAMUEL, GEORGE, MARY
(WEBSTER), ANN, DANIEL M., PHILIP, SARAH (COSNAHAN),
ISRAEL, WILLIAM, ELIZABETH, REBECCA.
Date in Pee Dee: 1760   Last Date: 1781
Origin: VIRGINIA
Location: CHERAWS DISTRICT
Source(s): COOK, GREGG, THOMAS.
Revolutionary War service: PRIVATE MARION'S BRIGADE.

CRUTCHLEY, JONATHAN   ID: 5256

Spouse: ELIZABETH [--?--]
Children: ELIZABETH.
Date in Pee Dee: 1739
Location: PRINCE FREDERICK PARISH
Source(s): RBPPFW.
Notes: HE SEEMS TO HAVE DIED BEFORE 1742 AS ELIZABETH
APPEARS AS WIFE OF WILLIAM MEGEE.

CULP, SEE KOLB, KOLP

CUMBESS, JOAN   ID: 5560
Date in Pee Dee: 1777
Location: ST. DAVID'S PARISH
Source(s): JVSDP.
Notes: BOUND BY PARISH AT AGE 5 TO FRANCIS ROBERTSON.
SHE, JOSIAH, AND MARY LIKELY SIBLINGS.

CUMBESS, JOSIAH   ID: 5559
Date in Pee Dee: 1770 DOB Last Date: 1782
Location: ST. DAVID'S PARISH
Source(s): JVSDP.
Notes: BOUND BY PARISH TO JOSEPH BOOTH FOR 9 YEARS.

CUMBESS, MARY   ID: 5561
Date in Pee Dee: 1776 DOB
Location: ST. DAVID'S PARISH
Source(s): JVSDP.
Notes: AT AGE 6 BOUND BY PARISH TO THOMAS LANKFORD.

CUNNINGHAM, ARTHUR   ID: 2336
Spouse: REBECCA ERVIN GORDON
Children: WILLIAM, DAVID, SARAH TAPHENAS (MCCREA).
Date in Pee Dee: 1758   Last Date: 1817
Location: WILLIAMSBURG
Source(s): MCCARTY, BODDIE.
Revolutionary War service: LIEUTENANT MARION'S BRIGADE.

CUNNINGHAM, JAMES   ID: 5204
Spouse: ELIZABETH SCOTT

Children: ALEXANDER.
Date in Pee Dee: 1780
Location: WILLIAMSBURG
Source(s): MCCARTY, BODDIE.
Notes: THIS IS PROBABLY 2ND JAMES CUNNINGHAM.
Revolutionary War service: PRIVATE MARION'S BRIGADE.

CUNNINGHAM, JOHN   ID: 267
Date in Pee Dee: 1740   Last Date: 1780
Location: CHERAW DISTRICT (PIDGEON CREEK (BUCKHOLDT'S))
Source(s): COOK, BODDIE.
Revolutionary War service: PRIVATE MARION'S BRIGADE.

CURRY, JANE   ID: 3739
Date in Pee Dee: 1760
Source(s): MOORE V.3.
Notes: PROBABLY WIFE OF JOHN #3738.

CURTIS, BENJAMIN   ID: 268
Date in Pee Dee: 1775
Location: ST. DAVID'S PARISH
Source(s): COOK.
Revolutionary War service: LIDE'S COMPANY.

CURTIS, JAMES   ID: 269
Date in Pee Dee: 1775
Location: ST. DAVID'S PARISH
Source(s): COOK.
Revolutionary War service: LIDE'S COMPANY.

CUSACK, ADAM   ID: 270
Spouse: FRANCIS ORAM
Children: SARAH.
Date in Pee Dee: 1778   Last Date: 1782
Location: CHERAWS DISTRICT
Source(s): COOK, CLEMENT, GREGG.
Notes: HANGED BY BRITISH.

DABBS, JOSEPH   ID: 1449
Spouse: HANNAH KOLB
Children: NANCY, SAMUEL, WILLIAM.
Date in Pee Dee: 1770   Last Date: 1770
Location: WELCH TRACT
Source(s): GREGG, JVSDP.

DAIGLE, JOHN   ID: 4937
Spouse: ROSALIE RICHARD
Children: JOHN BAPTIST.
Date in Pee Dee: 1756
Origin: NOVA SCOTIA
Location: WILLIAMSBURG
Source(s): BODDIE.
Notes: HE, WIFE, AND CHILDREN WERE ACADIANS TRANSPORTED
FROM NOVA SCOTIA.

DALE, THOMAS   ID: 272
Spouse: MARY BREWTON (WIDOW)
Date in Pee Dee: 1735   Last Date: 1742
Occupation: DOCTOR   Origin: NORTHERN IRELAND
Location: WILLIAMSBURG
Source(s): COOK, BODDIE, CLEMENS.
Notes: MARRIED 28 MARCH 1733 AT CHARLESTON.

DANIEL, AARON   ID: 1773
Date in Pee Dee: 1768   Last Date: 1778
Location: ST. DAVID'S PARISH
Source(s): GREGG, MOORE, RUDISILL, JVSDP.

Revolutionary War service: MILITIA KOLB'S COMPANY OF MARION'S BRIGADE.

DANIEL, JENNET   ID: 1587
Spouse: HUGH MONTGOMERY
Children: JOHN, NANCY, MARY, ELIZABETH, JOSEPH, HUGH, WILLIAM, MARGARET.
Date in Pee Dee: 1740
Origin: NORTHERN IRELAND
Location: WILLIAMSBURG
Source(s): WITHERSPOON.

DANIEL, JOHN   ID: 275
Spouse: SARAH RAVEN
Date in Pee Dee: 1730   Last Date: 1759
Location: KINGSTON TOWNSHIP BETWEEN PEE DEE AND WACCAMAW RIVERS.
Source(s): COOK, CLEMENS.
Notes: MARRIED 23 JANUARY 1736 AT CHARLESTON. SERVED IN FRENCH AND INDIAN WAR AS PRIVATE.

DANIEL, JOHN   ID: 5020
Date in Pee Dee: 1780
Location: WILLIAMSBURG
Source(s): BODDIE.
Revolutionary War service: PRIVATE MARION'S BRIGADE.

DANILLY, PATRICK   ID: 278
Spouse: ELIZABETH GRACEBERY
Date in Pee Dee: 1735   Last Date: 1740
Origin: NORTHERN IRELAND
Location: WILLIAMSBURG
Source(s): COOK, RBPPFW.
Notes: COOK GIVES DANNELL. MARRIED 24 SEPTEMBER 1740 AT PARISH OF PRINCE FREDERICK WINYAW.

DARBY, JACOB   ID: 2081
Date in Pee Dee: 1782
Source(s): GREGG P.406.

Early Pee Dee Settlers

--D--

Revolutionary War service: MILITIA

DARBY, PEGGY   ID: 4628
Date in Pee Dee: 1779
Location: ST. DAVID'S PARISH
Source(s): RWNBC.
Notes: PROBABLY WIFE OF OWEN.

DARGAN, DORCAS   ID: 3830
Spouse: [--?--] MILLER
Date in Pee Dee: 1766
Location: ST. MARK'S PARISH
Source(s): MOORE V.3.
Notes: SISTER OF JOHN DARGAN #279. SPOUSE NAME ALSO
SPELLED MILNER.

DARGAN, ELIZABETH   ID: 3826
Spouse: [--?--] COLLIATT
Date in Pee Dee: 1766
Location: ST. MARK'S PARISH
Source(s): MOORE V.3.
Notes: DAUGHTER OF JOHN #279.

DARGAN, JOHN   ID: 279
Spouse: ANN [--?--]
Children: ELIZABETH (COLLIATT), MARY, ALICE.
Date in Pee Dee: 1753   Last Date: 1768
Location: ST. MARK'S PARISH
Source(s): COOK, MOORE, GREGG.
Notes: BROTHER OF TIMOTHY DARGAN.

DARGAN, TIMOTHY   ID: 280
Date in Pee Dee: 1770   Last Date: 1780
Location: JEFFERIES CREEK.
Source(s): COOK, MOORE V.3.
Notes: BROTHER OF JOHN DARGAN.

DAUGHTERTY, EDWARD   ID: 5679
Date in Pee Dee: 1759

Location: ST. DAVID'S PARISH
Source(s): MUSTER ROLL.
Notes: SERVED IN FRENCH AND INDIAN WAR AS PRIVATE IN
PLEDGER'S COMPANY.

DAVID, AZARIAH   ID: 1405
Date in Pee Dee: 1750
Location: WELCH NECK
Source(s): GREGG.
Notes: GREGG SAYS LEFT PEE DEE EARLY. SON OF OWEN #284.

DAVID, EVANDER   ID: 281
Spouse: ANN [--?--]
Date in Pee Dee: 1781
Location: CHERAW DISTRICT
Source(s): COOK.

DAVID, EZEKIEL   ID: 2028
Date in Pee Dee: 1782
Source(s): GREGG P.406.
Revolutionary War service: PRIVATE IN MARION'S BRIGADE.

DAVID, JENKIN   ID: 1401
Spouse: RACHEL ROGERS
Children: JOHNUA, AZARIAH, OWENAMIN, JENKIN.
Date in Pee Dee: 1736   Last Date: 1768
Location: WELCH NECK, 1ST ON CATFISH CREEK.
Source(s): GREGG, MOORE, THOMAS, RWNBC.
Notes: DIED BEFORE REVOLUTION. SON OF OWEN #284

DAVID, JOHN   ID: 1404
Spouse: SARAH BOOTH
Date in Pee Dee: 1750   Last Date: 1784
Location: WELCH NECK
Source(s): GREGG, RWNBC, THOMAS.
Notes: SON OF DAVID #1401. SIX WIVES, MARY JONES,
ISABELLA ALLISON, SARAH STEPHENS.
Revolutionary War service: LIEUTENANT MARION'S BRIGADE.

DAVID, JOHUA   ID: 1407
Spouse: LUCY HODGE
Children: JOHN H., JESSE, SARAH, DINAH, JOSHUA, WELCOME,
BETSY.
Date in Pee Dee: 1750
Location: WELCH NECK
Source(s): GREGG, THOMAS.
Notes: SON OF OWEN #284.
Revolutionary War service: CAPTAIN

DAVID, OWEN   ID: 284
Spouse: CATHERINE VAUGHN
Children: JOHN, AZARIAH, OWEN, JENKIN.
Date in Pee Dee: 1736
Origin: ENGLAND
Location: LONG BLUFF, ABOVE SEVERAL MILES.
Source(s): COOK, GREGG, THOMAS.
Notes: SETTLED FIRST ON CATFISH CREEK. MARRIED 2ND DINAH
UNDERWOOD. CHILDREN SHOWN ARE HERS.

DAVID, OWEN   ID: 1406
Children: JOSHUA, JOSIAH, BENJAMIN, SARAH.
Date in Pee Dee: 1750
Location: WELCH NECK
Source(s): GREGG, THOMAS.
Notes: SON OF JENKIN #1401.

DAVIDSON, ALEXANDER   ID: 2839
Spouse: ELIZABETH BALL
Children: ALEXANDER, WILLIAM, ELIZABETH (GRINAN).
Date in Pee Dee: 1740   Last Date: 1766
Location: PRINCE FREDERICK PARISH
Source(s): MOORE, BODDIE, RBPPFW.
Notes: MARRIED 3 DECEMBER 1742 AT PARISH OF PRINCE
FREDERICK WINYAW. SON OF ALEXANDER #2839.

DAVIDSON, DAVID   ID: 1963
Date in Pee Dee: 1769
Location: ST. DAVID'S PARISH

Early Pee Dee Settlers
--D--

Source(s): GREGG, CLEMENS.
Notes: MAY HAVE MARRIED ELENOR HINSON.

DAVIDSON, ELIZABETH   ID: 3835
Spouse: [--?--] GRINAN
Date in Pee Dee: 1763
Location: PRINCE FREDRICK PARISH (LOWER)
Source(s): MOORE V.3.
Notes: DAUGHTER OF ALEXANDER #2839.

DAVIDSON, ELIZABETH   ID: 5430
Spouse: JOHN HAYNSWORTH
Date in Pee Dee: 1747
Location: PRINCE FREDERICK PARISH
Source(s): RBPPFW.

DAVIDSON, ROBERT   ID: 3838
Date in Pee Dee: 1763
Source(s): MOORE V.3, CLEMENS.
Notes: NEPHEW OF ALEXANDER DAVIDSON #2839. MAY HAVE
MARRIED MARY MACKEY.

DAVIDSON, WILLIAM   ID: 3834
Spouse: MARY [--?--]
Date in Pee Dee: 1763 Last Date: 1774
Location: PRINCE FREDRICK PARISH (MINGO)
Source(s): MOORE V.3, JVSDP.
Notes: SON OF ALEXANDER #2839.

DAVIS, ANN   ID: 4380
Spouse: [--?--] CANE
Date in Pee Dee: 1771
Location: UPPER PEE DEE RIVER
Source(s): MOORE V.3.
Notes: DAUGHTER OF THOMAS #4376.

DAVIS, ARTHUR   ID: 5645
Date in Pee Dee: 1759
Location: ST. DAVID'S PARISH

Source(s): MUSTER ROLL.
Notes: SERVED IN FRENCH AND INDIAN WAR AS PRIVATE WITH
LIDE'S COMPANY..

DAVIS, BENJAMIN   ID: 4267
Spouse: PORT RACHEL
Date in Pee Dee: 1748   Last Date: 1771
Location: ST. MARK'S PARISH (LOWER)
Source(s): MOORE V.3, RBPPFW.
Notes: SON OF DAVID #4265. MARRIED AT PARISH OF PRINCE
FREDERICK WINYAW 21 FEBRUARY 1748.

DAVIS, DAVID   ID: 2063
Date in Pee Dee: 1775
Location: ST. DAVID'S PARISH
Source(s): GREGG.
Revolutionary War service: IN MARION'S BRIGADE.

DAVIS, DAVID   ID: 4265
Spouse: MARY [--?--]
Children: JAMES, BENJAMIN, DOROTHY, RACHEL (MCDONALD),
LEAH (GAMBLE), MARY.
Date in Pee Dee: 1771   Last Date: 1771 DIED
Location: ST. MARK'S PARISH (LOWER)
Source(s): MOORE V.3.

DAVIS, DAVID SR.   ID: 4562
Children: WILLIAM.
Date in Pee Dee: 1775   Last Date: 1775 DIED
Source(s): MOORE V.3.

DAVIS, DOROTHY   ID: 4268
Spouse: [--?--] CANTEY
Date in Pee Dee: 1771
Location: ST. MARK'S PARISH (LOWER)
Source(s): MOORE V.3.
Notes: DAUGHTER OF DAVID #4265.

DAVIS, GEORGE   ID: 4947

Date in Pee Dee: 1759
Location: PRINCE FREDERICK PARISH
Source(s): BODDIE.
Notes: SERVED AS PRIVATE FRENCH AND INDIAN.

DAVIS, JAMES   ID: 4266
Date in Pee Dee: 1771   Last Date: 1780
Location: ST. MARK'S PARISH (LOWER)
Source(s): MOORE V.3, BODDIE.
Notes: SON OF DAVID #4265.
Revolutionary War service: LIEUTENANT IN MARION'S
BRIGADE.

DAVIS, JOHN   ID: 1786
Spouse: HANNAH [--?--]
Date in Pee Dee: 1738   Last Date: 1782
Location: ST. DAVID'S PARISH
Source(s): GREGG, JVSDP, BODDIE.
Notes: SERVED IN FRENCH AND INDIAN WAR AS PRIVATE.

DAVIS, LEAH   ID: 4270
Spouse: JOHN GAMBLE
Date in Pee Dee: 1771
Location: ST. MARK'S PARISH (LOWER)
Source(s): MOORE V.3.
Notes: DAUGHTER OF DAVID #4265.

DAVIS, RACHEL   ID: 4269
Spouse: JAMES MCDONALD
Children: SARAH.
Date in Pee Dee: 1771
Location: ST. MARK'S PARISH (LOWER)
Source(s): MOORE V.3.
Notes: DAUGHTER OF DAVID #4265.

DAVIS, ROBERT   ID: 5021
Date in Pee Dee: 1780
Location: WILLIAMSBURG
Source(s): BODDIE.

Revolutionary War service: PRIVATE MARION'S BRIGADE.

DAVIS, SAMUEL   ID: 5362
Spouse: MARGARET MATTHEWS (WIDOW)
Date in Pee Dee: 1741
Location: PRINCE FREDERICK PARISH (MUDDY CREEK)
Source(s): RBPPFW.
Notes: MARRIED 1 SEPTEMBER 1741 AT PARISH OF PRINCE
FREDERICK WINYAW.

DAVIS, THOMAS   ID: 2097
Spouse: MARY CROSS
Date in Pee Dee: 1765   Last Date: 1782
Location: PRINCE FREDERICK PARISH
Source(s): GREGG, CLEMENS, MOORE V.3.
Notes: MARRIED 5 FEBRUARY 1783 AT SANTEE.
Revolutionary War service: PRIVATE IN MARION'S BRIGADE.

DAVIS, THOMAS   ID: 4376
Spouse: ELIZABETH [--?--]
Children: NATHANIEL, GABRIELL, SARAH, ANN (CANE), DINA
(THOMPSON).
Date in Pee Dee: 1771   Last Date: 1771 DIED
Location: UPPER PEE DEE RIVER
Source(s): MOORE V.3, BODDIE.
Notes: PRIVATE IN FRENCH AND INDIAN WAR IN KOLB'S
COMPANY OF MARION'S BRIGADE.

DAVIS, THOMAS   ID: 5571
Children: THOMAS, FRANK.
Date in Pee Dee: 1784
Location: ST. DAVID'S PARISH
Source(s): JVSDP.
Notes: SUPPORTED BY PARISH.

DAVIS, WILLIAM   ID: 286
Spouse: MARGARET CAMPBELL
Date in Pee Dee: 1752   Last Date: 1776
Location: GEORGETOWN

Early Pee Dee Settlers
--D--

Source(s): COOK, CLEMENS, GREGG, MOORE.
Notes: MARRIED 11 MARCH 1775 AT CHARLESTON.
Revolutionary War service: CAPTAIN IN POWELL'S REGIMENT.

DEANE, THOMAS   ID: 2088
Date in Pee Dee: 1778
Location: ST. DAVID'S PARISH
Source(s): GREGG, COOK, RUDISILL.
Revolutionary War service: WISE'S COMPANY OF INFANTRY.

DEARMON, WILLIAM   ID: 5631
Date in Pee Dee: 1759
Location: ST. DAVID'S PARISH
Source(s): MUSTER ROLL.
Notes: SERVED IN FRENCH AND INDIAN WAR IN CAPTAIN GEORGE HICK'S COMPANY. LISTED AS DESERTER.

DEBAY, ANDREW   ID: 2667
Date in Pee Dee: 1780
Location: PRINCE GEORGE WINYAW PARISH
Source(s): ROGERS.
Notes: PROBABLY A TORY. SIGNED LOYALITY OATH.

DELAVILLITE, ANDREW   ID: 2734
Date in Pee Dee: 1746
Location: GEORGETOWN
Source(s): ROGERS.
Notes: FLED IN 1753 TO ESCAPE CREDITORS.

DENNIS, HENRY   ID: 5617
Date in Pee Dee: 1759
Location: ST. DAVID'S PARISH
Source(s): MUSTER ROLL.
Notes: SERVED IN FRENCH AND INDIAN WAR AS PRIVATE IN CAPTAIN ROBERT WEAVER'S COMPANY.

DENNIS, ISAIAH   ID: 5025
Date in Pee Dee: 1780
Location: WILLIAMSBURG

Source(s): BODDIE.
Revolutionary War service: PRIVATE MARION'S BRIGADE.

DESARRENCY, SAMUEL   ID: 295
Date in Pee Dee: 1775
Location: CHERAW DISTRICT
Source(s): COOK.
Revolutionary War service: WISE COMPANY INFANTRY.

DETRYMAPLE, JOHN   ID: 3388
Spouse: SUSANNAH [--?--]
Date in Pee Dee: 1762
Source(s): MOORE V.3.

DEVONALD, DANIEL   ID: 1349
Spouse: MARY [--?--]
Children: MARY, DANIEL.
Date in Pee Dee: 1737   Last Date: 1770 DIED
Location: PEE DEE RIVER WELCH TRACT
Source(s): GREGG, RWNBC, MOORE, JVSDP.
Notes: ORIGINAL WELCH NECK SETTLER.

DEVONALD, MARY   ID: 4180
Spouse: WILLIAM DEWITT
Children: JOHN, MARY (EDWARDS), SARAH, CHARLES M.,
ELEANOR, ELIZABETH, DANIEL, MARGARET, DOROTHEA, HARRIET.
Date in Pee Dee: 1770
Location: WELCH TRACT
Source(s): MOORE V.3, JENKINS.
Notes: DAUGHTER OF DANIEL #1349.

DEVONALDS, DANIEL   ID: 4699
Date in Pee Dee: 1768
Location: ST. DAVID'S PARISH
Source(s): RWNBC.
Notes: WIFE GAVE TWO ACRES FOR WELCH NECK BAPTIST CHURCH
SITE.

DEW, ABSALOM   ID: 2488

Spouse: [--?--] BERRY
Children: WILLIAM, ALEXANDER.
Date in Pee Dee: 1750
Location: PRESENT MARION COUNTY
Source(s): SELLERS.
Notes: WIFE WAS DAUGHTER OF ANDREW BERRY.

DEW, CHRISTOPHER   ID: 2487
Spouse: [--?--] BERRY
Children: HENRIETTA, WILSON, CHRISTOPHER, ABRAHAM,
MARINA, NANCY, MARY (POLLY), CHARITY.
Date in Pee Dee: 1750
Location: PRESENT MARION COUNTY
Source(s): SELLERS.
Notes: WIFE WAS DAUGHTER OF ANDREW BERRY.

DEWITT, CHARLES   ID: 1675
Spouse: [--?--] MCCALL
Date in Pee Dee: 1780
Location: WELCH TRACT
Source(s): GREGG.
Notes: SON OF THOMAS #1667.

DEWITT, CHARLES   ID: 5302
Spouse: SARAH TROUBLEFIELD
Children: WILLIAM.
Date in Pee Dee: 1743   Last Date: 1745
Location: PRINCE FREDERICK PARISH
Source(s): RBPPFW.
Notes: MARRIED 15 SEPTEMBER 1743 AT PARISH OF PRINCE
FREDERICK WINYAW.

DEWITT, DOROTHEA   ID: 1671
Spouse: JOHIAH J. EVANS
Date in Pee Dee: 1780
Location: WELCH TRACT
Source(s): GREGG.
Notes: DAUGHTER OF WILLIAM #297.

DEWITT, ELEANOR   ID: 1651
Spouse: ALLEN CHAPMAN
Date in Pee Dee: 1780
Location: WELCH TRACT
Source(s): GREGG.
Notes: DAUGHTER OF WILLIAM #297.

DEWITT, ELIZABETH   ID: 1652
Spouse: SAMUEL WILDS
Date in Pee Dee: 1780
Location: WELCH TRACT
Source(s): GREGG.
Notes: DAUGHTER OF WILLIAM #297.

DEWITT, HARRIS   ID: 1747
Spouse: ELIZABETH BROCKINGTON
Date in Pee Dee: 1770
Location: CHERAWS DISTRICT

DEWITT, JOHN   ID: 1646
Spouse: NANCY POWE
Children: MARTIN.
Date in Pee Dee: 1770   Last Date: 1780
Location: WELCH TRACT
Source(s): GREGG.
Notes: SON OF WILLIAM #297.

DEWITT, MARGARET   ID: 1653
Spouse: ENOCH HANFORD
Date in Pee Dee: 1780
Location: WELCH TRACT
Source(s): GREGG.
Notes: DAUGHTER OF WILLIAM #297.

DEWITT, MARTIN   ID: 296
Spouse: ELLEN DOUTHEL
Children: WILLIAM, HARRIS, THOMAS, JOHN.
Date in Pee Dee: 1760   Last Date: 1781
Origin: VIRGINIA

Location: BLACK CREEK
Source(s): COOK, JVSDP, GREGG.
Notes: GREGG SAYS HE WAS ACTIVE IN REVOLUTION ALTHOUGH
ADVANCED IN AGE.

DEWITT, MARY   ID: 1649
Spouse: EDWARD EDWARDS
Date in Pee Dee: 1775 DOB
Location: WELCH TRACT
Source(s): GREGG, JENKINS.
Notes: DAUGHTER OF WILLIAM #297.

DEWITT, SARAH   ID: 1650
Spouse: [--?--] JAMES
Date in Pee Dee: 1780
Location: WELCH TRACT
Source(s): GREGG.
Notes: DAUGHTER OF WILLIAM #297.

DEWITT, THOMAS   ID: 1667
Children: THOMAS, WILLIAM, CHARLES.
Date in Pee Dee: 1760
Origin: VIRGINIA
Location: WELCH TRACT
Source(s): GREGG.
Notes: PROBABLY BROTHER OF MARTIN.

DEWITT, WILLIAM   ID: 297
Spouse: MARY DEVONALD
Children: JOHN, MARY, SARAH, CHARLES M., ELIZABETH,
DANIEL, ELEANOR, MARGARET.
Date in Pee Dee: 1750 DOB Last Date: 1782 DIED
Origin: VIRGINIA
Location: ST. DAVID'S PARISH
Source(s): COOK, JENKINS, GREGG, JVSDP.
Notes: REPRESENTATIVE TO POST WAR LEGISLATURE. SON OF
MARTIN #296.
Revolutionary War service: MARION'S BRIGADE

DEXTER, JOHN ID: 298
Spouse: MARY BUCKELLS
Date in Pee Dee: 1741   Last Date: 1746
Location: PRINCE FREDERICK PARISH
Source(s): COOK, RBPPFW, MOORE.
Notes: MARRIED 14 FEBRUARY 1747 AT PARISH OF PRINCE
FREDERICK WINYAW.

DIAL, JOHN ID: 300
Date in Pee Dee: 1782
Location: CHERAWS DISTRICT
Source(s): COOK, BODDIE.
Revolutionary War service: PRIVATE MARION'S BRIGADE.

DIAL, SARAH ID: 4550
Spouse: JOHN FRIERSON
Children: AARON, MOSES, JOHN, THOMAS, MARY, CATHERINE.
Date in Pee Dee: 1741
Source(s): RBPPFW.

DIAL, THOMAS ID: 4549
Spouse: KATHERINE MCGINNEY
Children: SARAH, MARY, KATHERINE, THOMAS.
Date in Pee Dee: 1737   Last Date: 1759
Location: WILLIAMSBURG
Source(s): BODDIE, RBPPFW.
Notes: SPELLED DYAL IN PARISH RECORDS. SERVED IN FRENCH
AND INDIAN WAR. MARRIED 25 APRIL 1738.

DICK, GEORGE ID: 301
Spouse: ALLEIN MARY
Date in Pee Dee: 1735   Last Date: 1743
Location: PRINCE GEORGE PARISH ON BLACK RIVER.
Source(s): COOK, RBPPFW, MOORE V.1.
Notes: MARRIED 12 NOVEMBER 1743 AT PARISH OF PRINCE
FREDERICK WINYAW.

DICK, JENNETT ID: 3361
Spouse: [--?--] PACKER

Date in Pee Dee: 1760   Last Date: 1766
Location: PRINCE FREDERICK PARISH
Source(s): MOORE V.3.
Notes: DAUGHTER OF JOHN #303.

DICK, JOHN   ID: 303
Spouse: JANE (JEAN) MCCORMACK
Children: ROBERT, JOHN, WILLIAM, ELIZABETH (LEVISTON),
JENNET (PACKER), JANE, MARGARET (SCOTT), MARY (RAVNELS),
SUSANNA (WIRTER).
Date in Pee Dee: 1737   Last Date: 1749 DIED
Origin: NORTHERN IRELAND
Location: WILLIAMSBURG
Source(s): COOK, BODDIE, MOORE.
Notes: BODDIE SAYS MARY MARRIED RUNNELS.

DICK, JOHN   ID: 3814
Date in Pee Dee: 1765
Location: WILLIAMSBURG
Source(s): MOORE V.3.
Notes: INHERITED LAND CALLED RATTLESNAKE GULLY. SON OF
JOHN #303.

DICK, MARGARET   ID: 3817
Spouse: JOHN SCOTT
Date in Pee Dee: 1765
Location: WILLIAMSBURG
Source(s): MOORE V.3.
Notes: DAUGHTER OF JOHN #303.

DICK, MARY   ID: 3818
Spouse: [--?--] RAVNELS
Date in Pee Dee: 1765
Location: WILLIAMSBURG
Source(s): MOORE V.3.
Notes: DAUGHTER OF JOHN #303.

DICK, MARY   ID: 4318
Children: MARY.

Date in Pee Dee: 1772
Source(s): MOORE V.3.
Notes: A WIDOW IN 1772.

DICK, SUSANNA   ID: 3819
Spouse: [--?--] WINTER
Date in Pee Dee: 1765
Location: WILLIAMSBURG
Source(s): MOORE V.3.
Notes: DAUGHTER OF JOHN #303.

DICK, WILLIAM   ID: 1634
Spouse: MARGARET DUBOSE
Date in Pee Dee: 1756   Last Date: 1766
Location: LYNCHES CREEK
Source(s): GREGG.
Notes: PROBABLY SON OF JOHN #303. INHERITED LAND IN NC
FROM FATHER.

DICKEY, GEORGE   ID: 4522
Date in Pee Dee: 1771
Location: PRINCE FREDERICK PARISH
Source(s): MOORE V.3.
Notes: WIFE WAS PROBABLY JANET #4521.

DICKEY, JANET   ID: 4521
Date in Pee Dee: 1771
Location: PRINCE FREDERICK PARISH
Source(s): MOORE V.3.
Notes: GRAND-DAUGHTER OF JOHN FRIERSON AND JANET KING
#3434.

DICKEY, JOHN   ID: 306
Spouse: MARY PRIGG
Children: JOHN PRIGG.
Date in Pee Dee: 1775   Last Date: 1780
Location: PRINCE FREDERICK PARISH
Source(s): COOK, BODDIE.
Notes: MARRIED DAUGHTER OF JOHN PRIGG #4432.

Revolutionary War service: PRIVATE MARION'S BRIGADE.

DINKINS, WILLIAM   ID: 5338
Spouse: SARAH TOMPKINS
Date in Pee Dee: 1738
Location: PRINCE FREDERICK PARISH
Source(s): RBPPFW, BODDIE.
Notes: MARRIED 12 FEBRUARY 1738 AT PARISH OF PRINCE
FREDERICK WINYAW.

DOBBIN, ELIZABETH (WIDOW)   ID: 5191
Date in Pee Dee: 1780
Location: WILLIAMSBURG
Source(s): BODDIE.
Notes: SUPPLIED MARION.

DOBBIN, JANE   ID: 151
Spouse: [--?--] JAMES
Date in Pee Dee: 1753
Location: PRINCE FREDERICK PARISH
Source(s): MOORE.
Notes: GRAND-DAUGHTER OF THOMAS AND JANNETT MCCREE.

DOBIEN, WILLIAM   ID: 309
Children: JEAN.
Date in Pee Dee: 1750   Last Date: 1768
Location: WILLIAMSBURG
Source(s): COOK, MOORE.

DONALDLY, EDWARD   ID: 2523
Spouse: [--?--] BORDLINE
Children: SARAH.
Date in Pee Dee: 1744
Location: WILLIAMSBURG
Source(s): MOORE.

DONALDSON, JOHN   ID: 310
Date in Pee Dee: 1775
Location: CHERAW DISTRICT

Source(s): COOK, GREGG.
Revolutionary War service: LIEUTENANT IN WISE'S COMPANY.

DONALDSON, WILLIAM   ID: 3182
Date in Pee Dee: 1759   Last Date: 1759 DIED
Location: KINGSTON
Source(s): MOORE.
Notes: MINISTER OF PRESBYTERIAN CHURCH AT BRITTON'S
NECK.

DONEY, JOHN   ID: 2098
Date in Pee Dee: 1759   Last Date: 1782
Location: ST. DAVID'S PARISH
Source(s): GREGG P.407, MUSTER ROLL.
Notes: MAY HAVE BEEN ANOTHER WHO SERVED WITH MARION.
SERVED IN FRENCH AND INDIAN WAR.
Revolutionary War service: MILITIA PRIVATE.

DONOLDSON, JOHN   ID: 1633
Date in Pee Dee: 1756   Last Date: 1777
Location: LYNCHES CREEK
Source(s): GREGG, RUDISILL.
Notes: MOVED TO RICHMOND COUNTY NC, KILLED IN
REVOLUTION.
Revolutionary War service: COLONEL IN NC MILITIA.

DORMER, JAMES   ID: 314
Date in Pee Dee: 1761
Occupation: MINISTER   Origin: ENGLAND
Location: PRINCE FREDERICK PARISH
Source(s): COOK, RBPPFW.

DOUGLAS, DANIEL   ID: 5403
Spouse: MARGARET GANDY
Date in Pee Dee: 1745
Location: PRINCE FREDERICK PARISH
Source(s): RBPPFW.
Notes: MARRIED 24 FEBRUARY 1745 AT PARISH OF PRINCE
FREDERICK WINYAW.

DOUGLASS, JESSE ID: 316
Date in Pee Dee: 1781
Location: CHERAWS DISTRICT
Source(s): COOK, GREGG P.407.
Revolutionary War service: SERVED 110 DAYS IN MARION'S
BRIGADE.

DOUGLASS, JOSHUA ID: 1830
Date in Pee Dee: 1768   Last Date: 1781
Location: ST. DAVID'S PARISH
Source(s): GREGG, GREGG P.406.
Revolutionary War service: PRIVATE IN MARION'S BRIGADE.

DOWNES, RACHEL ID: 319
Date in Pee Dee: 1755   Last Date: 1759
Location: WELCH NECK
Source(s): COOK, RWNBC.
Notes: PROBABLY WIFE OF WALTER.

DOZIER, JOHN ID: 322
Spouse: ELIZABETH [--?--]
Date in Pee Dee: 1737   Last Date: 1775
Location: GEORGETOWN
Source(s): COOK, BODDIE, GREGG.
Notes: SERVED IN CAPTAIN POWELL'S REGIMENT DURING FRENCH
AND INDIAN WAR.

DRAKE, EDMUND ID: 2376
Date in Pee Dee: 1778
Location: ST. DAVID'S PARISH
Source(s): RUDISILL.
Notes: POSSIBLY MARRIED MARY MANN.

DRAPER, JOSEPH ID: 5580
Date in Pee Dee: 1759
Location: ST. DAVID'S PARISH
Source(s): MUSTER ROLL.
Notes: SERVED IN FRENCH AND INDIAN WAR AS PRIVATE IN
CAPTAIN DAVID EVANS' COMPANY.

DREW, NATHANIEL   **ID: 2695**
Spouse: MARGARET BARR
Children: SAMUEL.
Date in Pee Dee: 1737   Last Date: 1750 DIED
Location: WILLIAMSBURG
Source(s): MOORE, BODDIE.
Notes: BROTHER OF DAVID. TWO DAUGHTERS MARRIED JOHN
BROCKINGTON AND SAMUEL NESMITH.

DRIGGERS, WINSLER   **ID: 1751**
Date in Pee Dee: 1759   Last Date: 1771
Location: CHERAW DISTRICT
Source(s): GREGG, MUSTER ROLL.
Notes: AN OUTLAW KILLED BY A GROUP LED BY PHILLIP
PLEDGER. SERVED IN FRENCH AND INDIAN WAR.

DRING, AZARIAH   **ID: 1605**
Spouse: MARY [--?--]
Children: AZRIAH, PIERCE, THOMAS, BARSHERA, UNIS, MARY
NACY, ELIZABETH (BETSY).
Date in Pee Dee: 1756   Last Date: 1756 DIED
Location: CRAVEN COUNTY
Source(s): MOORE.

DROWHANNY, RENAIE   **ID: 4946**
Date in Pee Dee: 1756
Origin: NOVA SCOTIA
Location: WILLIAMSBURG
Source(s): BODDIE.
Notes: HE, WIFE, AND CHILDREN WERE ACADIANS TRANSPORTED
FROM NOVA SCOTIA.

DUBORDIEU, JOSEPH   **ID: 327**
Date in Pee Dee: 1735   Last Date: 1757
Location: NORTH SIDE OF SAMPIT RIVER
Source(s): COOK, MOORE, ROGERS.
Notes: FIRST CLERK OF INDIGO SOCIETY.

DUBOSE, ANDREW   **ID: 328**

Spouse: REBECCA DUBOSE
Children: BENJAMIN, HERBERT, ELIZABETH (BROWN), HUGH, JOSHUA, JOEL, MARGARET, SAMUEL.
Date in Pee Dee: 1735   Last Date: 1803
Location: ST. DAVID'S PARISH
Source(s): COOK, REMBERT, GREGG, BODDIE.
Notes: SON OF PETER JR. SHE WAS DAUGHTER OF JOHN DUBOSE.
Revolutionary War service: CAPTAIN IN LIDE'S COMPANY.

DUBOSE, DANIEL   ID: 329
Spouse: FRANCES SEMANS
Date in Pee Dee: 1781   Last Date: 1787
Location: LYNCHES CREEK
Source(s): COOK, CLEMENS, GREGG.
Notes: SON OF JOHN #336. MARRIED 11 NOVEMBER 1766 AT SANTEE.
Revolutionary War service: LIEUTENENT IN MARION'S BRIGADE.

DUBOSE, ELIAS   ID: 330
Spouse: LYDIA CASSELS
Children: JESSE, ISAIAH, JOHN.
Date in Pee Dee: 1784
Location: ST. DAVID'S
Source(s): COOK, GREGG.
Notes: SON OF JOHN #336.
Revolutionary War service: LIEUTENENT IN MARION'S BRIGADE.

DUBOSE, ELISHA   ID: 331
Date in Pee Dee: 1775
Location: ST. DAVID'S PARISH
Source(s): COOK.
Revolutionary War service: LIDE'S COMPANY.

DUBOSE, ESTHER   ID: 3569
Spouse: [--?--] COURTURIER
Date in Pee Dee: 1763
Location: SANTEE RIVER

Source(s): MOORE V.3.
Notes: DAUGHTER OF ESTHER #3565.

DUBOSE, ESTHER (WIDOW)   ID: 3565
Children: JONATHAN, JEPTHA, JOSHUA, ESTHER (COURTURIER).
Date in Pee Dee: 1763   Last Date: 1764 DIED
Location: SANTEE RIVER
Source(s): MOORE V.3.

DUBOSE, ISAAC   ID: 333
Date in Pee Dee: 1775   Last Date: 1782
Location: LYNCHES CREEK
Source(s): COOK, CLEMENS, GREGG.
Notes: SON OF JOHN #336. MAY HAVE MARRIED CATHERINE
DUBOSE.
Revolutionary War service: LIDE'S COMPANY.

DUBOSE, ISAAC ELBERT   ID: 332
Spouse: SARAH JAMES
Children: HOMER, ELISHA, SAMUEL, BENJAMIN JAMES, JAMES,
NANCY, REBECCA, ELIAS, MARY, SARAH, JOHN, ELIZABETH.
Date in Pee Dee: 1745   Last Date: 1824
Location: NORTH SIDE OF SANTEE RIVER
Source(s): COOK, REMBERT.
Notes: SON OF PETER JR.

DUBOSE, ISAIAH   ID: 1720
Spouse: GILLY BENTON
Date in Pee Dee: 1770
Location: CHERAW DISTRICT
Source(s): GREGG.

DUBOSE, JAMES   ID: 334
Date in Pee Dee: 1775
Location: ST. DAVID'S PARISH
Source(s): COOK.
Revolutionary War service: LIDE'S COMPANY.

DUBOSE, JOHN   ID: 335

Date in Pee Dee: 1759   Last Date: 1782
Location: CHERAWS DISTRICT
Source(s): COOK, BODDIE.
Notes: SERVED IN FRENCH AND INDIAN WAR.

DUBOSE, JOHN   ID: 336
Children: ISAAC, ELIAS, DANIEL, MARGARET, JOSEPH,
REBECCA.
Date in Pee Dee: 1732   Last Date: 1756
Location: PRINCE FREDRICK PARISH
Source(s): COOK, GREGG.
Notes: PLANTATION ON LYNCHES RIVER ABOUT 1756.

DUBOSE, MARGARET   ID: 1630
Spouse: WILLIAM DICK
Date in Pee Dee: 1760
Location: LYNCHES CREEK
Source(s): GREGG.
Notes: SON OF SON #336.

DUBOSE, PETER III   ID: 337
Spouse: MARY [--?--]
Children: CATHERINE (BOWERS) (O'HEARN), AMOS, PETER P.,
MARY (BELL), REUBEN.
Date in Pee Dee: 1782   Last Date: 1800
Location: CHERAWS DISTRICT
Source(s): COOK, REMBERT.
Notes: SON OF PETER II.

DUBOSE, PETER JR.   ID: 1629
Spouse: SARAH [--?--]
Children: ELIZABETH (HODGE), JAMES, AMOS, PETER, JOHN,
SARAH, ZACHARIAH, WILLIAM, ISAAC.
Date in Pee Dee: 1760   Last Date: 1777
Location: LYNCHES CREEK
Source(s): GREGG, BODDIE, REMBERT.
Notes: REMBERT REPORTS MOVED TO GEORGIA IN 1777. SON OF
PIERRE AND MADELAINE ROYER DUBOSE.
Revolutionary War service: PRIVATE MARION'S BRIGADE.

DUBOSE, SAMUEL   ID: 2101
Spouse: MARTHA WHITE (WIDOW)
Date in Pee Dee: 1782
Location: CHERAW DISTRICT
Source(s): GREGG, CLEMENS.
Notes: MARRIED IN CHARLESTON 6 DECEMBER 1801.
Revolutionary War service: PRIVATE IN MARION'S BRIGADE.

DUBOSE, STEPHEN   ID: 3550
Spouse: ELIZABETH [--?--]
Date in Pee Dee: 1736
Location: PRINCE FREDERICK PARISH
Source(s): BODDIE.

DUBOSE, WILLIAM   ID: 2102
Date in Pee Dee: 1782
Source(s): GREGG P.407.
Revolutionary War service: BENTON'S REGIMENT SERGEANT.

DUBOURIER, JOSEPH   ID: 4578
Spouse: MARY WHITE
Date in Pee Dee: 1746   Last Date: 1776
Location: PRINCE GEORGE WINYAH PARISH
Source(s): MOORE V.3, RBPPFW.
Notes: MARRIED 24 JUNE 1746 AT PARISH OF PRINCE
FREDERICK WINYAW.

DUBUSH, JOHN   ID: 4963
Date in Pee Dee: 1759
Location: WILLIAMSBURG
Source(s): BODDIE.
Notes: SERVED IN FRENCH AND INDIAN WAR.

DUBUSH, SUSANNAH   ID: 5421
Spouse: ROBERT LEWIS
Date in Pee Dee: 1747
Location: PRINCE FREDERICK PARISH
Source(s): RBPPFW.

Early Pee Dee Settlers
--D--

DUE, BENJAMIN   ID: 5587
Date in Pee Dee: 1759
Location: ST. DAVID'S PARISH
Source(s): MUSTER ROLL.
Notes: SERVED IN FRENCH AND INDIAN WAR AS PRIVATE IN
CAPTAIN DAVID EVANS' COMPANY.

DUETT, JOSEPH   ID: 5721
Date in Pee Dee: 1759
Location: ST. DAVID'S PARISH
Source(s): MUSTER ROLL.
Notes: LISTED AS A DESERTER FROM HITCHCOCK'S COMPANY
DURING FRENCH AND INDIAN WAR.

DUKE, BEN   ID: 5022
Spouse: RACHEL HIGGINS (WIDOW)
Date in Pee Dee: 1780
Location: WILLIAMSBURG
Source(s): BODDIE, CLEMENS.
Notes: MARRIED 30 AUGUST 1784 AT CHARLESTON.
Revolutionary War service: PRIVATE MARION'S BRIGADE.

DUKE, BENJAMIN   ID: 5296
Spouse: MARY [--?--]
Children: WILLIAM.
Date in Pee Dee: 1745
Location: PRINCE FREDERICK PARISH
Source(s): RBPPFW.

DUKE, WILLIAM   ID: 5023
Date in Pee Dee: 1780
Location: WILLIAMSBURG
Source(s): BODDIE.
Revolutionary War service: PRIVATE MARION'S BRIGADE.

DULING, JAMES   ID: 2103
Date in Pee Dee: 1782
Source(s): GREGG P.407.
Revolutionary War service: PRIVATE IN MARION'S BRIGADE.

DULING, JOHN   **ID: 2104**
Date in Pee Dee: 1782
Source(s): GREGG P.407.
Revolutionary War service: PRIVATE IN MARION'S BRIGADE.

DUNBAR, THOMAS   **ID: 1000**
Spouse: MARY WITHERS
Date in Pee Dee: 1784
Location: PRINCE GEORGE WINYAH PARISH
Source(s): CLEMENS.
Notes: MARRIED 2 SEPTEMBER 1784.

DUNLOP, MARY   **ID: 5473**
Spouse: WILLIAM PAULLING
Date in Pee Dee: 1757
Location: PRINCE FREDERICK PARISH
Source(s): RBPPFW.

DUNN, SILVESTER   **ID: 3201**
Date in Pee Dee: 1757
Location: ST. MARK'S PARISH
Source(s): MOORE, BODDIE.
Revolutionary War service: FRENCH AND INDIAN WAR

DUNNAM, EBENEZER   **ID: 339**
Spouse: FRANCES COMMANDER
Date in Pee Dee: 1745   Last Date: 1782
Location: PRINCE FREDERICK PARISH
Source(s): COOK, RBPPFW, MOORE V.3.
Notes: MARRIED 20 FEBRUARY 1745 AT PARISH OF PRINCE
FREDERICK WINYAW.

DUPONT, ALEXANDER   **ID: 5307**
Spouse: ANNE [--?--]
Children: ELIZABETH.
Date in Pee Dee: 1747
Location: PRINCE FREDERICK PARISH
Source(s): RBPPFW.

DUPRE, ANNE   ID: 5422
Spouse: GEORGE JR. PAWLEY
Date in Pee Dee: Last Date: 1746
Location: PRINCE FREDERICK PARISH
Source(s): RBPPFW.

DUPRE, JOSIAS GARNIER   ID: 341
Spouse: ANN [--?--]
Children: JOHN, JOHN ELDERS, RICHARD, LEWIS, SAMUEL.
Date in Pee Dee: 1730   Last Date: 1747
Location: PEE DEE BELOW LITTLE PEE DEE
Source(s): COOK, RBPPFW.
Notes: VESTRY MAN OF PARISH OF PRINCE FREDERICK WINYAW
IN 1731.

DURANT (DURONG), JOSEPH   ID: 4936
Spouse: ANN LAMBERT
Children: MARY, JOSSETTE, ANN, MARGARET, MARY ANN,
ROSALIE.
Date in Pee Dee: 1756
Location: WILLIAMSBURG
Source(s): BODDIE.
Notes: HE, WIFE AND CHILDREN WERE ACADIANS TRANSPORTED
FROM NOVA SCOTIA.

DURANT, THOMAS   ID: 345
Date in Pee Dee: 1783
Location: PRINCE FREDERICK'S PARRISH
Source(s): COOK.
Revolutionary War service: SERVED 40 DAYS IN MARION'S
BRIGADE.

DUTART, DANIEL   ID: 3288
Spouse: MARY [--?--]
Children: JOHN, DANIEL.
Date in Pee Dee: 1736   Last Date: 1736 DIED
Location: CRAVEN COUNTY
Source(s): MOORE V.1.

DUTART, JOHN   ID: 3290
Spouse: MARY BOINEAU
Date in Pee Dee: 1736   Last Date: 1764
Location: CRAVEN COUNTY
Source(s): MOORE V.1, CLEMENS.
Notes: SON OF DANIEL #3288.

DUTART, JOSEPH   ID: 3291
Date in Pee Dee: 1736
Location: CRAVEN COUNTY
Source(s): MOORE V.1.
Notes: BROTHER OF DANIEL #3288.

DWIGHT, DANIEL   ID: 346
Spouse: CHRISTIANA BROUGHTON
Date in Pee Dee: 1730   Last Date: 1747
Location: KINGSTON TOWNSHIP
Source(s): COOK, CLEMENS, SMITH, H..
Notes: MARRIED JANUARY 1747 AT CHARLESTON. SEEMS TO HAVE
MARRIED ESTHER CORDES IN 1747.

DWIGHT, JOHN   ID: 4162
Spouse: MARTHA LEWIS
Date in Pee Dee: 1770   Last Date: 1770 DIED
Location: ALL SAINT'S PARISH
Source(s): MOORE V.3.
Notes: BROTHER OF NATHANIEL AND SAMUEL.

DWIGHT, NATHANIEL   ID: 4163
Date in Pee Dee: 1770   Last Date: 1776 DIED
Location: WACCAMAW
Source(s): MOORE V.3.
Notes: BROTHER OF JOHN AND SAMUEL.

DWIGHT, SAMUEL   ID: 4164
Date in Pee Dee: 1770
Source(s): MOORE V.3.
Notes: BROTHER OF JOHN AND NATHANIEL.

Early Pee Dee Settlers
--D--

DWIGHT, TIMOTHY   ID: 347
Date in Pee Dee: 1782
Location: ALL SAINT'S PARISH
Source(s): COOK.
Notes: REPRESENTATIVE TO POST WAR SC LEGISLATURE.

DWYER, JUDITH   ID: 5466
Spouse: JAMES CAMPBELL
Date in Pee Dee: 1749
Location: PRINCE FREDERICK PARISH
Source(s): RBPPFW.

DYE, JOHN   ID: 5024
Date in Pee Dee: 1780
Location: WILLIAMSBURG
Source(s): BODDIE.
Revolutionary War service: PRIVATE MARION'S BRIGADE.

DYER, MARGARET   ID: 5436
Spouse: WILLIAM PROCTOR
Date in Pee Dee: 1747
Location: PRINCE FREDERICK PARISH
Source(s): RBPPFW.

EADDY, SEE ALSO EDIE, EADY, EDY, EADY, EDDY.

EADDY, DANIEL   ID: 5026
Date in Pee Dee: 1780
Location: WILLIAMSBURG
Source(s): BODDIE.
Revolutionary War service: PRIVATE IN MARION'S BRIGADE.

EADDY, HENRY   ID: 5027
Date in Pee Dee: 1780
Location: WILLIAMSBURG
Source(s): BODDIE.
Revolutionary War service: PRIVATE IN MARION'S BRIGADE.

EADDY, JAMES   ID: 2540
Spouse: SARAH [--?--]
Children: JAMES, SAMUEL.
Date in Pee Dee: 1753   Last Date: 1790
Location: SOUTH SIDE OF LYNCHES CREEK
Source(s): EADDY.
Revolutionary War service: MILITIA

EADDY, JAMES JR   ID: 2541
Spouse: MARY DRAKE
Children: HENRY, JAMES, EDWARD, JOHN, SARAH, MARY,
AGNES.

Date in Pee Dee: 1754
Location: SOUTH SIDE OF LYNCHES CREEK
Source(s): EADDY.
Notes: SON OF #2540.
Revolutionary War service: MILITIA

EDDY, WILLIAM   ID: 3603
Spouse: MARY HAMILTON
Date in Pee Dee: 1762
Location: PRINCE FREDERICK PARISH
Source(s): MOORE V.3.
Notes: ALSO SPELLED EADDY.

EDWARDS, ABEL   ID: 1447
Spouse: SARAH HARRY
Children: CATHERINE, EDWARD, SARAH.
Date in Pee Dee: 1760   Last Date: 1793 DIED
Location: WELCH TRACT
Source(s): GREGG, JVSDP, RWNBC.
Notes: SON OF JOSHUA #1444. SECOND MARRIED SARAH DOUTHEL
(DOUSNEL). KOLB'S COMPANY FRENCH AND INDIAN WAR.

EDWARDS, CATHERINE   ID: 1311
Spouse: TRASHLEY CHAPMAN
Date in Pee Dee: 1760
Location: ST. DAVID'S PARISH
Source(s): GREGG.
Notes: DAUGHTER OF JOSHUA #1444.

EDWARDS, CHARLES   ID: 4877
Spouse: SARAH DUGGAR
Date in Pee Dee: 1782   Last Date: 1790
Location: ST. MARK'S PARISH
Source(s): MOORE V.3, CLEMENS.

EDWARDS, EDWARD   ID: 1672
Spouse: MARY DEWITT
Children: ABEL.

Date in Pee Dee: 1760   Last Date: 1780
Location: WELCH TRACT
Source(s): GREGG.

EDWARDS, HENRY   ID: 5183
Spouse: ELIZABETH OLIVER
Date in Pee Dee: 1760
Location: ST. DAVID'S PARISH
Source(s): GREGG.
Notes: SON OF JOSHUA #1444.

EDWARDS, JOB   ID: 351
Spouse: MARY WILDS
Date in Pee Dee: 1737   Last Date: 1742
Location: WELCH NECK
Source(s): COOK, GREGG, RBPPFW.
Notes: MARRIED BY REV. FORDYCE IN PRINCE FREDERICK
PARISH 10 SEPTEMBER 1737.

EDWARDS, JOB   ID: 1854
Date in Pee Dee: 1768   Last Date: 1779
Location: ST. DAVID'S PARISH
Source(s): GREGG, RWNBC, MOORE V.3.
Notes: WIFE WAS PROBABLY MARY.

EDWARDS, JOHN   ID: 4385
Spouse: MARTHA [--?--]
Date in Pee Dee: 1773   Last Date: 1778
Location: ST. DAVID'S PARISH
Source(s): MOORE V.3, RWNBC.
Notes: SON OF WILLIAM #4384.

EDWARDS, JOHN   ID: 5182
Spouse: ELIZABETH BEVIL
Date in Pee Dee: 1760
Location: ST. DAVID'S PARISH
Source(s): GREGG.
Notes: SON OF JOSHUA #1444.

EDWARDS, JOSHUA   ID: 1444
Spouse: RACHEL [--?--]
Children: THOMAS, ABEL, RACHEL, PHOEBE, HENRY, ELIJAH,
JOHN, MARY.
Date in Pee Dee: 1749   Last Date: 1784
Occupation: MINISTER   Origin: DELAWARE
Location: WELCH TRACT
Source(s): GREGG, RWNBC, COOK.
Notes: THIRD PASTOR OF WELCH NECK CHURCH. MAY HAVE FIRST
MARRIED CATHERINE STEPHENS.

EDWARDS, JOSHUA   ID: 1446
Children: SARAH, THOMAS, PETER, ANN.
Date in Pee Dee: 1759   Last Date: 1780
Location: WELCH TRACT
Source(s): GREGG, RWNBC.
Notes: SON OF THOMAS #355. SERVED IN FRENCH AND INDIAN
WAR AS PRIVATE.

EDWARDS, MARY   ID: 53
Date in Pee Dee: 1755   Last Date: 1773
Location: WELCH NECK
Source(s): COOK, MOORE, RWNBC.
Notes: APPEARS TO HAVE DIED 2/5/1778. DAUGHTER OF
WILLIAM #4384.

EDWARDS, MARY   ID: 5185
Spouse: JOHN RODGERS
Date in Pee Dee: 1760
Location: ST. DAVID'S PARISH
Source(s): GREGG, JENKINS.
Notes: DAUGHTER OF JOSHUA #1444.

EDWARDS, ROBERT   ID: 4692
Date in Pee Dee: 1761
Location: ST. DAVID'S PARISH
Source(s): RWNBC.
Notes: MOVED TO CAPE FEAR ABOUT THIS TIME.

EDWARDS, SARAH   ID: 354
Spouse: JOHN MCDONALD
Date in Pee Dee: 1755   Last Date: 1759
Location: WELCH NECK
Source(s): COOK, GREGG, RWNBC.
Notes: DAUGHTER OF JOSHUA #1444.

EDWARDS, SARAH   ID: 1740
Spouse: JAMES HART
Children: JAMES, THOMAS.
Date in Pee Dee: 1770
Location: ST. DAVID'S PARISH.
Source(s): GREGG.

EDWARDS, THOMAS   ID: 355
Spouse: SARAH ROBLYN
Children: JOSHUA.
Date in Pee Dee: 1755   Last Date: 1770
Location: CASHAWAY
Source(s): COOK, RWNBC, GREGG.
Notes: SERVED IN FRENCH AND INDIAN WAR AS LIEUTENANT.
SON OF JOSHUA #1444.

EDWARDS, WILLIAM   ID: 4384
Children: JOHN, WILLIAM, ELIZABETH, MARY.
Date in Pee Dee: 1773   Last Date: 1773 DIED
Location: ST. DAVID'S PARISH
Source(s): MOORE V.3.

EDWARDS, WILLIAM   ID: 4876
Spouse: ELIZABETH [--?--]
Date in Pee Dee: 1782   Last Date: 1782 DIED
Location: PUDDEN (PUDDING) SWAMP
Source(s): MOORE V.3.
Notes: A NEPHEW, CHARLES EDWARDS.

EDWARDS, WILLIAM JR.   ID: 1796
Spouse: CATHERINE [--?--]
Date in Pee Dee: 1768   Last Date: 1778

Location: ST. DAVID'S PARISH
Source(s): GREGG, RWNBC, MOORE V.3.
Notes: SON OF WILLIAM #4384

ELLEBY, THOMAS   ID: 5258
Spouse: MARTHA [--?--]
Children: THOMAS.
Date in Pee Dee: 1743
Location: PRINCE FREDERICK PARISH
Source(s): RBPPFW.
Notes: SEE ELLERBE.

ELLERBE, JOHN   ID: 1374
Spouse: MARTHA POWE
Date in Pee Dee: 1780
Location: CHERAW DISTRICT
Source(s): GREGG, SELLERS.

ELLERBE, JOSEPH   ID: 1369
Spouse: ELIZABETH ELERBY
Date in Pee Dee: 1780
Location: CHERAW DISTRICT
Source(s): GREGG.

ELLERBE, THOMAS   ID: 358
Spouse: OBEDIENCE GALESPY
Children: THOMAS, JANE, MARY, WILLIAM, JAMES, JOSEPH,
REBECCA (MACFARLANE), JOHN.
Date in Pee Dee: 1743   Last Date: 1808 DIED
Location: CHERAW DISTRICT
Source(s): COOK, ELLERBE, GREGG, SELLERS.
Notes: MEMBER OF ORIGINAL BOARD OF ST. DAVID'S PARISH.
SON OF THOMAS #361.
Revolutionary War service: ELLERBE'S COMPANY.

ELLERBE, THOMAS M.   ID: 1371
Spouse: LESLIE PRINCE
Date in Pee Dee: 1769
Location: CHERAW DISTRICT

Source(s): ELLERBE.
Notes: SON OF THOMAS #358.

ELLERBE, WILLIAM   ID: 1874
Spouse: HANNAH FARR
Children: ESTHER, FARR, WILLIAM F., ELIZABETH F., MARTHA
E., ZACHARIAH, THOMAS F..
Date in Pee Dee: 1765   Last Date: 1830
Location: ST. DAVID'S PARISH
Source(s): GREGG, ELLERBE.

ELLERBE, WILLIAM E.   ID: 359
Spouse: ELIZABETH CRAWFORD
Children: ESTHER, THOMAS C., JOHN C., WILLIAM C.,
OBEDIENCE, ELIZABETH, ZACHARIAH, MARTHA E., MARY,
MICHAEL.
Date in Pee Dee: 1765   Last Date: 1830
Origin: NATIVE
Location: CHERAW DISTRICT
Source(s): COOK, ELLERBE, GREGG.
Notes: SON OF THOMAS #358.
Revolutionary War service: IN MARION'S BRIGADE.

ELLERBE, WILLIAM F.   ID: 360
Spouse: ANN ROBINSON
Date in Pee Dee: 1780
Location: CHERAW DISTRICT
Source(s): COOK, ELLERBE.
Notes: SON OF WILLIAM #1874.

ELLERBY, THOMAS   ID: 361
Spouse: MARTHA [--?--]
Children: WILLIAM, THOMAS, MARY, JUDITH.
Date in Pee Dee: 1737   Last Date: 1750
Origin: ENGLAND
Location: CHERAW DISTRICT
Source(s): COOK, ELLERBE, GREGG.
Notes: CHILDREN SPELL NAME ELLERBE.

ELLISON, JOSEPH   ID: 2099
Date in Pee Dee: 1759   Last Date: 1783
Location: CHERAW DISTRICT
Source(s): GREGG P.430, MOORE.
Notes: STEPSON OF HENRY KOLB #708. SERVED AS SERGEANT IN
KOLB'S COMPANY IN FRENCH AND INDIAN WAR.

ELLISON, MATTHEW   ID: 2947
Children: ROBERT.
Date in Pee Dee: 1750   Last Date: 1772
Location: WILLIAMSBURG
Source(s): MOORE.
Notes: SON OF ROBERT #4389.

ELLISON, ROBERT   ID: 2013
Date in Pee Dee: 1750   Last Date: 1783
Location: CHERAW DISTRICT
Source(s): GREGG P.416, MOORE.
Notes: SON OF ROBERT #4389.

ELLISON, ROBERT   ID: 4389
Children: MATTHEW, ROBERT, MARY (ERVIN), [--?--](ERVIN).
Date in Pee Dee: 1772   Last Date: 1772 DIED
Location: WILLIAMSBURG
Source(s): MOORE V.3.

ELMS, WILLIAM   ID: 3043
Spouse: SARAH FIELDS
Date in Pee Dee: 1784
Location: CHERAW DISTRICT
Source(s): CLEMENS.
Notes: MARRIED JULY 1784.

ELVES, JOHN   ID: 4418
Date in Pee Dee:
Source(s): MOORE V.3.
Notes: OWNED LAND ON LITTLE PEE DEE.

ERVIN, HUGH   ID: 366

Spouse: MARY ELLISON
Date in Pee Dee: 1759   Last Date: 1772
Location: WILLIAMSBURG
Source(s): COOK, BODDIE, MOORE V.3.
Notes: SERVED AS PRIVATE IN FRENCH AND INDIAN WAR.
MARION'S SECOND IN COMMAND.
Revolutionary War service: COLONEL IN MARION'S BRIGADE.

ERVIN, HUGH   ID: 5491
Spouse: ELIZABETH JAMES
Date in Pee Dee: 1750
Location: WILLIAMSBURG
Source(s): BODDIE.

ERVIN, JAMES ROBERT   ID: 5028
Spouse: ELIZABETH POWE
Date in Pee Dee: 1780
Location: WILLIAMSBURG
Source(s): BODDIE.
Revolutionary War service: PRIVATE IN MARION'S BRIGADE.

ERVIN, JOHN   ID: 368
Spouse: ELIZABETH ELLISON
Children: JOHN, ELIZABETH.
Date in Pee Dee: 1750   Last Date: 1760
Location: WILLIAMSBURG
Source(s): COOK, BODDIE, MOORE.

ERVIN, JOHN II   ID: 367
Spouse: JANE WITHERSPOON
Children: ELIZABETH, SAMUEL, JAMES ROBERT, HUGH AND JOHN
BY MARGARET ERVIN.
Date in Pee Dee: 1754 DOB Last Date: 1820 DIED
Location: PRINCE FREDERICK'S PARISH
Source(s): COOK, BODDIE.
Notes: MARRIED DAUGHTER OF ROBERT ELLISON. COMMANDED
BRITTON'S NECK REGIMENT.
Revolutionary War service: COLONEL OF MILITIA.

Early Pee Dee Settlers
--E--

ERVIN, SAMUEL   ID: 1670
Spouse: SARAH DEWITT
Date in Pee Dee: 1760
Location: WELCH TRACT
Source(s): GREGG.

ERVIN, SAMUEL   ID: 4954
Date in Pee Dee: 1759
Location: WILLIAMSBURG
Source(s): BODDIE.
Notes: PRIVATE IN FRENCH AND INDIAN WAR.

EVANS, ABEL   ID: 370
Spouse: ELEANOR [--?--]
Date in Pee Dee: 1740   Last Date: 1765 DIED
Location: LONG BLUFF
Source(s): COOK, RWNBC, GREGG.

EVANS, ANN   ID: 5354
Spouse: WILLIAM TELLAR
Date in Pee Dee: 1740
Location: PRINCE FREDERICK PARISH
Source(s): RBPPFW.

EVANS, BENJAMIN   ID: 2106
Date in Pee Dee: 1782
Source(s): GREGG P.407.
Revolutionary War service: WINDHAM'S COMPANY AS 1ST
LIEUTENANT.

EVANS, BURWELL   ID: 2105
Date in Pee Dee: 1782
Source(s): GREGG P.407.
Revolutionary War service: PRIVATE IN MARION'S BRIGADE.

EVANS, CHARLES JR   ID: 2059
Date in Pee Dee: 1775
Location: ST. DAVID'S PARISH
Source(s): GREGG.

Revolutionary War service: MILITIA

EVANS, DAVID   ID: 373
Spouse: MARTHA [--?--]
Date in Pee Dee: 1755   Last Date: 1762
Location: WELCH NECK
Source(s): COOK, SELLERS, RWNBC, GREGG, MOORE V.3, WNBC.
Notes: SON OF NATHAN EVANS. CAPTAIN IN FRENCH AND INDIAN
WAR.

EVANS, ELEANOR   ID: 374
Date in Pee Dee: 1755   Last Date: 1765 DIED
Location: WELCH NECK
Source(s): COOK, RWNBC.
Notes: WIFE OF ABEL.

EVANS, ELIZA   ID: 1637
Spouse: CHRISTOPHER PEGUES
Date in Pee Dee: 1770
Location: CHERAW DISTRICT
Source(s): GREGG.
Notes: DAUGHTER OF THOMAS EVANS.

EVANS, ENOCH   ID: 376
Date in Pee Dee: 1773   Last Date: 1787
Location: CHERAW
Source(s): COOK, GREGG, MOORE V.3.
Notes: SON OF THOMAS E. EVANS.
Revolutionary War service: LIEUTENANT IN MARION'S
BRIGADE.

EVANS, EZER   ID: 2107
Date in Pee Dee: 1780
Source(s): GREGG P.407.
Revolutionary War service: PRIVATE IN IRBY'S COMPANY.

EVANS, HANNAH   ID: 1708
Spouse: JOHN F. WILSON
Date in Pee Dee: 1770

Location: WELCH NECK
Source(s): GREGG.

EVANS, JOHN   ID: 379
Spouse: ELIZABETH [--?--]
Date in Pee Dee: 1740   Last Date: 1778
Location: CHERAW DISTRICT (PIDGEON CREEK (BUCKHOLDT'S))
Source(s): COOK, RWNBC, GREGG, JVSDP.

EVANS, JOHN   ID: 5224
Spouse: REBECCA [--?--]
Children: JOHN, JONATHAN.
Date in Pee Dee: 1741   Last Date: 1745
Location: PRINCE FREDERICK PARISH
Source(s): RBPPFW, BODDIE.

EVANS, JOHN JR   ID: 380
Spouse: MARGARET [--?--]
Date in Pee Dee: 1775   Last Date: 1779
Location: ST. DAVID'S PARISH
Source(s): COOK, RWNBC.
Revolutionary War service: LIDE'S COMPANY

EVANS, JOSHUA JAMES   ID: 1643
Spouse: DOROTHY DEWITT
Date in Pee Dee: 1780
Location: WELCH TRACT
Source(s): GREGG.
Notes: SON OF THOMAS #1638.
Revolutionary War service: MILTIA

EVANS, JOSIAH   ID: 383
Spouse: MARY [--?--]
Date in Pee Dee: 1768   Last Date: 1783
Location: ST. DAVID'S PARISH.
Source(s): COOK, RWNBC, GREGG, MOORE V.3.
Notes: GREGG SAYS MARRIED PHEOBE EDWARDS. MARY DIED IN
1784.

EVANS, JUDITH   ID: 4678
Spouse: [--?--] FERGUSON
Date in Pee Dee: 1740
Location: ST. DAVID'S PARISH
Source(s): SC WILLS.
Notes: APPEARS TO HAVE LIVED ELSEWHERE IN 1748.

EVANS, MARY   ID: 5471
Spouse: THOMAS CRAWFORD
Date in Pee Dee: 1753
Location: PRINCE FREDERICK PARISH
Source(s): RBPPFW.

EVANS, NATHAN   ID: 2476
Children: DAVID, NATHAN.
Date in Pee Dee: 1735   Last Date: 1750
Origin: WELCH
Location: CATFISH CREEK (PRESENT MARION COUNTY)
Source(s): SELLERS, GREGG.
Notes: MARRIED FIRST GODBOLD THEN ROGERS.

EVANS, PHILIP   ID: 389
Date in Pee Dee: 1755   Last Date: 1771 DIED
Location: WELCH NECK
Source(s): COOK, RWNBC.
Notes: DIED 12/5/1771. MAY HAVE MARRIED MARY CLAY.

EVANS, SARAH   ID: 398
Spouse: MCDANIEL DANIEL
Children: ELIZABETH, HANNAH.
Date in Pee Dee: 1742   Last Date: 1748
Location: ST. DAVID'S PARISH
Source(s): SC WILLS, RBPPFW.
Notes: DAUGHTER OF THOMAS.

EVANS, SARAH   ID: 5366
Spouse: JOHN BOODY
Date in Pee Dee: 1741
Location: PRINCE FREDERICK PARISH

Source(s): RBPPFW.

EVANS, THOMAS   ID: 395
Spouse: HANNAH [--?--]
Children: JUDITH (FERGUSION), SARAH (MCDANIEL), SAMUEL.
Date in Pee Dee: 1737   Last Date: 1751 DIED
Location: LONG BLUFF
Source(s): COOK, RWNBC, SC WILLS.
Notes: ONE OF ORIGINAL WELCH NECK SETTLERS. SHE DIED
1761.

EVANS, THOMAS JR   ID: 396
Spouse: ELIZABETH [--?--]
Date in Pee Dee: 1780
Location: CHERAW DISTRICT
Source(s): COOK, RWNBC.
Revolutionary War service: CAPTAIN OF MILITIA.

EVANS, THOMAS JR   ID: 1776
Date in Pee Dee: 1750
Location: GEORGETOWN
Source(s): COOK.
Notes: SERVED IN POWELL'S REGIMENT.

EVANS, THOMAS JR   ID: 1638
Spouse: ELIZABETH HODGE
Children: THOMAS, JOSIAH JAMES, ABEL, REBECCA, ELIZA.
Date in Pee Dee: 1737   Last Date: 1785 DIED
Location: CHERAW DISTRICT
Source(s): GREGG, RWNBC, COOK.
Notes: GREGG REFERS TO HIM AS COLONEL. ORIGINAL WELCH
NECK SETTLER.

EVANS, WILLIAM   ID: 400
Date in Pee Dee: 1740   Last Date: 1759
Location: CHERAW DISTRICT (PIDGEON CREEK (BUCKHOLDT'S))
Source(s): COOK, MUSTER ROLL.
Notes: SERVED IN FRENCH AND INDIAN WAR AS PRIVATE WITH
PLEDGER'S COMPANY.

EWBANK, JOHN   ID: 2008
Date in Pee Dee: 1775
Location: ST. DAVID'S PARISH
Source(s): GREGG.
Revolutionary War service: LIEUTENANT IN MARION'S
BRIGADE.

FALCONER, WILLIAM   ID: 1696
Spouse: MARY POWE
Date in Pee Dee: 1770
Location: WELCH NECK
Source(s): GREGG.

FAREWELL, THOMAS   ID: 403
Spouse: MARY [--?--]
Children: HENRY.
Date in Pee Dee: 1730   Last Date: 1738
Location: KINGSTON TOWNSHIP
Source(s): COOK, RBPPFW.

FARMER, ZACHARIAH   ID: 2113
Date in Pee Dee: 1782
Source(s): GREGG P.407.
Revolutionary War service: PRIVATE IN MARION'S BRIGADE.

FARWELL, HENRY   ID: 3164
Spouse: MARGARET WOODBERRY
Children: THOMAS, ANN.
Date in Pee Dee: 1756   Last Date: 1772 DIED
Location: PRINCE GEORGE WINYAW PARISH
Source(s): MOORE.

FATHERN, BENJAMIN   ID: 404
Date in Pee Dee: 1775
Location: CHERAW DISTRICT
Source(s): COOK.

Revolutionary War service: WISE'S COMPANY OF INFANTRY.

FAUCHERAUD, MARY   ID: 2511
Spouse: JOHN ALLSTON
Date in Pee Dee: 1764
Origin: CHARLESTON
Location: ALL SAINT'S PARISH
Source(s): SMITH, H..

FAULKNER, JOHN   ID: 2108
Date in Pee Dee: 1782
Source(s): GREGG P.407.
Revolutionary War service: PRIVATE IN MARION'S BRIGADE.

FAVRE, SUSANNAH   ID: 2682
Spouse: ABRAHAM JENNERET
Children: ABRAHAM, JOHN, STEPHEN, SUSANNAH.
Date in Pee Dee: 1744
Location: PRINCE FREDERICK PARISH
Source(s): MOORE.
Notes: DAUGHTER OF SIMEON FAVRE.

FEAGANS, JOHN   ID: 5557
Date in Pee Dee: 1780
Location: ST. DAVID'S PARISH
Source(s): JVSDP.
Notes: BOUND BY CHURCH TO JAMES SHIELDS FOR 10 YEARS TO
LEARN LEATHER WORKING.

FERDON, JAMES   ID: 4962
Date in Pee Dee: 1737   Last Date: 1759
Location: WILLIAMSBURG
Source(s): BODDIE.
Notes: SERVED IN FRENCH AND INDIAN WAR.

FERGUSON, HUGH   ID: 5029
Date in Pee Dee: 1780
Location: WILLIAMSBURG
Source(s): BODDIE.

Revolutionary War service: PRIVATE IN MARION'S BRIGADE.

FERGUSON, JOHN   ID: 5030
Date in Pee Dee: 1780
Location: WILLIAMSBURG
Source(s): BODDIE.
Revolutionary War service: PRIVATE IN MARION'S BRIGADE.

FERGUSON, MOSES   ID: 5032
Date in Pee Dee: 1780
Location: WILLIAMSBURG
Source(s): BODDIE.
Revolutionary War service: PRIVATE IN MARION'S BRIGADE.

FERGUSON, THOMAS   ID: 5031
Date in Pee Dee: 1780
Location: WILLIAMSBURG
Source(s): BODDIE.
Revolutionary War service: PRIVATE IN MARION'S BRIGADE.

FESCH, ANDREW   ID: 3422
Spouse: SOPHIA [--?--]
Children: SOPHIA.
Date in Pee Dee: 1761   Last Date: 1762 DIED
Location: PRINCE GEORGE WINYAW PARISH
Source(s): MOORE V.3.

FEWTHY, JAMES   ID: 3293
Spouse: ELIZABETH (YOUNG)
Children: ROBERT, MARGARET.
Date in Pee Dee: 1735   Last Date: 1735 DIED
Location: PRINCE FREDERICK PARISH
Source(s): MOORE V.1.

FIELDS, SARAH   ID: 4459
Spouse: WILLIAMS ELMS
Date in Pee Dee: 1784
Location: CHERAW DISTRICT
Source(s): CLEMENS.

Notes: MARRIED JULY 1784.

FINKE, JOHN A.   ID: 406
Date in Pee Dee: 1737   Last Date: 1773
Location: LOWER BLACK RIVER
Source(s): COOK, BODDIE, MOORE V.3.
Notes: COOK GIVES SECOND NAME AS ANGUS. HE WITNESSED A
WILL AS JOHN AUGUSTUS.

FINLAY, SARAH MARGARETA   ID: 5448
Spouse: JOHN BRYAN
Date in Pee Dee: 1747
Location: PRINCE FREDERICK PARISH
Source(s): RBPPFW.

FISHER, HUGH   ID: 3187
Date in Pee Dee: 1726
Location: NORTH OF SANTEE RIVER.
Source(s): MOORE V.1.
Notes: BROTHER OF JAMES.

FISHER, JAMES   ID: 3188
Date in Pee Dee: 1726
Location: NORTH OF SANTEE RIVER.
Source(s): MOORE V.1, BODDIE.
Notes: BROTHER OF HUGH #3187.

FITZGERALL, JOHN   ID: 4235
Spouse: MARY JOHNSON
Date in Pee Dee: 1771
Location: PRINCE FREDERICK PARISH
Source(s): MOORE V.3.

FITZPATRICK, JAMES   ID: 2109
Date in Pee Dee: 1782
Source(s): GREGG P.407.
Revolutionary War service: PRIVATE IN MARION'S BRIGADE.

FLADGER, HENRY   ID: 2714

Children: HUGH.
Date in Pee Dee: 1770
Location: BRITTON NECK
Source(s): SELLERS.
Notes: KILLED BY TORIES. SON OF #2713. SAID TO HAVE
SERVED IN MARION'S BRIGADE.

FLADGER, HUGH   ID: 2713
Children: HENRY.
Date in Pee Dee: 1735
Location: BRITTON NECK
Source(s): SELLERS.

FLAGER, WILLIAM GREGG   ID: 2340
Spouse: MARY PATTERSON
Children: ANDREW P., WILLIAM P., ROSA, JOHN A., JAMES,
MARGARET R., MARY J., WARREN, ROBERT A., ALONZO, SAMUEL,
MARTHA A., MARGARET G..
Date in Pee Dee: 1790   Last Date: 1845
Location: WILLIAMSBURG
Source(s): MCCARTY.
Notes: SON OF MARGARET GREGG #1462.

FLAGG, HENRY COLLINS   ID: 2691
Spouse: RACHEL nee MOORE ALLSTON
Children: EBENEZER.
Date in Pee Dee: 1742   Last Date: 1801
Occupation: PHYSICIAN   Origin: RHODE ISLAND
Location: PRINCE GEORGE WINYAW PARISH
Source(s): ROGERS, CLEMENS.
Notes: SURGEON TO GREENE'S ARMY. MARRIED 5 DECEMBER 1784
AT CHARLESTON.

FLAGLER, JOHN GREGG   ID: 2341
Spouse: ELIZABETH WHITE
Date in Pee Dee: 1788   Last Date: 1815
Location: PRESENT SUMTER COUNTY.
Source(s): MCCARTY.
Notes: SON OF MARGARET GREGG #1462. FOUR CHILDREN.

FLAGLER, WILLIAM   ID: 2333
Spouse: MARGARET GREGG
Children: JOHN GREGG, WILLIAM GREGG.
Date in Pee Dee: 1780   Last Date: 1820
Origin: NEW YORK
Location: DEEP CREEK (NOW CLARENDON COUNTY)
Source(s): MCCARTY.

FLANAGAN, JOHN   ID: 1853
Spouse: ELIZABETH [--?--]
Children: MARY.
Date in Pee Dee: 1768   Last Date: 1770 DIED
Location: ST. DAVID'S PARISH
Source(s): GREGG, MOORE V.3.
Notes: SPELLED FLANIGEN IN WILL.

FLEMING, AGNES   ID: 4033
Spouse: [--?--] COOPER
Children: JAMES, THOMAS, GEORGE, ELIZABETH.
Date in Pee Dee: 1768
Location: WILLIAMSBURG
Source(s): MOORE V.3.
Notes: BROTHER OF JOHN #4032.

FLEMING, CHRISTAIN   ID: 2917
Date in Pee Dee: 1750
Location: GEORGETOWN
Source(s): MOORE.
Notes: SISTER OF WILLIAM #413.

FLEMING, ELIZABETH   ID: 1516
Date in Pee Dee: 1773
Origin: NORTHERN IRELAND
Location: BLACK RIVER (FORKS)
Source(s): STEPHENSON.
Notes: BROTHER OF JOHN. AUNT OF SARAH G. FLEMING AND
HAMILTON BRADLEY.

FLEMING, ELIZABETH   ID: 2915

Spouse: JOHN BLAKELY
Date in Pee Dee: 1747   Last Date: 1750
Location: WILLIAMSBURG
Source(s): MOORE, BODDIE, COOK, WITHERSPOON.
Notes: DAUGHTER OF JOHN #1573. FOUR CHILDREN.

FLEMING, ISABELLA   ID: 1574
Spouse: JOHN PRESSLEY
Date in Pee Dee: 1734   Last Date: 1750
Origin: NORTHERN IRELAND
Location: WILLIAMSBURG
Source(s): WITHERSPOON, BODDIE, MOORE.
Notes: DAUGHTER OF JOHN #1573.

FLEMING, JAMES   ID: 2852
Spouse: JANNET STEWART
Children: JAMES, PETER, JANNET.
Date in Pee Dee: 1747   Last Date: 1780
Location: WILLIAMSBURG
Source(s): MOORE, BODDIE.
Revolutionary War service: PRIVATE IN MARION'S BRIGADE.

FLEMING, JAMES JR   ID: 411
Date in Pee Dee: 1780
Location: PRINCE FREDERICK PARISH
Source(s): COOK, BODDIE.
Notes: PROBABLY SON OF JAMES #2852.
Revolutionary War service: PRIVATE IN MARION'S BRIGADE.

FLEMING, JANET   ID: 3847
Spouse: [--?--] JAMES
Date in Pee Dee: 1750
Location: WILLIAMSBURG
Source(s): MOORE V.3, WITHERSPOON.
Notes: DAUGHTER OF JOHN #1573. HUSBAND APPEARS TO HAVE
BEEN JOHN OR WILLIAM.

FLEMING, JOHN   ID: 1500
Date in Pee Dee: 1773   Last Date: 1780

Origin: NORTHERN IRELAND
Location: BLACK RIVER (HEAD)
Source(s): STEPHENSON, BODDIE, MOORE V.3.
Notes: MAY BE SON OF JOHN #4032.
Revolutionary War service: PRIVATE IN MARION'S BRIGADE.

FLEMING, JOHN   ID: 4032
Spouse: ELIZABETH MCMULLIN
Date in Pee Dee: 1768   Last Date: 1768 DIED
Location: WILLIAMSBURG
Source(s): MOORE V.3, BODDIE.
Notes: SISTER AGNES COOPER. SON OF JOHN #412.

FLEMING, JOHN   ID: 1573
Spouse: JANET WITHERSPOON
Children: ISABELLA (PRESSLEY), JOHN (D.1750), ELIZABETH
(BLAKELY), JAMES, JANET, PENELOPE, WILLIAM.
Date in Pee Dee: 1734   Last Date: 1750 DIED
Origin: NORTHERN IRELAND
Location: WILLIAMSBURG
Source(s): WITHERSPOON, MOORE, BODDIE, COOK.
Notes: CHILDREN BORN IN NORTHERN IRELAND. BODDIE SAYS
JANET MARRIED [--?--] JAMES.

FLEMING, JOHN   ID: 412
Spouse: JANET STEWART
Date in Pee Dee: 1736
Origin: NORTHERN IRELAND
Location: WILLIAMSBURG
Source(s): COOK, BODDIE, MOORE.

FLEMING, WILLIAM   ID: 413
Spouse: ELIZABETH [--?--]
Date in Pee Dee: 1735   Last Date: 1750 DIED
Location: PRINCE GEORGE PARISH.
Source(s): COOK, ROGERS, MOORE.
Notes: DIED CIRCA 1750. BROTHER OF JOHN #412 AND
CHRISTIAN (SISTER).

FLEMING, WILLIAM   ID: 2901
Date in Pee Dee: 1747   Last Date: 1780
Location: PRINCE FREDERICK PARISH
Source(s): MOORE, BODDIE.
Notes: SON OF JOHN #412.
Revolutionary War service: PRIVATE IN MARION'S BRIGADE.

FLEMMING, SEE FLEMING.

FLETCHER, ELIZABETH   ID: 5443
Spouse: ABRAHAM GILES
Date in Pee Dee: 1747
Location: PRINCE FREDERICK PARISH
Source(s): RBPPFW.

FLIN, WILLIAM   ID: 4017
Spouse: MARY [--?--]
Date in Pee Dee: 1771   Last Date: 1771 DIED
Location: GEORGETOWN
Source(s): MOORE V.3.
Notes: SHE APPEARS TO HAVE MOVED TO PRINCE FREDERICK
PARISH.

FLOWERS, [--?--]   ID: 415
Date in Pee Dee: 1781
Location: CHERAW DISTRICT
Source(s): COOK.
Notes: KILLED AT BROWNS MILL BY TORIES.

FLOWERS, ARCHIBALD   ID: 2508
Date in Pee Dee: 1780
Location: PRESENT MARION COUNTY
Source(s): BODDIE.
Notes: THIS IS PROBABLY ARCHIE, SON OF HENRY.
Revolutionary War service: PRIVATE IN MARION'S BRIGADE.

FLOWERS, HENRY   ID: 2505
Spouse: PATSY SAVAGE

Children: ARCHIE, JAMES, BETSY, JOHN, JACOB, NANCY,
HENRY, BENNETT, SALLIE, WILLIAM, MOLLIE, OLIVE.
Date in Pee Dee: 1750
Location: PRESENT MARION COUNTY
Source(s): SELLERS.

FLOWERS, HENRY   ID: 2506
Date in Pee Dee: 1780
Location: PRESENT MARION COUNTY
Source(s): SELLERS, BODDIE.
Notes: SON OF HENRY #2505.
Revolutionary War service: PRIVATE IN MARION'S BRIGADE.

FLOWERS, JOHN   ID: 2507
Date in Pee Dee: 1780
Location: PRESENT MARION COUNTY
Source(s): SELLERS, RUDISILL, BODDIE.
Notes: SON OF HENRY #2505.
Revolutionary War service: PRIVATE IN MARION'S BRIGADE.

FOISSIN, ELIAS (I)   ID: 416
Spouse: ELIZABETH [--?--]
Children: ELIAS, PETER, ELIZABETH, SUSANNAH (HASSELL).
Date in Pee Dee: 1730   Last Date: 1767 DIED
Location: PRINCE GEORGE PARISH.
Source(s): COOK, MOORE V.3, ROGERS.

FOISSIN, ELIZABETH   ID: 4144
Spouse: PAUL TRAPIER
Date in Pee Dee: 1767
Location: PRINCE GEORGE WINYAH PARISH
Source(s): MOORE V.3, CLEMENS.
Notes: DAUGHTER OF ELIAS #416. MARRIED 19 NOVEMBER 1771
AT SANTEE.

FOISSIN, PETER JR   ID: 418
Date in Pee Dee: 1779
Source(s): COOK.

Revolutionary War service: LIEUTENANT SC CONTINENTAL
REGIMENT.

FOISSIN, SUSANNAH   ID: 4143
Spouse: JAMES HASSELL JR.
Date in Pee Dee: 1767
Source(s): MOORE V.3.
Notes: DAUGHTER OF ELIAS #416. HASSELL LIVED IN NORTH
CAROLINA.

FORBES, JOHN   ID: 2737
Spouse: JUDITH ROTHMAHLER
Date in Pee Dee: 1740   Last Date: 1760
Location: GEORGETOWN
Source(s): ROGERS, MOORE.

FORBES, WILLIAM   ID: 419
Spouse: CHARITY [--?--]
Children: WILLIAM, GRACE.
Date in Pee Dee: 1740   Last Date: 1750
Location: PRINCE GEORGE WINYAW
Source(s): COOK, RBPPFW, MOORE.

FORD, ALBERT   ID: 2110
Date in Pee Dee: 1782
Source(s): GREGG P.407.
Revolutionary War service: PRIVATE IN MARION'S BRIGADE.

FORD, ANN   ID: 4574
Spouse: MEREDITH HUGHES
Date in Pee Dee: 1776
Location: PRINCE GEORGE WINYAH PARISH
Source(s): MOORE V.3, CLEMENS.
Notes: DAUGHTER OF GEORGE #420. MARRIED 9 JANUARY 1772
AT SANTEE.

FORD, GEORGE   ID: 420
Spouse: ANN [--?--]

Children: GEORGE, STEPHEN, MARY (BONNEAU), ANN (HUGHES),
SARAH, ELIZABETH, REBECCA.
Date in Pee Dee: 1749   Last Date: 1776 DIED
Location: PRINCE GEORGE PARISH
Source(s): COOK, MOORE.
Notes: SON OF STEPHEN #425. OWNED SOUTH ISLAND.

FORD, GEORGE   ID: 4571
Spouse: BOONE MARY
Date in Pee Dee: 1776
Location: PRINCE GEORGE WINYAH PARISH
Source(s): MOORE V.3, CLEMENS.
Notes: SON OF GEORGE #420. MARRIED 13 OCTOBER 1778 AT
SANTEE. MAY HAVE LATER MARRIED KITTY WAYNE.

FORD, JAMES   ID: 422
Spouse: SARAH [--?--]
Children: SUSANNAH, MARY, JAMES.
Date in Pee Dee: 1742   Last Date: 1780
Location: GEORGETOWN
Source(s): COOK, RBPPFW, GREGG.
Notes: SERVED AS CAPTAIN IN POWELL'S REGIMENT.

FORD, JANE   ID: 3094
Spouse: JOHN SMITH
Date in Pee Dee: 1742   Last Date: 1749
Location: PRINCE GEORGE WINYAW PARISH
Source(s): MOORE, RBPPFW.
Notes: DAUGHTER OF STEPHEN #425. ABOUT 16 YEARS IN 1742.
MARRIED 10 SEPTEMBER 1742 AT PRINCE FREDERICK PARISH
WINYAW.

FORD, MARY   ID: 4573
Spouse: [--?--] BONNEAU
Children: ANN.
Date in Pee Dee: 1776
Location: PRINCE GEORGE WINYAH PARISH
Source(s): MOORE V.3.
Notes: DAUGHTER OF GEORGE #420.

FORD, REBECCA   ID: 4577
Spouse: SPENSER CALVIN
Date in Pee Dee: 1776
Location: PRINCE GEORGE WINYAH PARISH
Source(s): MOORE V.3, CLEMENS.
Notes: DAUGHTER OF GEORGE #420. MARRIED 21 AUGUST 1782
AT SANTEE.

FORD, SAMUEL   ID: 4955
Date in Pee Dee: 1759
Location: WILLIAMSBURG
Source(s): BODDIE.
Notes: SERVED AS PRIVATE IN FRENCH AND INDIAN WAR.

FORD, STEPHEN   ID: 425
Spouse: MARGARET WHITE
Date in Pee Dee: 1780
Location: PRINCE FREDERICK PARISH
Source(s): COOK, CLEMENS, ROGERS.
Notes: MARRIED 8 JULY 1779 AT SANTEE.

FORD, STEPHEN   ID: 426
Spouse: SARAH BARTON
Children: GEORGE, STEPHEN.
Date in Pee Dee: 1748   Last Date: 1790
Location: BLACK RIVER
Source(s): ROGERS, CLEMENS.
Notes: OPERATED PRINGLE'S FERRY OVER BLACK R. AT PRESENT
HIGHWAY 521.

FORDYCE, JOHN   ID: 429
Spouse: ELIZABETH [--?--]
Children: THOMAS, ISAAC, ELIZABETH.
Date in Pee Dee: 1735   Last Date: 1751 DIED
Location: RECTOR OF PRINCE FREDRICK PARISH CHURCH.
Source(s): COOK, RBPPFW, MOORE.
Notes: SECOND WIFE WAS MARY, WIDOW OF CRAFTON KERWIN.
ELIZABETH DIED 1747.

FORESTER, WILLIAM   ID: 4401
Spouse: ELIZABETH [--?--]
Children: ANTHONY, WILLIAM, JAMES, AGNES, ELIZABETH.
Date in Pee Dee: 1774   Last Date: 1774
Location: PRINCE FREDERICK PARISH
Source(s): MOORE V.3.

FORNISS, WILLIAM   ID: 1677
Date in Pee Dee: 1759   Last Date: 1770
Location: WELCH NECK
Source(s): GREGG, MUSTER ROLL.
Notes: SERVED IN FRENCH AND INDIAN WAR AS PRIVATE IN
LIDE'S COMPANY.

FORRIAT, MARGARET DAIGLE   ID: 4941
Children: LARION, PAUL, JOHN BAPTIST.
Date in Pee Dee: 1756
Origin: NOVA SCOTIA
Location: WILLIAMSBURG
Source(s): BODDIE.
Notes: HE, WIFE, AND CHILDREN WERE ACADIANS TRANSPORTED
FROM NOVA SCOTIA.

FOSTER, ARTHUR   ID: 433
Spouse: MARY [--?--]
Children: BLANCH.
Date in Pee Dee: 1731   Last Date: 1760
Location: PRINCE GEORGE PARISH.
Source(s): COOK, RBPPFW, MOORE V.3.
Notes: VESTRY MAN OF PRINCE FREDERICK PARISH WINYAW IN
1731.

FOULIS, JAMES   ID: 1967
Date in Pee Dee: 1768   Last Date: 1770
Location: ST. DAVID'S PARISH
Source(s): GREGG, JVSDP.
Notes: REMAINED A SHORT TIME AT ST. HELENA PARISH IN
1778. FIRST RECTOR OF ST. DAVID'S PARISH.

FOUNTAIN, WILLIAM   ID: 434
Date in Pee Dee: 1781   Last Date: 1783
Location: CHERAW DISTRICT
Source(s): COOK.
Revolutionary War service: SERVED 30 DAYS IN MARION'S
BRIGADE.

FOWLER, JAMES   ID: 3144
Spouse: ELIZABETH SCREVEN
Children: MARTHA.
Date in Pee Dee: 1757   Last Date: 1772 DIED
Location: PEE DEE RIVER, PRINCE GEORGE WINYAW PARISH
Source(s): MOORE, BODDIE.
Notes: SON OF RICHARD AND SARAH FOWLER. THEY AND SISTER
JOANNA IN ENGLAND.

FOX, HENRY   ID: 435
Spouse: MARTHA KEEN (WIDOW)
Children: TEMPERANCE.
Date in Pee Dee: 1735   Last Date: 1742
Location: CASHAWAY FERRY
Source(s): COOK, RBPPFW.
Notes: MARRIED 20 AUGUST 1738 AT PRINCE FREDERICK PARISH
WINYAW.

FOX, SAMUEL   ID: 5266
Spouse: GEORGE WILLOBY
Date in Pee Dee: 1743
Location: PRINCE FREDERICK PARISH
Source(s): RBPPFW.

FRANKS, SARAH   ID: 5405
Spouse: WILLIAM SAUNDERS
Date in Pee Dee: 1745
Location: PRINCE GEORGE WINYAH PARISH
Source(s): RBPPFW.

FRASER, [--?--]   ID: 5236
Spouse: ELIZABETH [--?--]

Children: PHILLIP.
Date in Pee Dee: 1742
Location: PRINCE FREDERICK PARISH
Source(s): RBPPFW.

FRASER, ANN   ID: 3576
Spouse: OWEN ROBERTS
Date in Pee Dee: 1772
Source(s): MOORE V.3.
Notes: DAUGHTER OF JUDITH #3572.

FRASER, JOHN   ID: 3574
Children: JOHN.
Date in Pee Dee: 1772
Source(s): MOORE V.3.
Notes: SON OF JUDITH #3572. HIS SON APPEARS IN THE
NINTY-SIX DISTRICT IN 1790.

FRASER, JUDITH (WIDOW)   ID: 3572
Children: ALEXANDER, JOHN, SUSANNA (LORIMER), ANN
(ROBERTS), JUDITH.
Date in Pee Dee: 1772   Last Date: 1772 DIED
Source(s): MOORE V.3.

FRASER, ROBERT   ID: 5036
Date in Pee Dee: 1780
Location: WILLIAMSBURG
Source(s): BODDIE.
Revolutionary War service: PRIVATE IN MARION'S BRIGADE.

FRASER, WILLIAM   ID: 436
Date in Pee Dee: 1737   Last Date: 1779
Location: PRINCE FREDERICK'S PARISH
Source(s): COOK, BODDIE.
Revolutionary War service: PRIVATE IN MARION'S BRIGADE.

FRASHER, [--?--]   ID: 2111
Date in Pee Dee: 1782
Source(s): GREGG P.407.

Revolutionary War service: PRIVATE IN MARION'S BRIGADE.

FRAZER, ISAAC   ID: 4744
Spouse: REBECCA [--?--]
Children: WILLIAM, ALEXANDER.
Date in Pee Dee: 1775   Last Date: 1775 DIED
Location: BRITTON'S NECK
Source(s): MOORE V.3.

FREEMAN, MARTHA   ID: 5387
Spouse: FRANCIS WHITTINGTON
Date in Pee Dee: 1743
Location: PRINCE FREDERICK PARISH
Source(s): RBPPFW.

FREEMAN, THOMAS   ID: 437
Spouse: MARY [--?--]
Children: JOHN.
Date in Pee Dee: 1736   Last Date: 1765
Location: BLACK CREEK
Source(s): COOK, RBPPFW, MOORE V.3.
Notes: SIGNED NAME WITH MARK.

FRIERSON, AARON   ID: 3432
Spouse: MARY CHANDLER
Children: AARON JR., MARY, SUSANNAH, SARAH, JOHN III.
Date in Pee Dee: 1743
Location: LYNCHES CREEK (ST. MARK'S PARISH)
Source(s): MOORE V.3, RBPPFW.
Notes: SON OF JOHN #3431. BORN NEAR PRESENT SHILOH
COMMUNITY.

FRIERSON, ABSOLEM   ID: 4852
Date in Pee Dee: 1777
Location: ST. MARK'S PARISH
Source(s): MOORE V.3, BODDIE.
Notes: SON OF JAMES SR. #3482.
Revolutionary War service: PRIVATE IN MARION'S BRIGADE.

FRIERSON, ELIZABETH   ID: 4853
Spouse: [--?--] BARNS
Date in Pee Dee: 1777
Location: ST. MARK'S PARISH
Source(s): MOORE V.3.
Notes: DAUGHTER OF JAMES SR. #3482.

FRIERSON, GEORGE   ID: 3483
Date in Pee Dee: 1755   Last Date: 1780
Location: WILLIAMSBURG
Source(s): MOORE V.3, BODDIE.
Notes: GRAND-SON OF JAMES MCNEALY #3479. SON OF JAMES
#3482.
Revolutionary War service: SERGEANT IN MARION'S BRIGADE.

FRIERSON, JAMES   ID: 3482
Spouse: [--?--] MCNEALY
Children: GEORGE, JAMES, ABSOLEM, LETITA, MARY,
ELIZABETH (BARNS).
Date in Pee Dee: 1755   Last Date: 1777 DIED
Location: WILLIAMSBURG
Source(s): MOORE V.3.
Notes: SON-IN-LAW OF JAMES MCNEALY #3479. PROBABLY SON
OF WILLIAM #1601.

FRIERSON, JAMES JR   ID: 3129
Date in Pee Dee: 1755   Last Date: 1780
Location: WILLIAMSBURG
Source(s): MOORE, BODDIE.
Notes: SON OF JAMES #3482.
Revolutionary War service: SERGEANT IN MARION'S BRIGADE.

FRIERSON, JANET   ID: 4520
Date in Pee Dee: 1771
Location: PRINCE FREDERICK PARISH
Source(s): MOORE V.3.
Notes: GRAND-SON OF JOHN FRIERSON AND JANET KING #3434.

FRIERSON, JOHN   ID: 3431

Spouse: SARAH DIAL
Children: AARON, JOHN, MOSES, THOMAS, MARY (PLAYER),
CATHERINE.
Date in Pee Dee: 1737   Last Date: 1760 DIED
Location: LYNCHES CREEK (ST. MARK'S PARISH, SHILOH)
Source(s): MOORE V.3, BODDIE, RBPPFW.
Notes: BODDIE NAMES A SON JAMES. MARRIED AT PRINCE
FREDERICK PARISH WINYAW 22 NOVEMBER 1741.

FRIERSON, JOHN   ID: 3481
Spouse: [--?--] MCNEALY
Date in Pee Dee: 1755   Last Date: 1780
Location: WILLIAMSBURG
Source(s): MOORE V.3, BODDIE.
Notes: SON-IN-LAW OF JAMES MCNEALY #3479. PROBABLY SON
OF WILLIAM #1601.
Revolutionary War service: LIEUTENANT IN MARION'S
BRIGADE.

FRIERSON, JOHN JR.   ID: 3434
Spouse: JANET KING
Date in Pee Dee: 1752   Last Date: 1774 DIED
Location: LYNCHES CREEK (ST. MARK'S PARISH)
Source(s): MOORE V.3.
Notes: SON OF JOHN #3431.

FRIERSON, JOSHUA   ID: 5033
Date in Pee Dee: 1780
Location: WILLIAMSBURG
Source(s): BODDIE.
Revolutionary War service: PRIVATE IN MARION'S BRIGADE.

FRIERSON, MARY   ID: 3436
Spouse: WILLIAM PLAYER
Date in Pee Dee: 1760   Last Date: 1774
Location: LYNCHES CREEK (ST. MARK'S PARISH)
Source(s): MOORE V.3.
Notes: DAUGHTER OF JOHN #3431.

FRIERSON, MARY   ID: **4226**
Spouse: ROGER WILSON
Children: THOMAS.
Date in Pee Dee: 1770   Last Date: 1770 DIED
Location: PRINCE FREDERICK PARISH
Source(s): MOORE V.3.
Notes: DAUGHTER OF THOMAS #3435.

FRIERSON, PHILIP   ID: **4217**
Date in Pee Dee: 1780
Location: WILLIAMSBURG
Source(s): BODDIE.
Revolutionary War service: CAPTAIN IN MARION'S BRIGADE.

FRIERSON, ROBERT   ID: **4224**
Date in Pee Dee: 1770   Last Date: 1780
Location: PRINCE FREDERICK PARISH
Source(s): MOORE V.3, BODDIE.
Notes: PROBABLY SON OF WILLIAM #1601.
Revolutionary War service: PRIVATE IN MARION'S BRIGADE.

FRIERSON, SARAH   ID: **4227**
Spouse: JOHN SCOTT
Date in Pee Dee: 1770
Location: PRINCE FREDERICK PARISH
Source(s): MOORE V.3.
Notes: DAUGHTER OF THOMAS #3435.

FRIERSON, THOMAS   ID: **3435**
Spouse: MARY [--?--]
Children: SARAH (SCOTT), MARY (WILSON).
Date in Pee Dee: 1760   Last Date: 1770 DIED
Location: PRINCE FREDERICK PARISH
Source(s): MOORE V.3.
Notes: SON OF JOHN #3431.

FRIERSON, WILLIAM   ID: **438**
Date in Pee Dee: 1770   Last Date: 1782
Location: PRINCE FREDERICK'S PARISH

Source(s): COOK, MOORE V.3.
Notes: GRAND-SON OF JOHN #3434.
Revolutionary War service: CAPTAIN IN MARION'S BRIGADE.

FRIERSON, WILLIAM   ID: 1601
Spouse: MARY [--?--]
Children: ROBERT, JOHN, JAMES, THOMAS.
Date in Pee Dee: 1736   Last Date: 1773 DIED
Origin: NORTHERN IRELAND
Location: WILLIAMSBURG
Source(s): WITHERSPOON, BODDIE, MOORE V.3.

FRIERSON, WILLIAM JR   ID: 5034
Date in Pee Dee: 1780
Location: WILLIAMSBURG
Source(s): BODDIE.
Revolutionary War service: PRIVATE IN MARION'S BRIGADE.

FRISBY, JOSIAH   ID: 1453
Date in Pee Dee: 1777
Location: ST. DAVID'S PARISH
Source(s): RUDISILL.
Notes: AN ORIGINAL SUBSCRIBER TO ST. DAVID'S SOCIETY.

FRYER, DRURY   ID: 439
Date in Pee Dee: 1782
Location: PRINCE FREDERICK'S PARISH
Source(s): COOK.
Revolutionary War service: MILITIA 94 DAYS

FULLER, JOHN   ID: 2112
Date in Pee Dee: 1782
Source(s): GREGG P.407.
Revolutionary War service: PRIVATE IN MARION'S BRIGADE.

FULLWOOD, WILLIAM   ID: 5035
Date in Pee Dee: 1780
Location: WILLIAMSBURG
Source(s): BODDIE.

Revolutionary War service: PRIVATE IN MARION'S BRIGADE.

FULTON, DAVID   ID: 2587
Spouse: REBECCAH [--?--]
Children: PAUL, SAMUEL.
Date in Pee Dee: 1735   Last Date: 1745 DIED
Location: WILLIAMSBURG
Source(s): MOORE, BODDIE.

FULTON, PAUL   ID: 2029
Spouse: MARY [--?--]
Children: JEAN.
Date in Pee Dee: 1742   Last Date: 1742 DIED
Location: PRINCE GEORGE WINYAW PARISH
Source(s): MOORE, BODDIE.
Notes: BROTHER OF SAMUEL #440. PROBABLY MARRIED MARY
THOMSON. SON OF DAVID #2587.

FULTON, SAMUEL   ID: 440
Children: DAVID.
Date in Pee Dee: 1742   Last Date: 1758
Location: WILLIAMSBURG
Source(s): COOK, BODDIE, MOORE.
Notes: SON OF DAVID #2587. BROTHER OF PAUL.

FURBISH, WILLIAM JR   ID: 2588
Spouse: [--?--] SOMERHOFFF
Date in Pee Dee: 1740
Location: PRINCE FREDERICK PARISH
Source(s): MOORE.
Notes: WIFE WAS DAUGHTER OF JOHN PETER #1171.

FURMAN, RICHARD   ID: 442
Spouse: ELIZABETH HAYNESWORTH
Date in Pee Dee: 1770
Location: MAY NEVER HAVE RESIDED IN THE PEE DEE.
Source(s): COOK, CLEMENS, JENKINS.
Notes: MARRIED 28 NOVEMBER 1774 AT CHARLESTON. NEXT
MARRIED MARIA BURN.

FUTHY, SEE ALSO FEWTHY.

FUTHY, FRANCIS   ID: 443
Spouse: MARGARET [--?--]
Children: HARTLY, SAMUEL, MARGERY.
Date in Pee Dee: 1735   Last Date: 1753 DIED
Location: PEE DEE RIVER, QUEENSBOROUGH TOWNSHIP
Source(s): COOK, BODDIE, MOORE.
Notes: BROTHER OF ROBERT AND JAMES.

FUTHY, HARDY   ID: 3364
Spouse: ELIZABETH [--?--]
Date in Pee Dee: 1736
Location: PRINCE FREDERICK PARISH
Source(s): BODDIE.

FUTHY, JAMES   ID: 444
Spouse: MARGARET GLENN
Children: FRANCIS, MARGARET.
Date in Pee Dee: 1735   Last Date: 1753
Location: NORTH SIDE OF SAMPIT RIVER
Source(s): COOK, RBPPFW, MOORE.
Notes: BROTHER OF ROBERT AND FRANCIS

FUTHY, JOHN   ID: 4410
Date in Pee Dee: 1771
Location: PRINCE FREDERICK PARISH
Source(s): MOORE V.3.
Notes: NEPHEW OF SAMUEL #1259.

FUTHY, MARGERY   ID: 1195
Spouse: RICHARD GREEN
Date in Pee Dee: 1753   Last Date: 1771
Location: PRINCE FREDERICK PARISH
Source(s): MOORE.
Notes: DAUGHTER OF FRANCIS #443.

FUTHY, ROBERT   ID: 2938
Children: ELIZABETH.

Date in Pee Dee: 1749   Last Date: 1753 DIED
Location: PRINCE FREDERICK PARISH (BLACK RIVER)
Source(s): MOORE.
Notes: WIFE WAS PROBABLY JANE. BROTHER OF JAMES AND
FRANCIS.

FYFFE, CHARLES   ID: 234
Date in Pee Dee: 1748   Last Date: 1782
Occupation: PHYSICIAN   Origin: DUNDEE, SCOTLAND
Location: GEORGETOWN
Source(s): LAMBERT, MOORE V.3, ROGERS.
Notes: BROTHER OF WILLIAM, JOHN, ELIZABETH AND
MAGDALENE. A TORY.

FYFFE, WILLIAM   ID: 2792
Date in Pee Dee: 1748   Last Date: 1771 DIED
Occupation: PHYSICIAN   Origin: DUNDEE, SCOTLAND
Location: PRINCE FREDERICK PARISH (NEAR GEORGETOWN)
Source(s): ROGERS, MOORE.
Notes: BROTHER OF CHARLES, JOHN, ELIZABETH AND
MAGDALENE.

GADSDEN, CHRISTOPHER   ID: 2738
Spouse: MARY HUSSEL
Children: THOMAS, PHILIP, MARY.
Date in Pee Dee: 1755   Last Date: 1782
Location: PRINCE GEORGE WINYAW PARISH
Source(s): ROGERS, MOORE V.3, COOK, CLEMENS.
Notes: REPRESENTATIVE TO CONTINENTAL CONGRESS. FIRST
MARRIED JANE GODFREY.

GADSDEN, THOMAS   ID: 2439
Children: JAMES, THOMAS.
Date in Pee Dee: 1737
Location: GEORGETOWN
Source(s): SMITH, H..

GAILLARD, BARTHOLOMEW   ID: 447
Date in Pee Dee: 1699
Location: NORTH OF SANTEE
Source(s): COOK.
Notes: FIRST KNOWN SETTLER IN PEE DEE AREA.

GAILLARD, JAMES   ID: 4038
Spouse: MARY JONES
Children: AN UNBORN CHILD AT HIS DEATH.
Date in Pee Dee: 1768   Last Date: 1768 DIED
Location: PRINCE FREDERICK PARISH
Source(s): MOORE V.3, CLEMENS.
Notes: COUSIN OF JOHN GAILLARD SR. MARRIED AT SANTEE 19
JULY 1763.

Early Pee Dee Settlers
--G--

GAILLARD, JOHN JR   ID: 4040
Spouse: SUSAN BOONE
Date in Pee Dee: 1768
Location: PRINCE FREDERICK PARISH
Source(s): MOORE V.3, CLEMENS.
Notes: MARRIED 10 NOVEMBER 1768 AT SANTEE.

GAILLARD, JOHN SR   ID: 4039
Date in Pee Dee: 1768
Location: PRINCE FREDERICK PARISH
Source(s): MOORE V.3.
Notes: COUSIN OF JAMES GAILLARD.

GAILLARD, PETER   ID: 448
Date in Pee Dee: 1780
Source(s): COOK.
Revolutionary War service: A TORY WHO LATER SIGNED
LOYALITY OATH AND SERVED WITH MARION.

GAILLARD, SUSANNA   ID: 797
Spouse: JAMES NICHOLAS MAYRANT
Children: JOHN.
Date in Pee Dee: 1720   Last Date: 1732
Location: SANTEE RIVER NORTH SIDE
Source(s): COOK, ROGERS.
Notes: SHE WAS A WIDOW IN 1732.

GAILLARD, THEODORE   ID: 2646
Spouse: CORNELIA MARSHALL
Date in Pee Dee: 1780
Location: PRINCE GEORGE WINYAW PARISH
Source(s): ROGERS, CLEMENS.
Notes: A TORY. MARRIED 3 NOVEMBER 1799 AT SANTEE.

GAILLARD, THEODORE (THEODORORUS)   ID: 449
Date in Pee Dee: 1732
Location: NORTH SIDE OF SANTEE RIVER
Source(s): COOK, MOORE V.1, ROGERS.
Notes: ONE OF THE FRENCH HUGUENOTS.

GAINEY, MICAJAH   ID: 2093
Date in Pee Dee: 1780
Location: CATFISH CREEK
Source(s): GREGG.
Notes: SON OF STEPHEN. A TORY LEADER.

GAINEY, STEPHEN   ID: 2092
Children: MICAJAH, STEPHEN.
Date in Pee Dee: 1760
Origin: ENGLAND
Location: CATFISH CREEK
Source(s): GREGG.

GALAVEN, JAMES   ID: 4413
Spouse: LEWEE [--?--]
Children: RICHARD.
Date in Pee Dee: 1774   Last Date: 1774 DIED
Location: GEORGETOWN
Source(s): MOORE V.3.

GALESPY, JAMES (ALSO GILLISPIE)   ID: 1366
Spouse: MARY YOUNG
Children: JAMES BORN 1754, FRANCIS, JANET, MARY,
OBEDIENCE.
Date in Pee Dee: 1742
Origin: IRELAND, NORTHERN
Location: CHERAW DISTRICT
Source(s): GREGG, ELLERBE.
Notes: DIED BEFORE REVOLUTION. ONE DAUGHTER MARRIED JOHN
WESTFIELD.

GALLOWAY, JAMES   ID: 2007
Date in Pee Dee: 1775
Location: ST. DAVID'S PARISH
Source(s): GREGG.
Revolutionary War service: SERVED IN MILITIA.

GAMBLE, HUGH   ID: 5038
Date in Pee Dee: 1780

Location: WILLIAMSBURG
Source(s): BODDIE.
Revolutionary War service: PRIVATE IN MARION'S BRIGADE.

GAMBLE, JAMES   ID: 5038
Date in Pee Dee: 1780
Location: WILLIAMSBURG
Source(s): BODDIE.
Revolutionary War service: PRIVATE IN MARION'S BRIGADE.

GAMBLE, JOHN   ID: 3823
Spouse: LEAH DAVIS
Date in Pee Dee: 1765   Last Date: 1780
Location: WILLIAMSBURG
Source(s): MOORE V.3, BODDIE.
Revolutionary War service: PRIVATE IN MARION'S BRIGADE.

GAMBLE, ROBERT   ID: 4971
Date in Pee Dee: 1780
Location: WILLIAMSBURG
Source(s): BODDIE.
Revolutionary War service: PRIVATE IN MARION'S BRIGADE.

GAMBLE, SAMUEL   ID: 5039
Date in Pee Dee: 1780
Location: WILLIAMSBURG
Source(s): BODDIE.
Revolutionary War service: PRIVATE IN MARION'S BRIGADE.

GAMBLE, STEPHEN   ID: 5040
Date in Pee Dee: 1780
Location: WILLIAMSBURG
Source(s): BODDIE.
Revolutionary War service: PRIVATE IN MARION'S BRIGADE.

GAMBLE, WILLIAM   ID: 2555
Date in Pee Dee: 1750   Last Date: 1780
Location: PRINCE FREDERICK PARISH
Source(s): ROGERS, BODDIE, MOORE.

Notes: COMMITTEE OF OBSERVATION AND INSPECTION. Revolutionary War service: LIEUTENANT IN MARION'S BRIGADE.

GANDY, MARGARET   ID: 5404
Spouse: DANIEL DOUGLAS
Date in Pee Dee: 1745
Location: PRINCE FREDERICK PARISH
Source(s): RBPPFW.

GANEY, ISAAC   ID: 5563
Date in Pee Dee: 1782
Location: ST. DAVID'S PARISH
Source(s): JVSDP.
Notes: AT AGE 15 BOUND BY PARISH TO THOMAS LANKFORD.

GARDNER, ISHAM   ID: 452
Date in Pee Dee: 1775
Location: CHERAW DISTRICT
Source(s): COOK.
Revolutionary War service: WISE'S COMPANY OF INFANTRY.

GARDNER, LEWIS   ID: 5625
Date in Pee Dee: 1759
Location: ST. DAVID'S PARISH
Source(s): MUSTER ROLL.
Notes: SERVED IN FRENCH AND INDIAN WAR AS SERGEANT IN CAPTAIN GEORGE HICK'S COMPANY.

GARDNER, STEPHEN   ID: 2114
Date in Pee Dee: 1782
Source(s): GREGG P.407.
Revolutionary War service: PRIVATE IN MILITIA.

GARDNER, WILLIAM   ID: 454
Spouse: SARAH [--?--]
Children: WILLIAM, MARY.
Date in Pee Dee: 1733   Last Date: 1769
Location: ST. DAVID'S PARISH

Source(s): COOK, RBPPFW, MOORE V.1, JVSDP.
Notes: SERVED IN FRENCH AND INDIAN WAR AS PRIVATE IN
CAPTAIN GEORGE HICK'S COMPANY.

GARDNER, WILLIAM JR   ID: 2115
Date in Pee Dee: 1768   Last Date: 1782
Location: ST. DAVID'S PARISH
Source(s): GREGG.
Revolutionary War service: PRIVATE IN MARION'S BRIGADE.

GARNER, SAMUEL   ID: 5041
Date in Pee Dee: 1780
Location: WILLIAMSBURG
Source(s): BODDIE.
Revolutionary War service: PRIVATE IN MARION'S BRIGADE.

GARNIER, JOHN   ID: 5194
Spouse: ANN KEEN
Date in Pee Dee: 1786
Location: GEORGETOWN
Source(s): CLEMENS.
Notes: MARRIED JULY 1786.

GARRISON, JOHN   ID: 4951
Date in Pee Dee: 1759
Location: WILLIAMSBURG
Source(s): BODDIE.
Notes: SERVED AS PRIVATE DURING FRENCH AND INDIAN WAR.

GASQUE, SAMUEL   ID: 2503
Spouse: [--?--] DOZIER
Children: ARBIE, ABSALOM, SAMUEL, HENRY, JOHN, NANCY.
Date in Pee Dee: 1761   Last Date: 1770
Location: PRESENT MARION COUNTY
Source(s): SELLERS, MOORE V.3.

GAY, [--?--]   ID: 2116
Date in Pee Dee: 1782
Source(s): GREGG P.407.

Early Pee Dee Settlers
--G--

Revolutionary War service: LIEUTENANT OF MILITIA.

GAYLE, JOSIAH   ID: 455
Date in Pee Dee: 1780
Source(s): COOK.
Notes: HANGED BY BRITISH AT CAMDEN.

GEE, CHARLES   ID: 2085
Spouse: CATHERINE BOND
Date in Pee Dee: 1778
Location: ST. DAVID'S PARISH
Source(s): GREGG, CLEMENS, RUDISILL.
Notes: MARRIED 24 APRIL 1770 AT SANTEE.

GEORGE, JESSE   ID: 5042
Date in Pee Dee: 1780
Location: WILLIAMSBURG
Source(s): BODDIE.
Revolutionary War service: PRIVATE IN MARION'S BRIGADE.

GEORGE, JOHN   ID: 5334
Spouse: MARY SKIPPER
Date in Pee Dee: 1738
Location: PRINCE FREDERICK PARISH
Source(s): RBPPFW.
Notes: MARRIED 17 AUGUST 1738 AT PARISH OF PRINCE
FREDERICK WINYAW.

GEORGE, RICHARD   ID: 1949
Date in Pee Dee: 1769   Last Date: 1784
Location: ST. DAVID'S PARISH
Source(s): GREGG, JVSDP, BODDIE.
Revolutionary War service: PRIVATE IN MARION'S BRIGADE.

GEORGE, WIILLIAM   ID: 5043
Date in Pee Dee: 1780
Location: WILLIAMSBURG
Source(s): BODDIE.
Revolutionary War service: PRIVATE IN MARION'S BRIGADE.

GERRALD, JAMES   ID: 3731
Spouse: MILDRED [--?--]
Children: GABRIEL.
Date in Pee Dee: 1760
Source(s): MOORE V.3.
Notes: HE DIED BEFORE 1762. SHE WAS FIRST MARRIED TO
WILLIAM STROTHER.

GEURIN, MARY   ID: 5417
Spouse: MARMADUKE BELL
Date in Pee Dee: 1746
Location: PRINCE FREDERICK PARISH
Source(s): RBPPFW.

GIBB, ROBERT   ID: 2640
Date in Pee Dee: 1754   Last Date: 1777
Origin: EDINBUROUGH
Location: PRINCE GEORGE WINYAW PARISH
Source(s): ROGERS, MOORE.
Notes: A TORY.

GIBBINS, MICHAEL   ID: 2594
Spouse: MARY GRIMES
Children: REBECCA, JEAN, SUSANNAH, UNBORN AT DEATH.
Date in Pee Dee: 1748   Last Date: 1748 DIED
Location: PRINCE FREDERICK PARISH
Source(s): MOORE.

GIBSON, GIDEON   ID: 461
Children: STEPHEN, SARAH, ROGER, TOBIAS.
Date in Pee Dee: 1735
Origin: VIRGINIA
Location: PEE DEE RIVER AT DUCK POND
Source(s): COOK, SELLERS, GREGG.
Notes: SON OF GIDEON #463.

GIBSON, GIDEON   ID: 463
Spouse: MARY [--?--]

Children: GIDEON, JORDAN, WILLIAM.
Date in Pee Dee: 1735   Last Date: 1743
Origin: VIRGINIA
Location: CASHAWAY
Source(s): COOK, RBPPFW, GREGG, JVSDP.

GIBSON, GILBERT   ID: 4551
Spouse: ELIZABETH [--?--]
Date in Pee Dee: 1767
Source(s): MOORE V.3.

GIBSON, JAMES   ID: 5044
Date in Pee Dee: 1780
Location: WILLIAMSBURG
Source(s): BODDIE.
Revolutionary War service: PRIVATE IN MARION'S BRIGADE.

GIBSON, JORDAN   ID: 462
Date in Pee Dee: 1735   Last Date: 1780
Origin: VIRGINIA
Location: WIGGINS LANDING
Source(s): COOK, SELLERS, GREGG.
Notes: BROTHER TO GIDEON. WENT WEST WITH DANIEL BOONE.
LATER RETURNED.

GIBSON, PAUL   ID: 87
Date in Pee Dee: 1779
Location: ST. DAVID'S PARISH
Source(s): ANDREWS.
Notes: RIGHT EAR CUT OFF AND WHIPPED, APPARENTLY FOR
TORY ACTIVITIES.

GIBSON, PHINEHAS   ID: 4253
Spouse: ELIZABETH [--?--]
Date in Pee Dee: 1771
Location: ST. MARK'S PARISH
Source(s): MOORE V.3.

GIBSON, ROBERT   ID: 1537

Date in Pee Dee: 1771   Last Date: 1778
Origin: NORTHERN IRELAND
Location: BLACK MINGO
Source(s): STEPHENSON, BODDIE, GREGG, MOORE V.3.
Revolutionary War service: PRIVATE IN MARION'S BRIGADE.

GIBSON, ROGER   ID: 465
Date in Pee Dee: 1742   Last Date: 1780
Origin: NORTHERN IRELAND
Location: WILLIAMSBURG
Source(s): COOK, BODDIE, MOORE.
Revolutionary War service: PRIVATE IN MARION'S BRIGADE.

GIBSON, STEPHEN   ID: 1423
Date in Pee Dee: 1760   Last Date: 1800
Source(s): GREGG.
Notes: SON OF GIDEON #461. MOVED TO GEORGIA 1800.

GIBSON, THOMAS JR   ID: 2118
Date in Pee Dee: 1782
Source(s): GREGG P.407.
Revolutionary War service: PRIVATE IN MARION'S BRIGADE.

GIBSON, THOMAS SR   ID: 2117
Date in Pee Dee: 1782
Source(s): GREGG P.407.
Revolutionary War service: PRIVATE OF MILITIA.

GIDDINS, JOHN   ID: 5578
Date in Pee Dee: 1759
Location: ST. DAVID'S PARISH
Source(s): MUSTER ROLL.
Notes: SERVED IN FRENCH AND INDIAN WAR AS PRIVATE IN
CAPTAIN DAVID EVANS' COMPANY.

GIDENS, HANNAH   ID: 5433
Spouse: EDWARD ROUSE
Date in Pee Dee: 1747

Location: PRINCE FREDERICK PARISH
Source(s): RBPPFW.

GILES, ABRAHAM   ID: 5442
Spouse: ELIZABETH FLETCHER (WIDOW)
Date in Pee Dee: 1737   Last Date: 1747
Location: PRINCE FREDERICK PARISH
Source(s): RBPPFW, BODDIE.
Notes: MARRIED AT PARISH OF PRINCE FREDERICK WINYAW 8
FEBRUARY 1747.

GILES, HUGH   ID: 2557
Date in Pee Dee: 1775
Location: PRINCE FREDERICK PARISH
Source(s): ROGERS, MOORE V.3.
Notes: COMMITTEE OF SAFETY.

GILLESPIE, ANDREW   ID: 5049
Date in Pee Dee: 1780
Location: WILLIAMSBURG
Source(s): BODDIE.
Revolutionary War service: PRIVATE IN MARION'S BRIGADE.

GILLESPIE, JAMES   ID: 466
Spouse: SARAH WILDS
Children: JAMES, FRANCIS, ELIZABETH, SAMUEL W., MARY,
JANNET, SARAH ANN.
Date in Pee Dee: 1754   Last Date: 1828
Location: CHERAW DISTRICT
Source(s): COOK, GREGG, ELLERBE.
Notes: SEEMS TO HAVE HAD TWO SONS NAMED JAMES. SON OF
#1366.

GILLESPIE, OBEDIENCE   ID: 4717
Spouse: THOMAS ELLERBE
Children: THOMAS, JANE, MARY, WILLIAM, JAMES, JOSEPH,
REBECCA (MACFARLANE), JOHN.
Date in Pee Dee: 1743   Last Date: 1821 DIED
Location: CHERAW DISTRICT

Source(s): COOK, ELLERBE, GREGG, SELLERS.

GILLESPIE, SAMUEL   ID: 2119
Date in Pee Dee: 1782
Source(s): GREGG P.408.
Revolutionary War service: PRIVATE IN ROBUCK'S REGIMENT.

GILLY, WILLIAM   ID: 5579
Date in Pee Dee: 1759
Location: ST. DAVID'S PARISH
Source(s): MUSTER ROLL.
Notes: SERVED IN FRENCH AND INDIAN WAR AS PRIVATE IN
CAPTAIN DAVID EVANS' COMPANY.

GILMAN, EDWARD   ID: 2351
Date in Pee Dee: 1777
Location: ST. DAVID'S PARISH
Source(s): RUDISILL, RWNBC.
Notes: AN ORIGINAL SUBSCRIBER TO ST. DAVID'S SOCIETY.

GLEN, JOHN   ID: 470
Spouse: ANNE (ANNA) THOMPSON
Children: ARCHIBALD, JOHN.
Date in Pee Dee: 1745   Last Date: 1773
Location: NEAR BLACK RIVER
Source(s): COOK, RBPPFW, MOORE V.3.
Notes: ANNE DIED 1752.

GODBOLD, JAMES   ID: 386
Spouse: MOURNING ELIZ BAKER
Children: JOHN, JAMES, ZACHARIAH, CADE, ABRAM, THOMAS.
Date in Pee Dee: 1740
Location: LIBERTY PRECINCT
Source(s): GREGG, SELLERS.
Notes: SON OF JOHN #471.
Revolutionary War service: PRIVATE IN MARION'S BRIGADE.

GODBOLD, JOHN   ID: 371
Spouse: PRISCILLA JONES

Children: ZACHARIAH, JOHN, JESSE.
Date in Pee Dee: 1740   Last Date: 1750
Origin: NATIVE BORN
Location: LIBERTY PRECINCT
Source(s): GREGG, SELLERS.
Notes: SON OF JOHN #471.

GODBOLD, JOHN   ID: 471
Spouse: ELIZABETH MCGURNEY
Children: JOHN, JAMES, THOMAS, ELIZABETH, ANNE.
Date in Pee Dee: 1734
Occupation: SAILOR   Origin: ENGLISH
Location: PEE DEE BELOW LITTLE PEE DEE
Source(s): COOK, GREGG, SELLERS.
Notes: DIED IN 1765, MORE THAN 100 YEARS OLD.

GODBOLD, JOHN   ID: 1380
Date in Pee Dee: 1750
Origin: NATIVE BORN
Location: LIBERTY PRECINCT
Source(s): GREGG, SELLERS.
Notes: SON OF JAMES #386.
Revolutionary War service: SERVED AS LIEUTENANT.

GODBOLD, THOMAS   ID: 387
Spouse: MARTHA HERRON
Children: STEPHEN, DAVID, THOMAS, ELY.
Date in Pee Dee: 1740
Location: LIBERTY PRECINCT
Source(s): GREGG, SELLERS.
Notes: SON OF JOHN #471.

GODBOLD, ZACHARIAH   ID: 1377
Date in Pee Dee: 1750
Origin: NATIVE BORN
Location: LIBERTY PRECINCT
Source(s): GREGG.
Notes: SON OF JOHN.
Revolutionary War service: CAPTAIN

GODBOLD, ZACHARIAH   ID: 1381
Date in Pee Dee: 1750
Origin: NATIVE BORN
Location: LIBERTY PRECINCT
Source(s): GREGG, SELLERS.
Notes: SON OF JAMES #386.
Revolutionary War service: SERVED AS LIEUTENANT.

GODBOLT, JOHN   ID: 5218
Spouse: ELIZABETH HAINS
Children: JOHN (ALIAS HAINS).
Date in Pee Dee: 1740
Location: PRINCE FREDERICK PARISH
Source(s): RBPPFW.

GODDARD, FRANCES   ID: 3100
Spouse: [--?--] WAINWRIGHT
Date in Pee Dee: 1737   Last Date: 1757
Location: BRITTON'S NECK
Source(s): MOORE, BODDIE.
Notes: SISTER OF FRANCIS AND WILLIAM GODDARD, JEAN
BRITTON, MARY BRITTON, MARTHA
Revolutionary War service: WITH ANDERSON.

GODDARD, FRANCIS   ID: 472
Spouse: MARY BRITTON
Children: PHILLIP, MARY.
Date in Pee Dee: 1735   Last Date: 1757
Origin: NORTHERN IRELAND
Location: WILLIAMSBURG
Source(s): COOK, MOORE.
Notes: BROTHER OF JEAN AND WILLIAM GODDARD #2860.

GODDARD, FRANCIS   ID: 3367
Children: JANE, WILLIAM, MARY, FRANCIS.
Date in Pee Dee: 1725   Last Date: 1777
Location: PRINCE GEORGE WINYAW PARISH
Source(s): MOORE.

Early Pee Dee Settlers
--G--

GODDARD, JEAN   ID: 3098
Spouse: [--?--] BRITTON
Date in Pee Dee: 1757   Last Date: 1757 DIED
Location: BRITTON'S NECK
Source(s): MOORE.
Notes: SISTER OF FRANCIS AND WILLIAM GODDARD, MARY
BRITTON, FRANCES WAINWRIGHT, MARTHA
Revolutionary War service: SERVED WITH ANDERSON.

GODDARD, MARTHA   ID: 3101
Spouse: [--?--] ANDERSON
Date in Pee Dee: 1757
Location: BRITTON'S NECK
Source(s): MOORE.
Notes: SISTER OF FRANCIS AND WILLIAM GODDARD, JEAN
BRITTON, AND MARY BRITTON

GODDARD, MARY   ID: 3099
Spouse: [--?--] BRITTON
Children: PHILLIP, WILLIAM.
Date in Pee Dee: 1757
Location: BRITTON'S NECK
Source(s): MOORE.
Notes: SISTER OF FRANCIS AND WILLIAM GODDARD, JEAN
BRITTON, FRANCES WAINWRIGHT, MARTHA

GODDARD, WILLIAM   ID: 2860
Spouse: ELIZABETH [--?--]
Children: FRANCIS.
Date in Pee Dee: 1749   Last Date: 1759 DIED
Location: PRINCE FREDERICK PARISH
Source(s): MOORE.
Notes: BROTHER OF JEAN AND FRANCIS GODDARD #472

GODFREY, JOHN   ID: 473
Spouse: MARY HARRINTON
Date in Pee Dee: 1737   Last Date: 1773
Location: LOWER PEE DEE

Source(s): COOK, RBPPFW, ROGERS, BODDIE.
Notes: LIEUTENANT IN LOWER PEE DEE MILITIA. MARRIED AT
PARISH OF PRINCE FREDERICK WINYAW 29 JULY 1761.

GODFREY, RICHARD   ID: 1723
Spouse: REBECCA GUY
Children: WILLIAM, WILSON, RICHARD, THOMAS.
Date in Pee Dee: 1760
Location: CHERAW DISTRICT
Source(s): GREGG, CLEMENS.
Notes: MARRIED 22 JANUARY 1743 AT ST. ANDREW'S PARISH.

GODFREY, THOMAS   ID: 1433
Spouse: NANCY HICKS
Children: SOPHIA, THOMAS, HARRIET, WILLIAM, MARY,
SAMUEL, RICHARD, ELIZABETH, WILSON, GEORGE.
Date in Pee Dee: 1760   Last Date: 1776 DIED
Location: PRINCE GEORGE WINYAH PARISH
Source(s): GREGG, MOORE V.3.
Notes: SON OF RICHARD

GODFREY, WILLIAM   ID: 474
Spouse: [--?--] BRITTON
Children: WILLIAM, WILSON, JEAN.
Date in Pee Dee: 1768
Location: ST. DAVID'S PARISH
Source(s): COOK, MOORE V.3, GREGG, JVSDP.
Notes: SON OF RICHARD

GODWIN, WILLIAM   ID: 5045
Date in Pee Dee: 1780
Location: WILLIAMSBURG
Source(s): BODDIE.
Revolutionary War service: PRIVATE IN MARION'S BRIGADE.

GOFF, JOHN   ID: 2581
Date in Pee Dee: 1780
Location: PRINCE GEORGE WINYAW PARISH
Source(s): ROGERS.

Early Pee Dee Settlers
--G--

Notes: PROBABLY A TORY. SIGNED LOYALITY OATH.

GOINGS, MIKE   ID: 476
Date in Pee Dee: 1781
Location: CHERAW DISTRICT
Source(s): COOK, GREGG.
Revolutionary War service: TORY PRIVATE WITH GAINEY.

GOODALL, WILLIAM   ID: 5221
Spouse: ELIZABETH GREENWOOD
Children: MARY.
Date in Pee Dee: 1740
Location: PRINCE FREDERICK PARISH
Source(s): RBPPFW.
Notes: MARRIED 24 DECEMBER 1739 AT PARISH OF PRINCE
FREDERICK WINYAW.

GOODSON, ARTHUR   ID: 2120
Date in Pee Dee: 1782
Source(s): GREGG P.408.
Revolutionary War service: PRIVATE IN ROBUCK'S REGIMENT.

GOODSON, JOHN   ID: 3146
Spouse: MARTHA [--?--]
Date in Pee Dee: 1757
Location: PEE DEE RIVER, PRINCE GEORGE WINYAW
Source(s): MOORE.

GOODSON, THOMAS   ID: 2121
Date in Pee Dee: 1782
Source(s): GREGG P.408.
Revolutionary War service: PRIVATE IN ROBUCK'S REGIMENT.

GOODWIN, JOHN   ID: 478
Spouse: LYDIA WILDS
Date in Pee Dee: 1740   Last Date: 1743
Location: WELCH NECK
Source(s): COOK, RBPPFW.

Notes: MARRIED BY REV. FORDYCE AT PARISH OF PRINCE
FREDERICK WINYAW 4 APRIL 1743. KOLB'S COMPANY DURING
FRENCH AND INDIAN WAR.

GOODWYN, BRITAIN   ID: 2122
Date in Pee Dee: 1782
Source(s): GREGG P.408.
Revolutionary War service: PRIVATE IN ROBUCK'S REGIMENT.

GOODWYN, DAVID   ID: 2123
Date in Pee Dee: 1782
Source(s): GREGG P.408.
Revolutionary War service: PRIVATE IN ROBUCK'S REGIMENT.

GOODWYN, FRANCIS   ID: 3871
Date in Pee Dee: 1767
Source(s): MOORE V.3.
Notes: BROTHER OF JESSE, THOMAS, BOSWELL, ROBERT,
JOSEPH, AND JAMES.

GOODWYN, JAMES   ID: 3870
Date in Pee Dee: 1767
Source(s): MOORE V.3.
Notes: BROTHER OF JESSE, THOMAS, BOSWELL, ROBERT,
JOSEPH, AND FRANCIS. SON OF JOHN #4723.

GOODWYN, JESSE   ID: 3866
Spouse: MARTHA (EPPS)
Children: MARTHA EPPS (WIFE'S PREVIOUS MARRIAGE.).
Date in Pee Dee: 1767   Last Date: 1767 DIED
Location: CEDAR CREEK, NORTH OF SANTEE RIVER
Source(s): MOORE V.3.
Notes: BROTHER OF THOMAS, JOSEPH, BOSWELL, ROBERT, JAMES
AND FRANCIS.

GOODWYN, JOHN   ID: 4723
Spouse: LUCY [--?--]
Children: WILLIAM, JOSEPH, BOSWELL, ROBERT, JAMES,
FRANCIS, MARTHA (RUSHEL).

Date in Pee Dee: 1775   Last Date: 1775 DIED
Source(s): MOORE V.3.
Notes: OWNED LAND IN DINWIDDIE COUNTY, VA.

GOODWYN, JOSEPH   ID: 3869
Date in Pee Dee: 1767
Source(s): MOORE V.3.
Notes: BROTHER OF JESSE, THOMAS, BOSWELL, ROBERT, JAMES,
AND FRANCIS. SON OF JOHN #4723.

GOODWYN, MARTHA   ID: 4725
Spouse: [--?--] RUSHEL
Date in Pee Dee: 1775   Last Date: 1775 DIED
Source(s): MOORE V.3.
Notes: DAUGHTER OF JOHN #4723.

GOODWYN, ROBERT   ID: 3872
Children: WILLIAM, HOWELL, JOHN.
Date in Pee Dee: 1767
Source(s): MOORE V.3.
Notes: BROTHER OF JESSE, THOMAS, BOSWELL, ROBERT, JAMES,
AND FRANCIS. SON OF JOHN #4723.

GOODWYN, THOMAS   ID: 3868
Date in Pee Dee: 1767
Source(s): MOORE V.3.
Notes: BROTHER OF JESSE, JOSEPH, BOSWELL, ROBERT, JAMES,
AND FRANCIS.

GOODWYN, WILLIAM   ID: 4726
Date in Pee Dee: 1775
Source(s): MOORE V.3.
Notes: BROTHER OF JESSE, JOSEPH, BOSWELL, ROBERT, JAMES,
AND FRANCIS. HE DOES NOT APPEAR IN JOHN'S WILL.

GOODYEAR, JACOB   ID: 5217
Spouse: MARY [--?--]
Children: JOHN, MARY, JACOB, FRANCES.
Date in Pee Dee: 1739   Last Date: 1746

Location: PRINCE FREDERICK PARISH
Source(s): RBPPFW.

GOODYEAR, WILLIAM   ID: 2482
Children: JOHN, LOVE.
Date in Pee Dee: 1750
Location: PRESENT MARION COUNTY
Source(s): SELLERS.

GORDON, ALEXANDER   ID: 479
Date in Pee Dee: 1758   Last Date: 1768
Location: ST. DAVID'S PARISH
Source(s): COOK, JVSDP, MOORE V.3.
Notes: CHURCH WARDEN.

GORDON, ALEXANDER   ID: 3184
Date in Pee Dee: 1726   Last Date: 1726   DIED
Location: NORTH OF SANTEE RIVER.
Source(s): MOORE V.1.
Notes: BROTHER OF WILLIAM.

GORDON, DAVID   ID: 4786
Children: WILLIAM, DAVID, JOHN.
Date in Pee Dee: 1772
Origin: SCOTLAND VIA PA.
Location: WILLIAMSBURG (BLACK MINGO CREEK)
Source(s): MCCARTY, BODDIE.
Notes: BROTHERS WILLIAM AND JOHN.

GORDON, ELIZABETH   ID: 2920
Spouse: SAMUEL BRADLEY
Children: JEAN.
Date in Pee Dee: 1750   Last Date: 1804 DIED
Location: WILLIAMSBURG
Source(s): MOORE, JENKINS.
Notes: DAUGHTER OF ROGER #485.

GORDON, JAMES   ID: 482
Children: COSMUS, PATRICK, CHARLES, JAMES, CLEMENTINE.

Date in Pee Dee: 1730   Last Date: 1739   DIED
Location: PRINCE GEORGE PARISH
Source(s): COOK, MOORE V.1, ROGERS.

GORDON, JAMES   ID: 2420
Spouse: MARY VAUX
Date in Pee Dee: 1739   Last Date: 1780
Location: GEORGETOWN
Source(s): LAMBERT, MOORE V.1, ROGERS, CLEMENS.
Notes: A TORY. SON OF JAMES #482. SERVED IN FRENCH AND
INDIAN WAR AS PRIVATE IN SCOTT'S COMPANY.
Revolutionary War service: LT. COL. IN LOYALIST MILITIA.

GORDON, JAMES   ID: 4979
Date in Pee Dee: 1780
Location: WILLIAMSBURG
Source(s): BODDIE.
Revolutionary War service: LIEUTENANT IN MARION'S
BRIGADE.

GORDON, JOHN   ID: 483
Date in Pee Dee: 1750   Last Date: 1780
Location: WILLIAMSBURG (INDIANTOWN)
Source(s): COOK, BODDIE, MOORE.
Notes: SON OF ROGER #485.
Revolutionary War service: PRIVATE IN MARION'S BRIGADE.

GORDON, MARGARET   ID: 2922
Date in Pee Dee: 1750
Location: WILLIAMSBURG
Source(s): MOORE, BODDIE.
Notes: DAUGHTER OF ROGER #485. SUPPLIED MARION.

GORDON, MARGARET   ID: 4896
Spouse: ROBERT WILSON
Children: ROGER.
Date in Pee Dee: 1740
Location: WILLIAMSBURG
Source(s): BODDIE.

GORDON, MOSES   ID: 484
Date in Pee Dee: 1750   Last Date: 1779
Location: WILLIAMSBURG (SALEM)
Source(s): COOK, MOORE, STEPHENSON, BODDIE.
Notes: SON OF ROGER #485.
Revolutionary War service: PRIVATE IN MARION'S BRIGADE.

GORDON, REBECCA ERVIN   ID: 2335
Spouse: ARTHUR CUNNINGHAM
Children: WILLIAM, DAVID, SARAH TAPHENAS, JOHN ERVIN
SCOTT.
Date in Pee Dee: 1780   Last Date: 1820
Location: WILLIAMSBURG
Source(s): MCCARTY.
Notes: DAUGHTER OF MARGARET GREGG #1462.

GORDON, ROGER   ID: 485
Spouse: MARY [--?--]
Children: JAMES, JOHN, MOSES, ELIZABETH, SARAH (MCGILL),
MARGARET (WILSON), JEAN, MARY.
Date in Pee Dee: 1732   Last Date: 1750 DIED
Origin: NORTHERN IRELAND
Location: WILLIAMSBURG
Source(s): COOK, MOORE, WITHERSPOON, BODDIE.
Notes: WIFE DIED IN 1761. LEADER OF GROUP THAT SETTLED
WILLIAMSBURG.

GORDON, ROGER   ID: 4980
Date in Pee Dee: 1780
Location: WILLIAMSBURG
Source(s): BODDIE.
Notes: GRAND-SON OF ORIGINAL ROGER. KILLED BY TORIES
AFTER SURRENDERING.
Revolutionary War service: LIEUTENANT IN MARION'S
BRIGADE.

GORDON, SAMUEL SCOTT   ID: 2338
Spouse: CARTHERINE MCCONNELL

Children: ELIZABETH H., MARGARET R., SAMUEL G., MARTHA R., CAROLINE R., MARTHA A., WILLIAM THOMAS.
Date in Pee Dee: 1783   Last Date: 1819
Location: WILLIAMSBURG
Source(s): MCCARTY.
Notes: SON OF MARAGRET GREGG #1462. THEY MOVED TO ALA. IN 1815.

GORDON, WILLIAM   ID: 2332
Spouse: MARGARET SCOTT Nee GREGG
Children: REBECCA ERVIN (CUNNINGHAM), MARY, SAMUEL SCOTT.
Date in Pee Dee: 1772   Last Date: 1783 DIED
Origin: PENNSYLVANIA
Location: JEFFERIES CREEK
Source(s): MCCARTY, BODDIE.
Notes: SON OF DAVID WHO WAS BROTHER OF WILLIAM.
Revolutionary War service: CAPTAIN IN MARION'S BRIGADE.

GORDON, WILLIAM   ID: 3185
Date in Pee Dee: 1726
Location: NORTH OF SANTEE RIVER.
Source(s): MOORE V.1.
Notes: BROTHER OF ALEXANDER #3184.

GOURDIN, LEWIS   ID: 2266
Spouse: MARIAN [--?--]
Children: PETER, THEODORE, WILLIAM, ISAAC.
Date in Pee Dee: 1754   Last Date: 1754 DIED
Location: CRAVEN COUNTY
Source(s): MOORE.

GOURDIN, PETER   ID: 2267
Spouse: ESTHER SULLIVAN
Children: PETER.
Date in Pee Dee: 1737   Last Date: 1774 DIED
Location: WILLIAMSBURG
Source(s): MOORE, BODDIE.
Notes: SON OF LEWIS #2266. SECOND MARRIED ANN LESTER.

GOURDIN, THEODORE   ID: 2268
Children: THEODORE, SAMUEL.
Date in Pee Dee: 1737   Last Date: 1773 DIED
Location: PRINCE FREDERICK PARISH
Source(s): MOORE, COOK, BODDIE, ROGERS.
Notes: SON OF LEWIS #2266. BROTHER OF ISAAC AND PETER.

GOURDIN, THEODORE JR   ID: 486
Spouse: ELIZABETH GAILLARD
Date in Pee Dee: 1780   Last Date: 1785
Location: PRINCE FREDERICK PARISH
Source(s): COOK, CLEMENS, MOORE V.3.
Notes: SON OF THEODORE #2268. MARRIED 20 OCTOBER 1785 AT
CHARLESTON.

GRACEBERRY, ELIZABETH   ID: 5352
Spouse: PATRICK DANILLY
Date in Pee Dee: 1740
Location: PRINCE FREDERICK PARISH
Source(s): RBPPFW.

GRACEBERRY, MARY   ID: 5377
Spouse: JOHN PERKINS
Date in Pee Dee: 1742
Location: PRINCE FREDERICK PARISH
Source(s): RBPPFW.

GRAHAM, DAVID   ID: 490
Spouse: ELIZABETH HUNTER
Date in Pee Dee: 1787
Location: WACCAMAW
Source(s): COOK, CLEMENS.
Notes: MARRIED 9 JANUARY 1770 AT SANTEE.

GRAHAM, JAMES   ID: 5046
Date in Pee Dee: 1780
Location: WILLIAMSBURG
Source(s): BODDIE.
Revolutionary War service: PRIVATE IN MARION'S BRIGADE.

GRAHAM, JOHN   ID: 3490
Spouse: [--?--] BOOTH
Date in Pee Dee: 1761   Last Date: 1780
Location: WELCH TRACT
Source(s): MOORE V.3, BODDIE.
Notes: MARRIED DAUGHTER OF JOHN BOOTH, EITHER MARY OR SARAH.
Revolutionary War service: CAPTAIN IN MARION'S BRIGADE.

GRAHAM, WILLIAM   ID: 5047
Date in Pee Dee: 1780
Location: WILLIAMSBURG
Source(s): BODDIE.
Revolutionary War service: PRIVATE IN MARION'S BRIGADE.

GRANT, JOHN   ID: 4895
Spouse: MARY CAMERON (WIDOW)
Date in Pee Dee: 1760   Last Date: 1785
Location: WILLIAMSBURG
Source(s): BODDIE, CLEMENS.
Notes: MARRIED JUNE 1785 IN CHARLESTON.

GRAVES, JAMES JR   ID: 5660
Date in Pee Dee: 1759
Location: ST. DAVID'S PARISH
Source(s): MUSTER ROLL.
Notes: SERVED IN FRENCH AND INDIAN WAR AS PRIVATE WITH MCINTOSH'S COMPANY.

GRAVES, JOHN   ID: 5674
Date in Pee Dee: 1759
Location: ST. DAVID'S PARISH
Source(s): MUSTER ROLL.
Notes: SERVED IN FRENCH AND INDIAN WAR AS PRIVATE WITH MCINTOSH'S COMPANY.

GRAVES, JOHN SR.   ID: 5675
Date in Pee Dee: 1759 DIED
Location: ST. DAVID'S PARISH

Source(s): MUSTER ROLL.
Notes: SERVED IN FRENCH AND INDIAN WAR AS PRIVATE WITH
MCINTOSH'S COMPANY. DIED IN SERVICE.

GRAVES, JOSEPH   ID: 2084
Spouse: MARY BENNET
Children: JOSEPH.
Date in Pee Dee: 1743   Last Date: 1775
Location: ST. DAVID'S PARISH
Source(s): GREGG, RBPPFW, MOORE V.3.
Notes: MOORE SPELLS GREAVES. MARRIED 29 APRIL 1743 AT
PARISH OF PRINCE FREDERICK WINYAW.
Revolutionary War service: LIEUTENANT IN MARION'S
BRIGADE.

GRAVES, ROBERT   ID: 5628
Date in Pee Dee: 1759
Location: ST. DAVID'S PARISH
Source(s): MUSTER ROLL.
Notes: SERVED IN FRENCH AND INDIAN WAR AS PRIVATE IN
CAPTAIN GEORGE HICK'S COMPANY.

GRAY, ROBERT   ID: 2031
Date in Pee Dee: 1774   Last Date: 1778
Location: ST. DAVID'S PARISH
Source(s): GREGG, LAMBERT, RUDISILL.
Notes: SPELLED GREY IN SOME BRITISH RECORDS.
Revolutionary War service: LT. COL. LOYALIST MILITIA.

GREAR, JOSEPH   ID: 2864
Spouse: BARBARA [--?--]
Children: JOSEPH, ANDREW, JEAN, MARY, BARBARA.
Date in Pee Dee: 1749   Last Date: 1749 DIED
Location: PRINCE GEORGE WINYAW PARISH
Source(s): MOORE.

GREEN, BENJAMIN   ID: 5048
Date in Pee Dee: 1780
Location: WILLIAMSBURG

Source(s): BODDIE.
Revolutionary War service: PRIVATE IN MARION'S BRIGADE.

GREEN, FRANCIS   ID: 2893
Date in Pee Dee: 1747
Location: PRINCE FREDERICK PARISH
Source(s): MOORE.
Notes: GRAND-SON OF JOHN AVANT #2887.

GREEN, GEORGE   ID: 5379
Spouse: MARY BRITT
Date in Pee Dee: 1737   Last Date: 1742
Location: PRINCE FREDERICK PARISH
Source(s): RBPPFW, BODDIE.
Notes: MARRIED 15 DECEMBER 1742 AT PARISH OF PRINCE
FREDERICK WINYAW.

GREEN, HANNAH   ID: 2928
Spouse: WILLIAM SMITH
Date in Pee Dee: 1749
Location: PRINCE GEORGE WINYAW PARISH
Source(s): MOORE.
Notes: DAUGHTER OF JOHN #495.

GREEN, JAMES   ID: 494
Date in Pee Dee: 1780
Location: PRINCE FREDERICK PARISH
Source(s): COOK, BODDIE.
Revolutionary War service: CAPTAIN IN MARION'S BRIGADE.

GREEN, JOHN   ID: 495
Spouse: ELIZABETH [--?--]
Children: JOHN, WILLIAM, RICHARD, ELIZABETH, SARAH,
HANNAH.
Date in Pee Dee: 1711   Last Date: 1743 DIED
Location: PRINCE GEORGE WINYAW PARISH (WACCAMAW)
Source(s): COOK, RBPPFW, MOORE, BODDIE.
Notes: SHE DIED IN 1765 ON BLACK RIVER. SIGNED WITH
MARK.

GREEN, JOHN   ID: 5718
Date in Pee Dee: 1759
Location: ST. DAVID'S PARISH
Source(s): MUSTER ROLL.
Notes: LISTED AS A DESERTER FROM HITCHCOCK'S COMPANY
DURING FRENCH AND INDIAN WAR.

GREEN, RICHARD   ID: 497
Spouse: MARGERY FUTHY
Date in Pee Dee: 1765   Last Date: 1780
Location: PRINCE FREDERICK PARISH
Source(s): COOK, MOORE V.3, ROGERS.
Notes: SON OF JOHN #495.
Revolutionary War service: MARION'S BRIGADE

GREEN, SARAH   ID: 2927
Spouse: DANIEL MCGINNEY
Date in Pee Dee: 1749   Last Date: 1765
Location: PRINCE GEORGE WINYAW PARISH
Source(s): MOORE.
Notes: DAUGHTER OF JOHN #495.

GREEN, WILLIAM   ID: 498
Spouse: JANE THOMPSON
Date in Pee Dee: 1737   Last Date: 1779
Location: PRINCE FREDERICK PARISH
Source(s): COOK, BODDIE, MOORE.
Notes: GRAND-SON OF JOHN AVANT #2887. BROTHER OF
FRANCIS. MARRIED AT PARISH OF PRINCE FREDERICK WINYAW 19
AUGUST 1752.
Revolutionary War service: PRIVATE IN MARION'S BRIGADE.

GREEN, WILLIAM   ID: 2925
Spouse: LYDIA AVANT
Children: JOHN (DIED 1743), LYDIA (DAUGHTER OF JANE DIED
1766).
Date in Pee Dee: 1741   Last Date: 1765
Location: PRINCE GEORGE WINYAW PARISH
Source(s): MOORE, BODDIE, RBPPFW.

Notes: SON OF JOHN #495. LYDIA DIED 1751. MARRIED 31
MARCH 1741 AT PARISH OF PRINCE FREDERICK WINYAW.

GREENING, MASON   ID: 4807
Spouse: MARGARET [--?--]
Children: JOHN, ELIZABETH, SUSANNAH.
Date in Pee Dee: 1776   Last Date: 1776 DIED
Location: ST. MARK'S PARISH
Source(s): MOORE V.3.

GREENLAND, ANN   ID: 4554
Children: WILLIAM, THOMAS, ELIZABETH (CAHUSAC), JOHN.
Date in Pee Dee: 1777   Last Date: 1777 DIED
Location: PRINCE FREDERICK PARISH
Source(s): MOORE V.3.

GREENLAND, ELIZABETH   ID: 4557
Spouse: ROBERT CAHUSAC
Date in Pee Dee: 1777
Location: PRINCE FREDERICK PARISH
Source(s): MOORE V.3.
Notes: DAUGHTER OF ANN #4554.

GREENLAND, JOHN   ID: 4817
Children: MARY.
Date in Pee Dee: 1776   Last Date: 1776 DIED
Location: PRINCE FREDERICK PARISH
Source(s): MOORE V.3.
Notes: SON OF ANN. BROTHER-IN-LAW JOHN OF SEIGHTON.

GREENLAND, MARY   ID: 4559
Spouse: PETER SIMMONS
Date in Pee Dee: 1777
Location: PRINCE FREDERICK PARISH
Source(s): MOORE V.3, CLEMENS.
Notes: GRAND-DAUGHTER OF ANN GREENLAND #4554. DAUGHTER
OF JOHN. MARRIED 30 DECEMBER 1770.

GREENWOOD, ELIZABETH   ID: 5348

Spouse: WILLIAM GOODALL
Date in Pee Dee: 1739
Location: PRINCE FREDERICK PARISH
Source(s): RBPPFW.

GREGG, ALEXANDER   ID: 2193
Spouse: MARY GORDON
Children: REBECCA, MARGARET, EUNICE, ELEANOR, MARY E,
SARAH, JENNETT, JOHN B, SAMUEL D., ALEXANDER W, ROBERT
B. SPENCER.
Date in Pee Dee: 1778   Last Date: 1832 DIED
Location: MARS BLUFF
Source(s): MCCARTY.
Notes: SON OF JOHN #1460. MARY GORDON WAS A COUSIN.

GREGG, ALEXANDER SR   ID: 2346
Spouse: ANNA (NANCY) SPRING
Children: MARTHA, ALEXANDER LEWIS, ANN MARGARET
(CUNNINGHAM).
Date in Pee Dee: 1767   Last Date: 1823
Location: WILLOW CREEK, LATER COLUMBIA.
Source(s): MCCARTY.
Notes: SON OF JOSEPH #2344.

GREGG, ELIZABETH   ID: 2270
Spouse: ROBERT WILLIAM WILSON
Children: SARAH, WILLIAM W..
Date in Pee Dee: 1796   Last Date: 1821
Location: MARS BLUFF
Source(s): MCCARTY.
Notes: DAUGHTER OF JOHN #1460 AND PROBABLY MISS SPRINGS.

GREGG, ELIZABETH   ID: 2329
Spouse: WILLIAM DAVIDSON HALL
Children: JAMES G., SAMUEL W., ERMINA, THOMAS P., ELIAS
G., WILLIAM MARSHALL, RICHARD K., SARAH, JOHN E.,
ROBERT, CORNELIA.
Date in Pee Dee: 1788   Last Date: 1844
Location: MARS BLUFF, LATER NC

Source(s): MCCARTY.
Notes: DAUGHTER OF JOHN #1460.

GREGG, HUGH   ID: 2345
Date in Pee Dee: 1762   Last Date: 1793
Origin: NORTHERN IRELAND
Location: WILLIAMSBURG (ON BLACK MINGO)
Source(s): MCCARTY.
Notes: BROTHER OF JOHN #1455 AND JOSEPH #2344.

GREGG, JAMES   ID: 500
Spouse: ELIZABETH WILSON
Children: JENNET, ELIAS, JOHN, MARY, DAVID, SARAH,
JAMES, MARGARET, ELIZABETH.
Date in Pee Dee: 1752   Last Date: 1802 DIED
Location: JEFFERIES CREEK
Source(s): COOK, GREGG, MCCARTY, DAR.
Notes: PROBABLY CAME FROM N. IRELAND AS INFANT.
Revolutionary War service: CAPTAIN IN MARION'S BRIGADE.

GREGG, JAMES   ID: 5201
Spouse: CORNELIA MANNING MAXCY
Children: MAXCY, EDWARD FISHER, JULIA, CORNELIA.
Date in Pee Dee: 1787   Last Date: 1852 DIED
Location: MARS BLUFF
Source(s): MCCARTY.
Notes: SON OF JAMES #500.

GREGG, JAMES   ID: 5203
Spouse: MARY MULDROW
Children: JOHN, ELLEN, DAVID.
Date in Pee Dee: 1786
Location: MARS BLUFF
Source(s): MCCARTY.
Notes: SON OF JOHN #1460. MOVED TO ALABAMA. SECOND
MARRIED MISS DAVIS.

GREGG, JANE   ID: 2313
Spouse: JOHN COOPER

Children: ELEANOR MCKNIGHT, JANE, SAMUEL, ROBERT
DRAYTON, JOHN MILTON, FRANK, AMELIA, SUSANNAH ELIZA.
Date in Pee Dee: 1774
Location: MARS BLUFF
Source(s): MCCARTY.
Notes: DAUGHTER OF JOHN #1460.

GREGG, JANNET   ID: 2328
Spouse: JOHN GREGG
Children: EZRA, ELIZA, JOHN WILSON, DAVID REESE, MARY
E., EVANDER A., HENRY SMILIE, EPHRIAM, SARAH A..
Date in Pee Dee: 1779   Last Date: 1844
Location: MARS BLUFF
Source(s): MCCARTY.
Notes: DAUGHTER OF JOHN #1460.

GREGG, JANNETT   ID: 2321
Spouse: JAMES HUDSON
Children: JAMES WILSON, ELIZABETH HARRIET, JANNET
CAMPAIN, JOHN NELSON, MARY GREGG.
Date in Pee Dee: 1771   Last Date: 1844
Location: MARS BLUFF LATER BISHOPVILLE
Source(s): MCCARTY.
Notes: DAUGHTER OF JAMES #500.

GREGG, JENNET   ID: 1465
Spouse: JAMES BIGHAM
Children: ROBERT JAMES, BOYD, WILLIAM GORDON, WILLIAM,
GADSDEN, LEVI, WILDS, SUZANNAH, ELIZA.
Date in Pee Dee: 1780
Location: JEFFERIES CREEK
Source(s): GREGG, MCCARTY.
Notes: DAUGHTER OF JOHN #1455.

GREGG, JOHN   ID: 1455
Spouse: ELEANOR [--?--]
Children: JAMES, MARY, JOHN, WILLIAM, MARGARET, JENNET,
ROBERT.
Date in Pee Dee: 1752   Last Date: 1775 DIED

Origin: NORTHERN IRELAND
Location: JEFFERIES CREEK
Source(s): BODDIE, GREGG, MCCARTY, DAR.
Notes: OVERSEER OF POOR FOR PARISH OF PRINCE FREDERICK
WINYAW DURING 1762-63.

GREGG, JOHN   ID: 2327
Spouse: JANNET GREGG
Children: EZRA, ELIZA, JOHN WILSON, DAVID REESE, MARY
E., EVANDER A., HENRY SMILIE, EPHRIAM, SARAH A..
Date in Pee Dee: 1781   Last Date: 1839
Location: MARS BLUFF
Source(s): MCCARTY.
Notes: SON OF JAMES #500.

GREGG, JOHN II   ID: 1460
Spouse: ELEANOR MCKNIGHT
Children: JANE, WILLIAM, JOHN, SAMUEL, JANET, AXEXANDER,
JAMES, JANET, MARGARET, ROBERT.
Date in Pee Dee: 1765
Location: JEFFERIES CREEK
Source(s): GREGG, MCCARTY, DAR.
Notes: SON OF JOHN #1455 SECOND MARRIED A MISS SPRING.
Revolutionary War service: LIEUTENANT IN MARION'S
BRIGADE.

GREGG, JOSEPH   ID: 2344
Spouse: SARAH ATKINS
Children: ALEXANDER, JANNET, ROBERT, MARY, SARAH,
MARGARET, JOSEPH.
Date in Pee Dee: 1752   Last Date: 1829
Origin: NORTHERN IRELAND
Location: WILLOW CREEK
Source(s): MCCARTY.
Notes: BROTHER OF JOHN #1455 AND HUGH #2345.

GREGG, JOSEPH II   ID: 2348
Spouse: HARRIET JAMES

Children: AMANDA C., CHARLES M., GEORGE C., JOHN DAVIS, ROWENA, HARRIET, SARAH, MARY, LOUISE, JAMES P..
Date in Pee Dee: 1796   Last Date: 1864
Location: WILLOW CREEK
Source(s): MCCARTY.
Notes: SON OF JOSEPH #2344.

GREGG, MARGARET   ID: 1462
Spouse: SAMUEL SCOTT
Children: ELIZABETH, JOHN, REBECCA, WILLIAM, MARY, JANNET, SAMUEL.
Date in Pee Dee: 1765
Location: JEFFERIES CREEK
Source(s): GREGG, MCCARTY.
Notes: DAUGHTER OF JOHN #1455. MARRIED 2ND WILLIAM GORDON THEN WILLIAM FLAGLER.

GREGG, MARGARET   ID: 2165
Spouse: WILLIAM BIGHAM
Children: SARAH, JOHN H., EUNICE, AMBROSE, ELIZA, MILINDA.
Date in Pee Dee: 1786   Last Date: 1822
Location: MARS BLUFF
Source(s): MCCARTY.
Notes: DAUGHTER OF JOHN #1460.

GREGG, MARGARET   ID: 2326
Spouse: SAMUEL HALL
Children: OLIVIA, MARY MARSHALL, SOPHIA, ELIZABETH GREGG, SAMUEL PIKE.
Date in Pee Dee: 1776
Location: MARS BLUFF LATER COVINGTON TENN.
Source(s): MCCARTY.
Notes: DAUGHTER OF JAMES #500. HALL WAS FROM IREDELL COUNTY NC.

GREGG, MARGARET LOUISA   ID: 2347
Spouse: ROBERT CHARLES HUDSON

Children: MARGARET LOUISE, THOMAS MCDONOUGH, WILLIAM S., SARAH JANE.
Date in Pee Dee: 1787   Last Date: 1828
Location: WILLOW CREEK, LATER WILLIAMSBURG.
Source(s): MCCARTY.
Notes: DAUGHTER OF JOSEPH #2344.

GREGG, MARY   ID: 1458
Spouse: SAMUEL ASKINS
Children: SAMUEL, JOHN, ROBERT, WILSON.
Date in Pee Dee: 1765
Location: CHERAW DISTRICT
Source(s): GREGG, MCCARTY.
Notes: DAUGHTER OF JOHN #1455.

GREGG, MARY   ID: 2324
Spouse: ADAM MARSHALL
Children: WILLIAM, ELIZABETH, SARAH, MARY.
Date in Pee Dee: 1773   Last Date: 1819
Location: MARS BLUFF, LATER SOCIETY HILL
Source(s): MCCARTY.
Notes: DAUGHTER OF JAMES #500.

GREGG, ROBERT   ID: 1466
Spouse: MARY ANN MCSWAIN
Children: MARY ANN MARGARET (GORDON).
Date in Pee Dee: 1759   Last Date: 1813 DIED
Location: JEFFERIES CREEK
Source(s): GREGG, MCCARTY.
Notes: SON OF JOHN #1455. GREGG REPORTS WOUNDED IN REVOLUTION BUT DOES NOT APPEAR ON DAR LIST.

GREGG, ROBERT H.   ID: 2087
Spouse: ELIZABETH HICKS STROTHER
Children: ROBERT S., LUCY, JANE, OLIVER H. P., ELIZABETH, CHARLES A., MARY, HARRIET, SAMUEL G., SARAH, ROBERT H..
Date in Pee Dee: 1790   Last Date: 1862 DIED
Location: MARS BLUFF

Source(s): MCCARTY.
Notes: SON OF JOHN #1460. MOVED TO ALA. ELIZABETH WAS
DAUGHTER OF WILLIAM STROTHER. FIRST WIFE WAS [--?--]
COVINGTON.

GREGG, SAMUEL   ID: 5202
Spouse: ANNA SCOTT
Date in Pee Dee: 1784
Location: MARS BLUFF
Source(s): MCCARTY.
Notes: DAUGHTER OF JOHN #1460. MOVED TO MISS.

GREGG, SARAH   ID: 2323
Spouse: ALEXANDER JONES
Date in Pee Dee: 1775
Source(s): MCCARTY.
Notes: DAUGHTER OF JAMES #500. MOVED TO LINCOLN COUNTY
NC.

GREGG, WILLIAM   ID: 1464
Spouse: JANE MCILVEEN
Children: ROBERT JAMES, BOYD, WILLIAM GORDON, WILLIAM,
GADSDEN, LEVI, WILDS, SUZANNAH, ELIZA.
Date in Pee Dee: 1770   Last Date: 1816
Location: JEFFERIES CREEK
Source(s): GREGG, MCCARTY.
Notes: SON OF JOHN #1455.

GREGG, WILLIAM   ID: 2316
Spouse: ISABELLA MCDOWELL
Children: SUSAN, SELINA, ISABELLA, MARGARET, JULIA, MARY
C., GEORGE COOPER, ROBERT G., SAMUEL T, WILLIAM P.
Date in Pee Dee: 1782   Last Date: 1837 DIED
Location: MARS BLUFF
Source(s): MCCARTY.
Notes: SON OF JOHN #1460.

GREGG, WILLIAM   ID: 2808
Date in Pee Dee: 1742   Last Date: 1750

Location: PRINCE FREDERICK PARISH
Source(s): MOORE.
Notes: WITNESS TO WILLIAM HEATHLY AND TIMOTHY BRITTON'S
WILLS.

GRIER, AGNES   ID: 2870
Spouse: [--?--] BAXTER
Date in Pee Dee: 1749   Last Date: 1768
Location: PRINCE GEORGE WINYAW PARISH
Source(s): MOORE.
Notes: SISTER OF PATRICK, THOMAS (IN NORTHERN IRELAND),
SAMUEL, JOHN, JOSEPH, JANNET, AND MARY.

GRIER, AGNES   ID: 4425
Spouse: JOHN MCDOUGAL
Date in Pee Dee: 1772
Location: PEE DEE RIVER
Source(s): MOORE V.3.
Notes: DAUGHTER OF SAMUEL #4043.

GRIER, ANDREW   ID: 4790
Spouse: BARBARA [--?--]
Children: MARY, JANE.
Date in Pee Dee: 1774   Last Date: 1774 DIED
Source(s): MOORE V.3.
Notes: WILL MENTIONS BROTHERS JOHN AND JOSEPH.

GRIER, ANDREW SR   ID: 3717
Spouse: MARGARET [--?--]
Children: JOSEPH, SAMUEL, JEAN.
Date in Pee Dee: 1765   Last Date: 1765 DIED
Location: KINGSTON
Source(s): MOORE V.3.
Notes: BROTHER OF JOSEPH JR. NEPHEW OF PATRICK AND
SAMUEL GRIER.

GRIER, JANNET   ID: 4045
Spouse: [--?--] WILLSON
Date in Pee Dee: 1768

Location: PRINCE GEORGE WINYAH PARISH
Source(s): MOORE V.3.
Notes: SISTER OF THOMAS (IN IRELAND),PATRICK, SAMUEL,
JOSEPH, JOHN, AGNES, AND MARY.

GRIER, JOHN   ID: 4044
Date in Pee Dee: 1768
Location: PRINCE GEORGE WINYAH PARISH
Source(s): MOORE V.3.
Notes: BROTHER OF THOMAS (IRELAND),PATRICK, SAMUEL,
JOSEPH, JANNET, AGNES, AND MARY.

GRIER, JOSEPH   ID: 501
Spouse: REBECCA GRIER
Date in Pee Dee: 1765   Last Date: 1787
Location: PRINCE GEORGE WINYAW
Source(s): COOK, MOORE V.3.
Notes: BROTHER OF ANDREW SR. AND PATRICK. MARRIED AT
CHARLESTON AUGUST 1785.

GRIER, JOSEPH   ID: 3721
Spouse: AGNES [--?--]
Date in Pee Dee: 1765
Location: KINGSTON
Source(s): MOORE V.3.
Notes: SON OF ANDREW SR. #3717. DIED BEFORE 1772.

GRIER, JOSEPH JR   ID: 3718
Spouse: SUSANNA WESTON
Date in Pee Dee: 1765   Last Date: 1768 DIED
Location: KINGSTON
Source(s): MOORE V.3.
Notes: SON OF ANDREW SR. #3717.

GRIER, MARY   ID: 4046
Spouse: WILLIAM RIDGILL
Children: WILLIAM, ANN.
Date in Pee Dee: 1768
Location: PRINCE GEORGE WINYAH PARISH

Source(s): MOORE V.3.
Notes: SISTER OF THOMAS (IN NORTHERN IRELAND),PATRICK,
SAMUEL, JOSEPH, JOHN, AGNES, AND JANNET.

GRIER, MARY ANN   ID: 4042
Spouse: ANTHONY MITCHELL
Date in Pee Dee: 1768
Location: PRINCE GEORGE WINYAH PARISH
Source(s): MOORE V.3.
Notes: DAUGHTER OF PATRICK #3722.

GRIER, PATRICK   ID: 3722
Spouse: JUDITH [--?--]
Children: SAMUEL, JAMES, MARY ANN (MITCHELL).
Date in Pee Dee: 1765   Last Date: 1768 DIED
Location: KINGSTON
Source(s): MOORE V.3.
Notes: BROTHER OF THOMAS (IN NORTHERN IRELAND), SAMUEL,
JOHN, JOSEPH, JANNET (WILLSON), AGNES (BAXTER), MARY
(RIDGELL).

GRIER, SAMUEL   ID: 3720
Date in Pee Dee: 1765
Location: KINGSTON
Source(s): MOORE V.3.
Notes: UNCLE OF ANDREW SR. #3717. SON OF PATRICK #3722.

GRIER, SAMUEL   ID: 4043
Children: JOHN, WILLIAM, AGNES (MCDOUGAL), ELIZABETH.
Date in Pee Dee: 1768   Last Date: 1772 DIED
Location: PRINCE GEORGE WINYAH PARISH
Source(s): MOORE V.3.
Notes: BROTHER OF THOMAS (IN NORTHERN IRELAND),PATRICK,
JOHN, JOSEPH, JANNET, AGNES, AND MARY.

GRIER, SARAH   ID: 4052
Date in Pee Dee: 1768
Source(s): MOORE V.3.

Notes: NIECE OF PATRICK GRIER #3722.

GRIFFIN, JAMES   ID: 5294
Spouse: ELIZABETH [--?--]
Children: ANNE.
Date in Pee Dee: 1745
Location: PRINCE FREDERICK PARISH
Source(s): RBPPFW.

GRIFFIN, JOHN   ID: 3048
Date in Pee Dee: 1742   Last Date: 1754
Location: PRINCE FREDERICK PARISH
Source(s): MOORE, RBPPFW.
Notes: SON OF JOSEPH #3627. DOB 8 OCTOBER 1719.

GRIFFIN, JOSEPH   ID: 3627
Spouse: JOYCE [--?--]
Children: JOHN.
Date in Pee Dee: 1742   Last Date: 1763
Location: PRINCE FREDERICK PARISH
Source(s): MOORE V.3, RBPPFW.
Notes: PROBABLY HERE AS EARLY AS 1719.

GRIFFITH, JANE   ID: 3285
Spouse: [--?--] MOSTYN
Date in Pee Dee: 1733
Location: WACCAMAW
Source(s): MOORE V.1.

GRIFFITH, JOHN   ID: 1818
Date in Pee Dee: 1768
Location: ST. DAVID'S PARISH
Source(s): GREGG, JVSDP.
Notes: SERVED IN FRENCH AND INDIAN WAR AS SERGEANT WITH
CAPTAIN PLEDGER'S COMPANY.
Revolutionary War service: PRIVATE IN MARION'S BRIGADE.

GRIFFITH, JOSEPH   ID: 2124
Date in Pee Dee: 1782

Source(s): GREGG P.408.
Revolutionary War service: CAPTAIN IN MARION'S BRIGADE.

GRIFFITH, MICHAEL   ID: 1943
Date in Pee Dee: 1759   Last Date: 1769
Location: ST. DAVID'S PARISH
Source(s): GREGG, JVSDP.
Notes: SERVED IN FRENCH AND INDIAN WAR AS PRIVATE IN
CAPTAIN GEORGE HICK'S COMPANY.

GRIMES, JAMES   ID: 2125
Date in Pee Dee: 1780
Source(s): GREGG P.408.
Revolutionary War service: PRIVATE IN IRBY'S COMPANY.

GRIMES, JOHN JR   ID: 5637
Date in Pee Dee: 1759
Location: ST. DAVID'S PARISH
Source(s): MUSTER ROLL.
Notes: SERVED IN FRENCH AND INDIAN WAR AS PRIVATE WITH
LIDE'S COMPANY.

GRIMES, JOHN SR.   ID: 5636
Date in Pee Dee: 1759
Location: ST. DAVID'S PARISH
Source(s): MUSTER ROLL.
Notes: SERVED IN FRENCH AND INDIAN WAR AS PRIVATE WITH
LIDE'S COMPANY.

GRIMES, WILLIAM   ID: 3438
Date in Pee Dee: 1759
Location: ST. MARK'S PARISH
Source(s): MOORE V.3, BODDIE.
Notes: SERVED IN FRENCH AND INDIAN WAR.

GROOM, WILLIAM   ID: 5259
Spouse: JUDITH [--?--]
Children: SUSANNAH.
Date in Pee Dee: 1743

Location: PRINCE FREDERICK PARISH
Source(s): RBPPFW.

GROVES, G. WILLIAM   ID: **5534**
Date in Pee Dee: 1773
Location: ST. DAVID'S PARISH
Source(s): JVSDP.
Notes: THREE CHILDREN AT DEATH. TWO BOYS BOUND TO JOHN
HURD.

GUERRY, JAMES   ID: **504**
Spouse: MARY JANE (MARIE) REMBERT
Children: THEODORE, JOHN, PETER.
Date in Pee Dee: 1717   Last Date: 1756
Location: NORTH SIDE OF SANTEE RIVER
Source(s): COOK, REMBERT, MOORE.
Notes: SON OF JAMES #3302.

GUERRY, JAMES (JACQUE GUERY)   ID: **3302**
Spouse: JEANE REMBERT
Children: JOHN, JAMES, ESTHER (BY 2ND WIFE), JANE.
Date in Pee Dee: 1700   Last Date: 1728 DIED
Location: CRAVEN COUNTY
Source(s): MOORE V.1, REMBERT.
Notes: BROTHER OF PETER #505. SECOND MARRIED ESTHER
MICHAU. MAY HAVE LIVED SOUTH OF SANTEE.

GUERRY, JANE   ID: **3306**
Spouse: STEPHEN DUMAY
Date in Pee Dee: 1728
Location: CRAVEN COUNTY
Source(s): MOORE V.1, REMBERT.
Notes: DAUGHTER OF JAMES #3302.

GUERRY, JOHN   ID: **3303**
Children: STEPHEN, MARY.
Date in Pee Dee: 1715
Location: CRAVEN COUNTY
Source(s): MOORE V.1, REMBERT.

Notes: SON OF JAMES #3302.

GUERRY, PETER   ID: 505
Spouse: MARGUERITE REMBERT
Children: ELIZABETH (GAILLARD), ANNE (DUPONT), ELISHA,
MARGARET, ANDRE, PIERRE, MADELAINE (JEANNERETT), LYDIA
(STEEL).
Date in Pee Dee: 1700   Last Date: 1732
Location: NORTH SIDE OF SANTEE RIVER
Source(s): COOK, REMBERT, MOORE V.1.
Notes: BROTHER OF JAMES. SON OF 1ST PETER.

GUERRY, PETER   ID: 606
Spouse: ELIZABETH CROFT
Date in Pee Dee: 1756
Location: ALONG SANTEE RIVER
Source(s): CLEMENS, BOODIE.
Notes: MARRIED AT SANTEE 30 JULY 1778. SON OF PETER
#505.

GUNSON, THOMAS   ID: 5635
Date in Pee Dee: 1759
Location: ST. DAVID'S PARISH
Source(s): MUSTER ROLL.
Notes: SERVED IN FRENCH AND INDIAN WAR AS SERGEANT WITH
LIDE'S COMPANY.

GWINN, WILLIAM   ID: 508
Date in Pee Dee: 1781
Source(s): COOK, BODDIE.
Revolutionary War service: SERVED IN MARION'S BRIGADE.

HAGIN, DAVID   ID: 2126
Date in Pee Dee: 1782
Source(s): GREGG P.408.
Revolutionary War service: SERVED AS PRIVATE IN BENTON'S
REGIMENT.

HAINS, ELIZABETH   ID: 5219
Spouse: JOHN GODBOLT
Children: JOHN (ALIAS HAINS).
Date in Pee Dee: 1740
Location: PRINCE FREDERICK PARISH
Source(s): RBPPFW.
Notes: MARRIED 24 APRIL 1740.

HALES, SILAS   ID: 2127
Date in Pee Dee: 1782
Source(s): GREGG P.408.
Revolutionary War service: SERVED AS PRIVATE IN BENTON'S
REGIMENT.

HALEY, EDWARD   ID: 5661
Date in Pee Dee: 1759
Location: ST. DAVID'S PARISH
Source(s): MUSTER ROLL.
Notes: SERVED IN FRENCH AND INDIAN WAR AS PRIVATE WITH
MCINTOSH'S COMPANY.

HALL, JOHN   ID: 5253
Spouse: MARY [--?--]

Children: ELIZABETH.
Date in Pee Dee: 1742
Location: PRINCE FREDERICK PARISH
Source(s): RBPPFW.

HALL, JOHN JR.   ID: 3742
Spouse: ANN HUNT
Children: JOHN HENRY, LEWEY CANNON.
Date in Pee Dee: 1766   Last Date: 1766 DIED
Location: ST. DAVID'S PARISH
Source(s): MOORE V.3.
Notes: PARENTS WERE JOHN AND ANN HALL.

HALL, THOMAS   ID: 5213
Spouse: GRACE [--?--]
Children: EDWARD.
Date in Pee Dee: 1737   Last Date: 1739
Location: PRINCE FREDERICK PARISH
Source(s): RBPPFW, BODDIE.

HAM, JACOB   ID: 5696
Date in Pee Dee: 1759
Location: ST. DAVID'S PARISH
Source(s): MUSTER ROLL.
Notes: SERVED IN FRENCH AND INDIAN WAR AS PRIVATE WITH
KOLB'S COMPANY.

HAM, JOHN   ID: 5695
Date in Pee Dee: 1759
Location: ST. DAVID'S PARISH
Source(s): MUSTER ROLL.
Notes: SERVED IN FRENCH AND INDIAN WAR AS PRIVATE WITH
KOLB'S COMPANY.

HAMILTON, CHARLES   ID: 3597
Spouse: MARGARET [--?--]
Children: JOHN, JAMES, CHARLES, WILLIAM, MARY (EDDY).
Date in Pee Dee: 1762   Last Date: 1765 DIED
Origin: PENNSYLVANIA

Location: PRINCE FREDERICK PARISH
Source(s): MOORE V.3.

HAMILTON, JAMES   ID: 3600
Date in Pee Dee: 1762   Last Date: 1780
Location: PRINCE FREDERICK PARISH
Source(s): MOORE V.3, BODDIE.
Notes: SON OF CHARLES #3597.
Revolutionary War service: SERVED AS LIEUTENANT IN
MARION'S BRIGADE.

HAMILTON, JOHN   ID: 511
Spouse: CHRISTAIN MCCLELAND
Date in Pee Dee: 1742   Last Date: 1744 DIED
Origin: NORTHERN IRELAND
Location: WILLIAMSBURG
Source(s): COOK, BODDIE, MOORE.

HAMILTON, JOHN   ID: 3599
Date in Pee Dee: 1762
Location: PRINCE FREDERICK PARISH
Source(s): MOORE V.3, BODDIE.
Notes: SON OF CHARLES #3597. APPEARS TO HAVE SERVED WITH
MARION LATER. FRANCIS MARION WAS VERY QUICK TO FORGIVE
HIS ENEMIES, MANY OF WHOM THOUGHT BETTER OF THE
SITUATION, SIGNED A LOYALITY OATH AND JOINED HIM IN THE
FIELD.
Revolutionary War service: TORY MAJOR

HAMILTON, MARY   ID: 3602
Spouse: WILLIAM EDDY
Date in Pee Dee: 1762
Location: PRINCE FREDERICK PARISH
Source(s): MOORE V.3.
Notes: DAUGHTER OF CHARLES #3597.

HAMILTON, WILLIAM   ID: 3601
Date in Pee Dee: 1762   Last Date: 1782
Location: PRINCE FREDERICK PARISH

Source(s): MOORE V.3, BODDIE.
Notes: SON OF CHARLES #3597. LEFT AT END OF WAR
Revolutionary War service: TORY MAJOR

HAMLITON, JAMES JR.   ID: 2655
Spouse: ELIZABETH Nee LYNCH HARLESTON
Date in Pee Dee: 1780
Location: GEORGETOWN
Source(s): ROGERS.

HANDLEN, JOHN   ID: 1326
Spouse: MARGARETT [--?--]
Children: JOHN, THOMAS, BENJAMIN, WILLIAM, ELIZABETH,
MARGARETT.
Date in Pee Dee: 1738   Last Date: 1753 DIED
Location: WILLIAMSBURG
Source(s): MOORE, RBPPFW.
Notes: ALSO SPELLED HANDLIN AND HENLIN.

HANDLEN, MERCY   ID: 5426
Spouse: JAMES (II) BELIN
Date in Pee Dee: 1747
Location: PRINCE FREDERICK PARISH
Source(s): RBPPFW.
Notes: DAUGHTER OF EDWARD #514.

HANDLEN, THOMAS   ID: 2838
Spouse: ELIZABETH KING
Date in Pee Dee: 1746
Location: PRINCE FREDERICK PARISH
Source(s): MOORE, RBPPFW.
Notes: MARRIED AT PARISH OF PRINCE FREDERICK WINYAW 5
SEPTEMBER 1749.

HANDLIN, EDWARD   ID: 514
Spouse: ELIZABETH [--?--]
Children: THOMAS, PARMENAS, EDWARD, ROBERT, MARY,
CHAMPINO, MERCY.
Date in Pee Dee: 1730   Last Date: 1746 DIED
Location: BLACK MINGO CREEK

Source(s): COOK, RBPPFW, MOORE.
Notes: APPEARS TO HAVE BEEN MARRIED TO MARY UNTIL 1742.
VESTRY MAN OF PARISH OF PRINCE FREDERICK WINYAW IN 1731.

HANDYMAN, THOMAS   ID: 515
Date in Pee Dee: 1776
Location: GEORGETOWN
Source(s): COOK.
Revolutionary War service: SERVED AS CAPTAIN IN POWELL'S
REGIMENT.

HANLEY, THOMAS   ID: 5495
Date in Pee Dee: 1729
Location: PRINCE FREDERICK PARISH
Source(s): RBPPFW.
Notes: GAVE ONE COW TO THE PARISH IN 1729. NO OTHER
REFERENCE. MAY BE SAME AS HANDLEN.

HARBIN, FRANCIS   ID: 4917
Spouse: ANN VAREEN
Children: ELIZABETH.
Date in Pee Dee: 1750
Location: WILLIAMSBURG
Source(s): BODDIE.

HARDEE, JOHN   ID: 516
Spouse: SARAH [--?--]
Date in Pee Dee: 1775
Location: ST. DAVID'S PARISH
Source(s): COOK, MOORE V.3.
Revolutionary War service: LIDE'S COMPANY

HARDEN, SAMUEL   ID: 5681
Date in Pee Dee: 1759
Location: ST. DAVID'S PARISH
Source(s): MUSTER ROLL.
Notes: SERVED IN FRENCH AND INDIAN WAR AS PRIVATE IN
PLEDGER'S COMPANY.

HARDIN, CHARLES   ID: 517

Date in Pee Dee: 1781
Source(s): COOK, BODDIE.
Revolutionary War service: SERVED AS MAJOR IN MARION'S
BRIGADE.

HARDYMAN, JOSEPH   ID: 1999
Date in Pee Dee: 1775
Location: ST. DAVID'S PARISH
Source(s): GREGG.
Revolutionary War service: MILITIA

HARGRAVE, ROBERT   ID: 519
Date in Pee Dee: 1776
Location: GEORGETOWN
Source(s): COOK.
Revolutionary War service: CAPTAIN

HARGRAVE, SAMUEL   ID: 520
Date in Pee Dee: 1776
Location: GEORGETOWN
Source(s): COOK.
Revolutionary War service: LIEUTENANT

HARGROVE, HOWEL   ID: 5705
Date in Pee Dee: 1759
Location: ST. DAVID'S PARISH
Source(s): MUSTER ROLL.
Notes: LISTED AS DESERTER FROM KOLB'S COMPANY DURING
FRENCH AND INDIAN WAR.

HARLOW, BENJAMIN   ID: 2019
Date in Pee Dee: 1775
Location: ST. DAVID'S PARISH
Source(s): GREGG.
Revolutionary War service: IN MARION'S BRIGADE.

HARRALL, LEVI   ID: 2128
Date in Pee Dee: 1782
Source(s): GREGG P.408.

Revolutionary War service: SERVED AS PRIVATE IN BENTON'S
REGIMENT.

HARRINGTON, HARRIET   ID: 1732
Spouse: BELAH STRONG
Date in Pee Dee: 1770
Location: CHERAW
Source(s): GREGG.
Notes: DAUGHTER OF HENRY WILLIAM #1730.

HARRINGTON, HENRY WILLIAM   ID: 1730
Spouse: ROSANNA AULD
Children: ROSANNA, HENRY WILLIAM, JAMES AULD, HARRIET.
Date in Pee Dee: 1760   Last Date: 1766
Origin: ENGLAND VIA JAMAICA
Location: CHERAW
Source(s): GREGG.
Notes: IN 1766 MOVED TO RICHMOND COUNTY NORTH CAROLINA.
Revolutionary War service: GENERAL

HARRINGTON, JAMES AULD   ID: 1734
Spouse: ELEANOR WILSON
Date in Pee Dee: 1770
Location: CHERAW
Source(s): GREGG.
Notes: SON OF HENRY WILLIAM #1730.

HARRINGTON, ROSANNA   ID: 1731
Spouse: ROBERT TROY
Date in Pee Dee: 1770
Location: CHERAW
Source(s): GREGG.
Notes: DAUGHTER OF HENRY WILLIAM #1730.

HARRINGTON, THOMAS   ID: 522
Spouse: HANNAH [--?--]
Children: MARY, SARAH WHITMEL, THOMAS, HANNAH.
Date in Pee Dee: 1737   Last Date: 1745
Location: WILLIAMSBURG
Source(s): COOK, BODDIE, RBPPFW.

Notes: BROTHER OF WHITMELL. BODDIE GIVES WIFE AS MARY.

HARRINGTON, WHITMELL   ID: 5247
Spouse: JANNET SHAW
Children: MARY, JANNET.
Date in Pee Dee: 1741   Last Date: 1745 DIED
Location: PRINCE FREDERICK PARISH
Source(s): RBPPFW, MOORE.
Notes: MARRIED 2 FEBRUARY 1742 AT PARISH OF PRINCE
FREDERICK WINYAW.

HARRINGTON, WILLIAM HENRY   ID: 1776
Date in Pee Dee: 1776
Location: GEORGETOWN
Source(s): COOK.
Notes: FIRST SHERIFF OF CHERAW DISTRICT UNDER
CONSTITUTION OF 1776.

HARRINTON, MARY   ID: 5475
Spouse: JOHN GODFREY
Date in Pee Dee: 1761
Location: PRINCE FREDERICK PARISH
Source(s): RBPPFW.

HARRIS, ANGELICO   ID: 3309
Spouse: [--?--] HANLEY
Date in Pee Dee: 1735
Location: NORTH OF SANTEE
Source(s): MOORE V.1.
Notes: DAUGHTER OF FRANCIS #3307.

HARRIS, FRANCIS   ID: 3307
Spouse: SARAH [--?--]
Children: MARY (BROWN), ANGELICO (HANLEY).
Date in Pee Dee: 1735   Last Date: 1735 DIED
Location: NORTH OF SANTEE
Source(s): MOORE V.1.

HARRIS, GRIFFITH   ID: 5643

Date in Pee Dee: 1759
Location: ST. DAVID'S PARISH
Source(s): MUSTER ROLL.
Notes: SERVED IN FRENCH AND INDIAN WAR AS PRIVATE WITH
LIDE'S COMPANY.

HARRIS, MARY   ID: 3308
Spouse: [--?--] BROWN
Date in Pee Dee: 1735
Location: NORTH OF SANTEE
Source(s): MOORE V.1.
Notes: DAUGHTER OF FRANCIS #3307.

HARRISON, HENRY   ID: 2129
Date in Pee Dee: 1782
Source(s): GREGG P.408.
Revolutionary War service: SERVED AS PRIVATE IN MARION'S
BRIGADE.

HARRISON, JOHN   ID: 2393
Date in Pee Dee: 1779
Origin: VIRGINIA
Location: LYNCHES CREEK (SPARROW SWAMP)
Source(s): LAMBERT.
Notes: SERVED AS BRITISH SPY. BROTHERS ROBERT AND SAMUEL
SERVED WITH HIM AS CAPTAINS.
Revolutionary War service: MAJOR WITH SOUTH CAROLINA
RANGERS.

HARRY, DAVID   ID: 525
Spouse: MARY [--?--]
Children: DAVID.
Date in Pee Dee: 1737   Last Date: 1772 DIED
Location: LONG BLUFF, ABOVE SEVERAL MILES.
Source(s): COOK, RWNBC, GREGG, MOORE.
Notes: BROTHER OF GEORGE AND DAVID. ORIGINAL SETTLER OF
THE WELCH NECK.

HARRY, ELEANOR   ID: 527

Spouse: [--?--] JONES
Date in Pee Dee: 1745   Last Date: 1745 DIED
Location: WELCH NECK
Source(s): COOK, RWNBC.

HARRY, JAMES   ID: 529
Spouse: MARY [--?--]
Date in Pee Dee: 1755   Last Date: 1759
Location: WELCH NECK
Source(s): COOK, RWNBC.
Notes: SERVED IN FRENCH AND INDIAN WAR AS PRIVATE WITH
PLEDGER'S COMPANY.

HARRY, JOHN   ID: 530
Date in Pee Dee: 1737   Last Date: 1759
Location: LONG BLUFF, ABOVE SEVERAL MILES.
Source(s): COOK, MUSTER ROLL, RWNBC.
Notes: ORIGINAL WELCH NECK SETTLER. SERVED AS PRIVATE IN
LIDE'S COMPANY DURING FRENCH AND INDIAN WAR

HARRY, NAOMI   ID: 532
Spouse: [--?--] UNDERWOOD
Date in Pee Dee: 1755
Location: WELCH NECK
Source(s): COOK, RWNBC.

HARRY, SARAH   ID: 1448
Spouse: ABEL EDWARDS
Children: CATHERINE, EDWARD, SARAH.
Date in Pee Dee: 1760
Location: WELCH TRACT
Source(s): GREGG.

HARRY, THOMAS   ID: 533
Date in Pee Dee: 1737   Last Date: 1778
Location: SEVERAL MILES ABOVE LONG BLUFF.
Source(s): COOK, JVSDP, RWNBC.
Notes: ORIGINAL WELCH NECK SETTLER. PRIVATE WITH
PLEDGER'S COMPANY IN FRENCH AND INDIAN WAR.

Early Pee Dee Settlers
--H--

HARRY, WILLIAM   ID: 5682
Date in Pee Dee: 1759
Location: ST. DAVID'S PARISH
Source(s): MUSTER ROLL.
Notes: SERVED IN FRENCH AND INDIAN WAR AS PRIVATE IN
PLEDGER'S COMPANY.

HART, ARTHUR   ID: 1738
Spouse: [--?--] IRBY
Children: JAMES, MARY, SARAH, ELIZABETH, SALLY, POLLY.
Date in Pee Dee: 1767   Last Date: 1777 DIED
Origin: ENGLAND VIA VIRGINIA
Location: LONG BLUFF
Source(s): GREGG, MOORE V.3, COOK.
Notes: MARRIED [--?--] IN VIRGINIA. THEN ELIZABETH
WILLIAMS.

HART, JAMES   ID: 1319
Spouse: SARAH EDWARDS
Children: JAMES, THOMAS.
Date in Pee Dee: 1770
Location: ST. DAVID'S
Source(s): GREGG.
Notes: SON OF ARTHUR #1738.

HART, JOHN   ID: 5714
Date in Pee Dee: 1759
Location: ST. DAVID'S PARISH
Source(s): MUSTER ROLL.
Notes: LISTED AS A DESERTER FROM HITCHCOCK'S COMPANY
DURING FRENCH AND INDIAN WAR.

HART, MARY   ID: 1493
Spouse: RICHARD BROCKINGTON
Date in Pee Dee: 1765
Location: CHERAW DISTRICT
Source(s): GREGG.
Notes: WIFE OF RICHARD #1489. DAUGHTER OF ARTHUR #1738.

HART, PETER   ID: 5715
Date in Pee Dee: 1759
Location: ST. DAVID'S PARISH
Source(s): MUSTER ROLL.
Notes: LISTED AS A DESERTER FROM HITCHCOCK'S COMPANY
DURING FRENCH AND INDIAN WAR.

HART, SARAH   ID: 1739
Spouse: NICHOLAS ROGERS
Date in Pee Dee: 1770
Location: ST. DAVID'S
Source(s): GREGG.
Notes: DAUGHTER OF ARTHUR #1738.

HARWELL, LONDEN   ID: 2721
Spouse: MARY HODGE
Children: LONDEN.
Date in Pee Dee: 1780
Origin: NORTH CAROLINA
Location: MARLBORO DISTRICT
Source(s): THOMAS.

HASELDEN, ROBERT   ID: 5051
Date in Pee Dee: 1780
Location: WILLIAMSBURG
Source(s): BODDIE.
Revolutionary War service: SERVED AS PRIVATE IN MARION'S
BRIGADE.

HASELDEN, SEE HAZELTON, HASELTON

HASELDEN, WILLIAM   ID: 5052
Date in Pee Dee: 1780
Location: WILLIAMSBURG
Source(s): BODDIE.
Revolutionary War service: SERVED AS PRIVATE IN MARION'S
BRIGADE.

HASELL, THOMAS   ID: 539
Spouse: ELIZABETH ASHBY
Date in Pee Dee: 1722
Source(s): COOK, CLEMENS.
Notes: MARIED 21 JANUARY 1714 AT CHARLESTON.

HASELL, THOMAS   ID: 540
Spouse: MARGARET SUMMERS
Date in Pee Dee: 1741   Last Date: 1780
Location: PRINCE GEORGE PARISH.
Source(s): COOK, MOORE, ROGERS, CLEMENS.
Notes: SIGNED LOYALITY OATH IN 1780. MARRIED AT SANTEE 2
FEBRUARY 1772.

HASELL, THOMAS   ID: 3122
Spouse: ALICE MORRITT
Children: THOMAS, MARY, ELIZABETH.
Date in Pee Dee: 1756   Last Date: 1756 DIED
Location: PRINCE GEORGE WINYAW PARISH
Source(s): MOORE, RBPPFW, CLEMENS.
Notes: ONE SOURCE GIVES A DAUGHTER MARGARET. MARRIED 26
APRIL 1744 AT ST. THOMAS PARISH.

HASELTON, SAMUEL   ID: 1925
Date in Pee Dee: 1759   Last Date: 1769
Location: ST. DAVID'S PARISH
Source(s): GREGG, BODDIE.
Notes: SERVED IN FRENCH AND INDIAN WAR AS PRIVATE IN
MCINTOSH'S COMPANY.

HASKEW, JOHN   ID: 2719
Date in Pee Dee: 1775
Source(s): THOMAS.
Notes: MAY BE SPELLED ASKEW. BROTHER OF ZACHEUS.
Revolutionary War service: MARION'S BRIGADE.

HASKEW, ZACHEUS   ID: 2720
Date in Pee Dee: 1775
Location: MARION DISTRICT

Early Pee Dee Settlers
--H--

Source(s): THOMAS.
Notes: BROTHER OF JOHN.

HASSEL, THOMAS JR.   ID: 5413
Spouse: ALICE MORRITT
Date in Pee Dee: 1744
Location: PRINCE FREDERICK PARISH
Source(s): RBPPFW.
Notes: MARRIED 26 APRIL 1744 AT PARISH OF PRINCE
FREDERICK WINYAW.

HAWKINS, ABIGAIL   ID: 5368
Spouse: ISAAC KERR
Date in Pee Dee: 1741
Location: PRINCE FREDERICK PARISH
Source(s): RBPPFW.

HAWKINS, ANNE   ID: 5429
Spouse: THOMAS HUGHES
Date in Pee Dee: 1747
Location: PRINCE FREDERICK PARISH
Source(s): RBPPFW.

HAWKINS, EDWARD   ID: 4787
Spouse: MARTHA [--?--]
Date in Pee Dee: 1774   Last Date: 1774 DIED
Location: GEORGETOWN
Source(s): MOORE V.3.

HAWKINS, JOHN   ID: 2666
Date in Pee Dee: 1780
Location: PRINCE GEORGE WINYAW PARISH
Source(s): ROGERS.
Notes: PROBABLY A TORY. SIGNED LOYALITY OATH.

HAY, PETER   ID: 4101
Spouse: ELIZABETH [--?--]
Date in Pee Dee: 1768   Last Date: 1768 DIED
Source(s): MOORE V.3.
Notes: WIFE WAS PREVIOUSLY MARRIED TO GILBERT GIBSON.

HAY, WILLIAM   ID: 3780
Spouse: SARAH MURPHY
Date in Pee Dee: 1762
Location: LITTLE RIVER
Source(s): MOORE V.3.

HAYES, JOHN   ID: 541
Date in Pee Dee: 1726   Last Date: 1745
Location: PRINCE FREDERICK PARISH
Source(s): COOK, RBPPFW.
Notes: REFUSED TO PAY PEW SUBSCRIPTION TO PRINCE
FREDERICK PARISH.

HAYNSWORTH, JOHN   ID: 3440
Spouse: ELIZABETH DAVIDSON
Date in Pee Dee: 1747   Last Date: 1756
Location: PRINCE FREDERICK PARISH
Source(s): MOORE V.3, RBPPFW.
Notes: SON OF RICHARD #3439. MARRIED 5 JULY 1747 AT
PARISH OF PRINCE FREDERICK WINYAW.

HAYNSWORTH, RICHARD   ID: 3439
Spouse: ELIZABETH HESSE
Children: JOHN, HENRY, MARGARET, MARY, ELIZABETH.
Date in Pee Dee: 1742   Last Date: 1762 DIED
Location: PRINCE FREDERICK PARISH
Source(s): MOORE V.3, RBPPFW.

HAYRNE, ELIZABETH   ID: 2700
Spouse: DANIEL TUCKER
Children: JOHN HAYRNE TUCKER.
Date in Pee Dee: 1775
Location: PRINCE GEORGE WINYAW PARISH
Source(s): ROGERS.

HAYS, ISAAC   ID: 5668
Date in Pee Dee: 1759
Location: ST. DAVID'S PARISH

Source(s): MUSTER ROLL.
Notes: SERVED IN FRENCH AND INDIAN WAR AS PRIVATE WITH MCINTOSH'S COMPANY.

HAYS, JACOB   ID: 5673
Date in Pee Dee: 1759
Location: ST. DAVID'S PARISH
Source(s): MUSTER ROLL.
Notes: SERVED IN FRENCH AND INDIAN WAR AS PRIVATE WITH MCINTOSH'S COMPANY.

HEADWIR, ELIZABETH   ID: 5341
Spouse: STEPHEN BOAREE
Date in Pee Dee: 1738
Location: PRINCE FREDERICK PARISH
Source(s): RBPPFW.
Notes: MARRIED 27 FEBRUARY 1738.

HEAPE, MARY ANN   ID: 4755
Children: HENRY, CHARLES, MARY ANN, ELIZABETH, AMELIA.
Date in Pee Dee: 1775   Last Date: 1775 DIED
Location: CHERAW
Source(s): MOORE V.3.

HEARD, JOHN   ID: 543
Date in Pee Dee: 1775   Last Date: 1778
Location: CHERAW
Source(s): COOK, RUDISILL.
Revolutionary War service: WISE'S COMPANY OF INFANTRY.

HEATHLEY, ROBERT   ID: 5053
Date in Pee Dee: 1780
Location: WILLIAMSBURG
Source(s): BODDIE.
Revolutionary War service: SERVED AS PRIVATE IN MARION'S BRIGADE.

HEATHLEY, WILLIAM   ID: 2621
Spouse: MARY [--?--]

Children: WILLIAM, ELIZABETH, MARY.
Date in Pee Dee: 1742   Last Date: 1742 DIED
Location: PRINCE FREDERICK PARISH
Source(s): MOORE, BODDIE.

HEATLY, WILLIAM   ID: 5227
Spouse: MARY [--?--]
Children: WILLIAM, ELIZABETH.
Date in Pee Dee: 1741
Location: PRINCE FREDERICK PARISH
Source(s): RBPPFW.
Notes: PREVIOUS WIFE SUSANNAH DIED 1730.

HEMSWORTH, WILLIAM JR   ID: 5639
Date in Pee Dee: 1759
Location: ST. DAVID'S PARISH
Source(s): MUSTER ROLL.
Notes: SERVED IN FRENCH AND INDIAN WAR AS PRIVATE WITH
LIDE'S COMPANY.

HEMSWORTH, WILLIAM SR.   ID: 5228
Spouse: NAOMI [--?--]
Children: WILLIAM.
Date in Pee Dee: 1742   Last Date: 1759
Location: PRINCE FREDERICK PARISH
Source(s): RBPPFW, MUSTER ROLL.
Notes: SERVED IN FRENCH AND INDIAN WAR AS PRIVATE IN
LIDE'S COMPANY.

HENDLEY, JESSE   ID: 2130
Date in Pee Dee: 1782
Source(s): GREGG P.408.
Revolutionary War service: SERVED AS PRIVATE IN MILITIA.

HENDLEY, THOMAS   ID: 2665
Date in Pee Dee: 1780
Location: PRINCE GEORGE WINYAW PARISH
Source(s): ROGERS.
Notes: PROBABLY A TORY. SIGNED LOYALITY OATH.

HENDRICKS, WILLIAM   ID: 2131
Date in Pee Dee: 1782
Source(s): GREGG P.408.
Revolutionary War service: SERVED AS CAPTAIN IN MARION'S
BRIGADE.

HENEGAN, JOHN S.   ID: 1602
Date in Pee Dee: 1770
Location: DARLINGTON DISTRICT
Source(s): GREGG.
Notes: GREGG REPORTS ORIGINAL NAME SWEENEY.

HENNING, GRACE   ID: 4431
Spouse: JOHN HENNING
Children: SEE JOHN HENNING.
Date in Pee Dee: 1774   Last Date: 1774 DIED
Location: PRINCE GEORGE WINYAH PARISH
Source(s): MOORE V.3, RBPPFW.
Notes: FIVE GRAND CHILDREN WITH SURNAME LANE.

HENNING, JOHN   ID: 3546
Spouse: GRACE [--?--]
Children: URSILLA, JOSEPH, ABRAHAM, PETER, DANIEL,
THOMAS.
Date in Pee Dee: 1737   Last Date: 1742
Location: PRINCE FREDERICK PARISH
Source(s): RBPPFW, MOORE.

HENNING, URSILLA   ID: 5472
Spouse: JAMES LANE
Date in Pee Dee: 1757
Location: PRINCE FREDERICK PARISH
Source(s): RBPPFW.

HENNINGS, THOMAS   ID: 548
Spouse: SARAH BOSSARD
Date in Pee Dee: 1734   Last Date: 1770
Location: PEE DEE BELOW LITTLE PEE DEE

Early Pee Dee Settlers

--H--

Source(s): COOK, MOORE V.3, SMITH, H..
Notes: PROBABLY SON OF GRACE.

HEPBURN, JAMES   ID: 549
Spouse: ELIZABETH BROCKINTON
Date in Pee Dee: 1735   Last Date: 1759
Location: PEE DEE RIVER. IN QUEENSBOROUGH TOWNSHIP.
Source(s): COOK, BODDIE, MOORE.

HERIOT, GEORGE   ID: 2561
Spouse: SALLEY TUCKER
Children: MARIA.
Date in Pee Dee: 1775
Occupation: MERCHANT   Origin: SCOTLAND
Location: GEORGETOWN
Source(s): CLEMENS, ROGERS, REMBERT.
Notes: BROTHER OF JAMES, SON OF GEORGE OF HADDINGTON,
SCOTLAND.

HERIOT, ROBERT   ID: 550
Spouse: MARY (POLLY) OULDFIELD
Children: JOHN OULDFIELD, ROBERT, SUSAN.
Date in Pee Dee: 1760   Last Date: 1792
Origin: SCOTLAND
Location: ALL SAINT'S PARISH
Source(s): COOK, REMBERT, ROGERS, MOORE.
Notes: BROTHER OF WILLIAM, SON OF JAMES AND JANET
HORSBURGH OF DIRLETON, SCOTLAND.

HERIOT, WILLIAM   ID: 2688
Spouse: MARY THOMAS
Children: EDWARD, THOMAS, WILLIAM, FRANCIS.
Date in Pee Dee: 1760   Last Date: 1807
Origin: SCOTLAND
Location: PRINCE GEORGE WINYAW PARISH
Source(s): ROGERS, REMBERT.
Notes: BROTHER OF ROBERT.

HERON, ROBERT   ID: 551

Date in Pee Dee: 1734 Last Date: 1736
Occupation: MINISTER Origin: NORTHERN IRELAND
Location: WILLIAMSBURG
Source(s): COOK, WITHERSPOON.
Notes: FIRST PASTOR OF WILLIAMSBURG PRESBYTERIAN CHURCH
LOCATED IN PRESENT TOWN OF KINGSTREE.

HERRENDINE, SILAS   ID: 5627
Date in Pee Dee: 1759
Location: ST. DAVID'S PARISH
Source(s): MUSTER ROLL.
Notes: SERVED IN FRENCH AND INDIAN WAR AS PRIVATE IN
CAPTAIN GEORGE HICK'S COMPANY.

HESE, ELIZABETH   ID: 3446
Spouse: RICHARD HAYNSWORTH
Children: JOHN, HENRY, MARGARET, MARY, UNKNOWN.
Date in Pee Dee: 1756
Location: PRINCE FREDERICK PARISH
Source(s): MOORE V.3.

HEWSON, EDWARD   ID: 5600
Date in Pee Dee: 1759
Location: ST. DAVID'S PARISH
Source(s): MUSTER ROLL.
Notes: SERVED IN FRENCH AND INDIAN WAR AS PRIVATE IN
CAPTAIN JAMES THOMSON'S COMPANY.

HEWSON, WILLIAM   ID: 4618
Spouse: ELIZABETH [--?--]
Date in Pee Dee: 1779
Location: ST. DAVID'S PARISH
Source(s): RWNBC.

HEWSTESS, JAMES   ID: 2132
Date in Pee Dee: 1779 Last Date: 1782
Location: ST. DAVID'S PARISH
Source(s): GREGG P.408, RWNBC.

Revolutionary War service: SERVED AS SERGEANT IN
MARION'S BRIGADE.

HEWSTESS, JOHN   ID: 1871
Spouse: AGNES [--?--]
Date in Pee Dee: 1773   Last Date: 1779
Location: ST. DAVID'S PARISH
Source(s): GREGG, RWNBC.

HICKMAN, ISAAC   ID: 5251
Spouse: ELIZABETH [--?--]
Children: SARAH, WILLIAM.
Date in Pee Dee: 1743   Last Date: 1759
Location: PRINCE FREDERICK PARISH
Source(s): RBPPFW.
Notes: SERVED IN FRENCH AND INDIAN WAR AS PRIVATE IN
CAPTAIN ROBERT WEAVER'S COMPANY.

HICKMAN, JOHN   ID: 3522
Spouse: ANN WINGATE
Children: JOHN.
Date in Pee Dee: 1758
Location: PRINCE GEORGE WINYAW PARISH
Source(s): MOORE V.3.

HICKMAN, JOSHUA   ID: 1858
Date in Pee Dee: 1759   Last Date: 1768
Location: ST. DAVID'S PARISH
Source(s): GREGG, MUSTER ROLL.
Notes: SERVED IN FRENCH AND INDIAN WAR AS PRIVATE IN
CAPTAIN ROBERT WEAVER'S COMPANY.

HICKMAN, PARIS   ID: 5612
Date in Pee Dee: 1759
Location: ST. DAVID'S PARISH
Source(s): MUSTER ROLL.
Notes: SERVED IN FRENCH AND INDIAN WAR AS ENSIGN IN
CAPTAIN ROBERT WEAVER'S COMPANY.

HICKMAN, SAMUEL   ID: 5623

Date in Pee Dee: 1759
Location: ST. DAVID'S PARISH
Source(s): MUSTER ROLL.
Notes: SERVED IN FRENCH AND INDIAN WAR IN CAPTAIN ROBERT
WEAVER'S COMPANY. LISTED AS DESERTER.

HICKS, BENJAMIN   ID: 554
Spouse: ELIZABETH HICKS
Date in Pee Dee: 1750   Last Date: 1787
Origin: VIRGINIA
Location: CHERAW
Source(s): COOK, MOORE V.3.
Notes: SON OF ROBERT.
Revolutionary War service: SECOND SERGEANT IN WISE'S
COMPANY OF INFANTRY.

HICKS, BENJAMIN   ID: 3449
Date in Pee Dee: 1761
Location: WELCH TRACT
Source(s): MOORE V.3.
Notes: GRAND-SON OF GEORGE #3448.

HICKS, CHARLOTTE   ID: 1431
Spouse: JOHN WILSON
Children: GEORGE, BENJAMIN, ELEANOR, SARAH J., ANNE.
Date in Pee Dee: 1760
Location: WELCH TRACT
Source(s): GREGG.
Notes: DAUGHTER OF GEORGE #556.

HICKS, DANIEL   ID: 1437
Date in Pee Dee: 1760
Location: WELCH TRACT
Source(s): GREGG.
Notes: SON OF WILLIAM #1427. MOVED TO RICHMOND COUNTY
NORTH CAROLINA.

HICKS, ELIZABETH   ID: 1434
Spouse: BENJAMIN HICKS

Children: BETSY.
Date in Pee Dee: 1760
Location: WELCH TRACT
Source(s): GREGG.
Notes: DAUGHTER OF GEORGE #556.

HICKS, ELIZABETH   ID: 3450
Date in Pee Dee: 1761
Location: WELCH TRACT
Source(s): MOORE V.3.
Notes: GRAND-DAUGHTER OF GEORGE #3448.

HICKS, GEORGE   ID: 556
Spouse: SARAH JAMES
Children: GEORGE, BENJAMIN, MARY, ELIZABETH, LUCY,
NANCY, CHARLOTTE.
Date in Pee Dee: 1747   Last Date: 1791
Origin: VIRGINIA
Location: UPPER ST. DAVID PARISH
Source(s): COOK, RWNBC, GREGG.
Notes: BROTHER OF WILLIAM. BENJAMIN DIED YOUNG, GEORGE
JR. WENT WEST. JUSTICE OF PEACE IN 1756.
Revolutionary War service: COLONEL IN MARION'S BRIGADE.

HICKS, GEORGE   ID: 3448
Children: GEORGE, ROBERT.
Date in Pee Dee: 1761   Last Date: 1762 DIED
Location: WELCH TRACT
Source(s): MOORE V.3.

HICKS, GEORGE   ID: 3593
Date in Pee Dee: 1765
Location: UPPER PEE DEE RIVER
Source(s): MOORE V.3.
Notes: BROTHER OF ROBERT #3588.

HICKS, GEORGE JR.   ID: 555
Spouse: ELIZABETH HICKS
Date in Pee Dee: 1784

Location: CHERAW DISTRICT
Source(s): COOK.
Notes: SON OF GEORGE #555.

HICKS, JOHN   ID: 1904
Spouse: OBEDIENCE [--?--]
Children: FRANCES.
Date in Pee Dee: 1743   Last Date: 1768
Location: ST. DAVID'S PARISH
Source(s): GREGG, JVSDP, RBPPFW.

HICKS, LUCY   ID: 1750
Spouse: WILLIAM STROTHER
Children: ELIZABETH, MARY, GEORGE, HARRIET, CHARLOTTE.
Date in Pee Dee: 1772
Location: CHERAW
Source(s): GREGG.
Notes: DAUGHTER OF GEORGE #556. SHE SURVIVED HIM AND
MOVED TO ALABAMA.

HICKS, MARY   ID: 1435
Spouse: MALACHI MURPHY
Date in Pee Dee: 1760
Location: WELCH TRACT
Source(s): GREGG.
Notes: DAUGHTER OF GEORGE #556. SECOND MARRIED WILLIAM
PEGUES.

HICKS, NANCY   ID: 1432
Spouse: THOMAS GODFREY
Children: SOPHIA, THOMAS, HARRIET, WILLIAM, MARY,
SAMUEL, RICHARD, ELIZABETH, WILSON, GEORGE.
Date in Pee Dee: 1760
Location: WELCH TRACT
Source(s): GREGG.
Notes: DAUGHTER OF GEORGE #556.

HICKS, ROBERT   ID: 3588
Spouse: MARY [--?--]

Children: BENJAMIN, ROBERT, ELIZABETH, MARY.
Date in Pee Dee: 1765   Last Date: 1765 DIED
Location: UPPER PEE DEE RIVER
Source(s): MOORE V.3, RWNBC.
Notes: SON OF GEORGE #3448. SERVED IN FRENCH AND INDIAN
WAR AS CLERK IN CAPTAIN GEORGE HICK'S COMPANY.

HICKS, SARAH (SALLIE)   ID: 2571
Spouse: WILLIAM PEGUES
Children: CLAUDE, SAMUEL BUTLER, CHARLOTTE, JOHN MURRAY.
Date in Pee Dee: 1770
Location: ST. DAVID'S PARISH
Source(s): ELLERBE.
Notes: DAUGHTER OF COLONEL GEORGE HICKS.

HICKS, WILLIAM   ID: 1427
Children: CHARLES, BENJAMIN, DANIEL.
Date in Pee Dee: 1747   Last Date: 1768
Origin: VIRGINIA
Location: WELCH TRACT
Source(s): GREGG, JVSDP, MOORE.
Notes: BROTHER OF GEORGE #556.

HICKSON, JOHN   ID: 2133
Date in Pee Dee: 1782
Source(s): GREGG P.408.
Revolutionary War service: SERVED AS PRIVATE IN MARION'S
BRIGADE.

HILL, CHARLES   ID: 1732
Spouse: ELIZABETH [--?--]
Date in Pee Dee: 1735
Location: BLACK MINGO CREEK
Source(s): COOK.

HILLBURN, THOMAS   ID: 3606
Spouse: REBECCA TOMPLING
Date in Pee Dee: 1765   Last Date: 1765 DIED
Location: NORTHEAST SIDE OF UPPER PEE DEE RIVER

Early Pee Dee Settlers
--H--

Source(s): MOORE V.3.

HINDLEY, EDWARD   ID: 2134
Date in Pee Dee: 1782
Source(s): GREGG P.408.
Revolutionary War service: SERVED AS PRIVATE IN BENTON'S
REGIMENT.

HINDS, JAMES   ID: 2410
Date in Pee Dee: 1777
Location: ST. DAVID'S PARISH
Source(s): RUDISILL.
Notes: AN ORIGINAL SUBSCRIBER TO ST. DAVID'S SOCIETY.

HINDS, JOHN   ID: 2135
Date in Pee Dee: 1782
Location: WILLIAMSBURG
Source(s): GREGG, BODDIE.
Revolutionary War service: SERVED AS LIEUTENANT IN
MARION'S BRIGADE.

HINES, SAMUEL   ID: 2136
Date in Pee Dee: 1782
Location: ST. DAVID'S PARISH
Source(s): GREGG P.408, MUSTER ROLL.
Notes: SERVED IN FRENCH AND INDIAN WAR AS PRIVATE IN
LIDE'S COMPANY.
Revolutionary War service: LIEUTENANT IN MARION'S
BRIGADE.

HINSON, CLAYBURN   ID: 2137
Date in Pee Dee: 1781
Source(s): GREGG P.408.
Revolutionary War service: COMMANDER OF PRISONER
DETACHMENT.

HINSON, WILLIAM   ID: 2138
Date in Pee Dee: 1779
Source(s): GREGG P.408.

Revolutionary War service: SERVED AS PRIVATE IN MARION'S BRIGADE.

HIRD, JOHN   ID: 2139
Date in Pee Dee: 1782
Source(s): GREGG P.408.
Revolutionary War service: LIEUTENANT OF MILITIA.

HITCHCOCK, JOHN   ID: 562
Date in Pee Dee: 1736
Location: PEE DEE RIVER AT BEAUTY SPOT
Source(s): COOK, MUSTER ROLL.
Notes: LISTED AS A DESERTER FROM HIS OWN COMPANY DURING FRENCH AND INDIAN WAR.

HITCHCOCK, JOHN   ID: 1929
Date in Pee Dee: 1759   Last Date: 1769
Location: ST. DAVID'S PARISH
Source(s): GREGG, JVSDP, MOORE, MUSTER ROLL.
Notes: SERVED IN FRENCH AND INDIAN WAR AS PRIVATE WITH LIDE'S COMPANY.

HITTS, DURHAM   ID: 1981
Date in Pee Dee: 1768
Location: ST. DAVID'S PARISH
Source(s): GREGG, JVSDP, COOK.
Notes: COOK SPELLS HITT. CLERK OF VESTRY OF ST. DAVID'S. CLERK OF LIDE'S COMPANY DURING FRENCH AND INDIAN WAR.

HODGE, BENJAMIN   ID: 5054
Date in Pee Dee: 1780
Location: WILLIAMSBURG
Source(s): BODDIE.
Revolutionary War service: SERVED AS PRIVATE IN MARION'S BRIGADE.

HODGE, EDMUND   ID: 564
Date in Pee Dee: 1775
Location: CHERAW
Source(s): COOK.

Revolutionary War service: WISE'S COMPANY OF INFANTRY.

HODGE, ELIAS   ID: 2140
Date in Pee Dee: 1779
Source(s): GREGG P.408.
Revolutionary War service: SERVED AS PRIVATE IN MARION'S
BRIGADE.

HODGE, JAMES   ID: 2141
Spouse: ELIZABETH DUBOSE
Date in Pee Dee: 1782
Location: WILLIAMSBURG
Source(s): GREGG, BODDIE, REMBERT.
Notes: REMBERT REPORTS, BUT DOES NOT NAME FIVE CHILDREN.
Revolutionary War service: SERVED AS PRIVATE IN
PLEDGER'S COMPANY.

HODGE, JOSEPH   ID: 2142
Date in Pee Dee: 1782
Source(s): GREGG P.408.
Revolutionary War service: SERVED AS PRIVATE IN HICK'S
REGIMENT.

HODGE, THOMAS   ID: 2722
Children: LUCY, MARY.
Date in Pee Dee: 1780   Last Date: 1782
Origin: NORTH CAROLINA
Location: MARLBORO DISTRICT
Source(s): THOMAS, GREGG.
Revolutionary War service: SERVED AS PRIVATE IN MILITIA.

HODGE, WILLIAM   ID: 688
Date in Pee Dee: 1771
Location: CHERAW
Source(s): GREGG.
Notes: AN OUTLAW KILLED BY A GROUP LED BY PHILLIP
PLEDGER.

HODGES, HENRY   ID: 3104

Spouse: LYDIA [--?--]
Children: RICHARD (UNDER 18).
Date in Pee Dee: 1757   Last Date: 1757 DIED
Location: CRAVEN COUNTY
Source(s): MOORE.

HODGES, ISHAM   ID: 1766
Date in Pee Dee: 1770   Last Date: 1775
Location: ST. DAVID'S PARISH (CHERAW)
Source(s): GREGG, COOK.
Revolutionary War service: WISE'S COMPANY OF INFANTRY.

HODGES, JOHN   ID: 1767
Spouse: REBECCA [--?--]
Date in Pee Dee: 1757   Last Date: 1775
Location: ST. DAVID'S PARISH
Source(s): GREGG, RWNBC, MOORE.

HODGES, JOHN   ID: 3556
Spouse: REBECCA [--?--]
Date in Pee Dee: 1736
Location: PRINCE FREDERICK PARISH
Source(s): BODDIE.

HODGES, RICHARD   ID: 3105
Spouse: LYDIA [--?--]
Children: RICHARD (UNDER 18).
Date in Pee Dee: 1757
Location: CRAVEN COUNTY
Source(s): MOORE.
Notes: SON OF HENRY #3104.

HODGES, WELCOME   ID: 2144
Date in Pee Dee: 1780
Location: ST. DAVID'S PARISH
Source(s): GREGG P.409, RWNBC.
Notes: GREGG SPELLS HODGE. WIFE WAS PROBABLY ELIZABETH.
Revolutionary War service: SERGEANT IN BENTON'S
REGIMENT.

HOLDER, JOHN   ID: 4767
Date in Pee Dee: 1776
Location: PRINCE FREDERICK PARISH (LOWER)
Source(s): MOORE V.3.
Notes: SON OF MARY #4766.

HOLDER, MARY   ID: 4766
Children: JOHN, MARY, SARAH (JOHNSTON).
Date in Pee Dee: 1776   Last Date: 1776 DIED
Location: PRINCE FREDERICK PARISH (LOWER)
Source(s): MOORE V.3.

HOLDER, SARAH   ID: 4769
Spouse: THOMAS JOHNSTON
Children: JOSEPH.
Date in Pee Dee: 1776
Location: PRINCE FREDERICK PARISH (LOWER)
Source(s): MOORE V.3.
Notes: DAUGHTER OF MARY #4766.

HOLDING, MATTHEW   ID: 2027
Date in Pee Dee: 1775
Location: ST. DAVID'S PARISH
Source(s): GREGG.
Revolutionary War service: MILITIA

HOLLIDAY, GILES   ID: 3313
Spouse: ELIZABETH [--?--]
Date in Pee Dee: 1738   Last Date: MOORE V.1
Location: PRINCE GEORGE WINYAW PARISH
Source(s): MOORE V.1.

HOLLINGSWORTH, MARY   ID: 569
Date in Pee Dee: 1755   Last Date: 1784 DIED
Location: WELCH NECK
Source(s): COOK, RWNBC.
Notes: PROBABLY WIFE OF WILLIAM HOLLINGSWORTH. SHE DIED
SEPTEMBER 1784.

HOLLINGSWORTH, SAMUEL   ID: 570
Children: SAMUEL.
Date in Pee Dee: 1740   Last Date: 1753 DIED
Location: LONG BLUFF, ABOVE SEVERAL MILES.
Source(s): COOK, MOORE.
Notes: BROTHER OF VOLENTINE HOLLINGSWORTH AND ANN
SUTTON.

HOLLINGSWORTH, SARAH   ID: 571
Date in Pee Dee: 1755
Location: WELCH NECK
Source(s): COOK.
Notes: DIED 12/14/1759.

HOLLINSWORTH, VOLUNTINE   ID: 572
Date in Pee Dee: 1755   Last Date: 1760 DIED
Location: WELCH NECK
Source(s): COOK, RWNBC.
Notes: DIED 3/26/1760. BROTHER OF SAMUEL HOLLINGSWORTH
AND ANN SUTTON. A PERSON OF THIS NAME APPLIED FOR LAND
IN BURKE COUNTY, GEORGIA IN 1772. COULD IT POSSIBLY BE A
SON?

HOLLIS, MOSES   ID: 2145
Date in Pee Dee: 1783
Source(s): GREGG P.409.
Revolutionary War service: LIEUTENANT OF MILITIA.

HOLLYBUSH, ALICE   ID: 2515
Spouse: WESTON PLOWDEN
Children: CHARLES WESTON.
Date in Pee Dee: 1775   Last Date: 1827
Location: PRINCE GEORGE WINYAW PARISH
Source(s): ROGERS, CLEMENS.
Notes: MARRIED 18 JULY 1762 AT CHARLESTON.

HOOLE, JAMES   ID: 4889
Spouse: HANNAH BROCKINTON

Date in Pee Dee: 1737   Last Date: 1750
Location: LOWER BLACK RIVER.
Source(s): BODDIE.

HOPTON, WILLIAM   ID: 1047
Spouse: SARAH LYNCH
Date in Pee Dee: 1751
Source(s): BODDIE.
Notes: SHE PREVIOUSLY MARRIED GIBSON CLAPP.

HORRY, BENJAMIN   ID: 2659
Children: BENJAMIN, MARY M..
Date in Pee Dee: 1775
Location: GEORGRTOWN
Source(s): ROGERS.
Notes: KILLED IN REVOLUTION. LAFAYETTE LANDED AT HIS
HOUSE ON NORTH ISLAND.

HORRY, DANIEL   ID: 574
Spouse: HARRIET PINCKNEY
Date in Pee Dee: 1779   Last Date: 1781
Location: ALL SAINT'S
Source(s): COOK, CLEMENS.
Revolutionary War service: TORY COLONEL.

HORRY, DANIEL   ID: 2512
Spouse: JUDITH SERRI
Date in Pee Dee: 1736   Last Date: 1750
Location: SANTEE RIVER
Source(s): CLEMENS, ROGERS, MOORE V.1.
Notes: SON OF ELIAS (I) #2623.

HORRY, DANIEL   ID: 2658
Spouse: SARAH FORD
Children: DANIEL.
Date in Pee Dee: 1758   Last Date: 1764 DIED
Location: ST. MARK'S PARISH
Source(s): CLEMENS, ROGERS, MOORE V.3.

Notes: SON OF DANIEL, BROTHER OF BENJAMIN, ISSAC, AND JOHN.

HORRY, ELIAS   ID: 2752
Spouse: MARGARET LYNCH
Children: THOMAS, ELIAS.
Date in Pee Dee: 1707
Location: ON SANTEE RIVER
Source(s): ROGERS, CLEMENS, MOORE V.1.

HORRY, ELIAS III   ID: 576
Spouse: ELIZABETH BRANFORD
Children: MARGARET, ELIAS.
Date in Pee Dee: 1753   Last Date: 1785
Location: NORTH SIDE OF SANTEE
Source(s): COOK, ROGERS, SMITH, H., CLEMENS.
Notes: COOK PLACES AT BRITTON'S NECK IN 1735. THIS IS DOUBTFUL. MARRIED 15 NOVEMBER 1770.

HORRY, ELIAS SR   ID: 2623
Spouse: MARGARET HUGER
Children: DANIEL, ELIAS, JOHN, PETER, JOHN, MARGARET, HENRIETTA, MAGDALENE.
Date in Pee Dee: 1700   Last Date: 1736 DIED
Origin: CHARENTON
Location: SANTEE RIVER
Source(s): ROGERS, MOORE V.1, BALDWIN.
Notes: HUGUENOT IMMIGRANT BEFORE JULY 1695. MARRIED 17 AUGUST 1704.

HORRY, HENRIETTA   ID: 3311
Spouse: [--?--] BONNEAU
Date in Pee Dee: 1736
Location: PRINCE GEORGE WINYAW PARISH
Source(s): MOORE V.1.
Notes: DAUGHTER OF ELIAS SR. #2623.

HORRY, HUGH   ID: 577
Date in Pee Dee: 1758   Last Date: 1780

Location: PRINCE GEORGE WINYAW PARISH
Source(s): COOK, MOORE V.3.
Notes: SON OF DANIEL #2658.
Revolutionary War service: COLONEL

HORRY, ISSAC   ID: 2706
Date in Pee Dee: 1775
Location: GEORGRTOWN
Source(s): ROGERS.
Notes: SON OF DANIEL THE IMMIGRANT AND BROTHER OF
DANIEL, BENJAMIN, AND JOHN.

HORRY, JOHN   ID: 2514
Children: JOHN, PETER, HUGH.
Date in Pee Dee: 1736   Last Date: 1770 DIED
Location: SANTEE RIVER
Source(s): ROGERS, MOORE V.1.
Notes: SON OF ELIAS (I) #2623. ONE OF THE JOHNS MARRIED
ANN ROYER AT SANTEE JULY, 1759.

HORRY, JOHN   ID: 2707
Children: PETER, JONAH, HUGH.
Date in Pee Dee: 1775
Location: GEORGETOWN
Source(s): ROGERS, MOORE V.3.
Notes: SON OF DANIEL THE IMMIGRANT AND BROTHER OF
DANIEL, BENJAMIN, AND ISSAC.

HORRY, MAGDALENE   ID: 2755
Spouse: PAUL TRAPIER
Date in Pee Dee: 1743
Location: GEORGETOWN
Source(s): ROGERS.

HORRY, PETER   ID: 578
Date in Pee Dee: 1780   Last Date: 1784
Location: PRINCE GEORGE WINYAW PARISH
Source(s): COOK.

Notes: REPRESENTATIVE TO POST WAR SOUTH CAROLINA
LEGISLATURE.
Revolutionary War service: COLONEL IN MARION'S BRIGADE.

HORRY, THOMAS   ID: 2517
Spouse: NANCY BRANFORD
Children: ELIAS (IV).
Date in Pee Dee: 1748   Last Date: 1820
Location: SANTEE RIVER
Source(s): ROGERS, CLEMENS.
Notes: SON OF ELIAS (III) #2576. MARRIED AT CHARLESTON
13 JUNE 1772.

HOSKINS, JOHN   ID: 1582
Spouse: SARAH TAYLOR
Date in Pee Dee: 1747
Location: PRINCE FREDERICK PARISH
Source(s): RBPPFW.
Notes: MARRIED AT PARISH OF PRINCE FREDERICK WINYAW 9
APRIL 1747.

HOW, JOB   ID: 580
Date in Pee Dee: 1726
Location: BLACK RIVER AND LYNCH'S LAKE
Source(s): COOK.
Notes: MINISTER OF CIRCULAR CHURCH.

HOWARD, BENJAMIN   ID: 5055
Date in Pee Dee: 1780
Location: WILLIAMSBURG
Source(s): BODDIE.
Revolutionary War service: SERVED AS PRIVATE IN MARION'S
BRIGADE.

HOWARD, EDWARD   ID: 582
Spouse: REBECCA MCKELVY
Date in Pee Dee: 1735   Last Date: 1773
Location: BLACK MINGO CREEK
Source(s): COOK, RBPPFW, MOORE.

Notes: APPEARS TO HAVE HAD A SON EDWARD. SON OF GEORGE #3219. MARRIED 25 APRIL 1738 AT PARISH OF PRINCE FREDERICK WINYAW.

HOWARD, EDWARD   ID: 5056
Date in Pee Dee: 1780
Location: WILLIAMSBURG
Source(s): BODDIE.
Revolutionary War service: SERVED AS PRIVATE IN MARION'S BRIGADE.

HOWARD, GEORGE   ID: 3219
Children: EDWARD.
Date in Pee Dee: 1758   Last Date: 1765
Location: ST. MARK'S PARISH
Source(s): MOORE, BODDIE.

HOWARD, JOHN   ID: 5057
Date in Pee Dee: 1780
Location: WILLIAMSBURG
Source(s): BODDIE.
Revolutionary War service: SERVED AS PRIVATE IN MARION'S BRIGADE.

HOWARD, ROBERT   ID: 4727
Spouse: CATHERINE [--?--]
Children: WILLIAM, JAMES, ROBERT, THOMAS SMITH, JOSEPH.
Date in Pee Dee: 1775   Last Date: 1776 DIED
Source(s): MOORE V.3.

HOWEL, JAMES   ID: 4453
Spouse: PRISCILLA [--?--]
Children: JAMES, JESSE, ELIZABETH, MARY, SARAH.
Date in Pee Dee: 1773   Last Date: 1773 DIED
Location: WELCH NECK
Source(s): MOORE V.3.

HOWELL, HANNAH   ID: 5530
Date in Pee Dee: 1760 DOB Last Date: 1773

Location: ST. DAVID'S PARISH
Source(s): JVSDP.
Notes: BOUND BY PARISH TO ABEL CULP (KOLB) UNTIL 18
YEARS AGE OR MARRIED.

HOWELL, JAMES   ID: 584
Spouse: ANN [--?--]
Date in Pee Dee: 1711
Location: WACCAMAW
Source(s): COOK.

HOWELL, WILLIAM   ID: 585
Spouse: MARTHA [--?--]
Children: SARAH.
Date in Pee Dee: 1724   Last Date: 1757 DIED
Location: WACCAMAW RIVER
Source(s): COOK, MOORE.
Notes: APPEARS TO HAVE MOVED TO BROAD RIVER BY 1757.

HOWZE, ANN   ID: 3670
Date in Pee Dee: 1763
Location: WILLIAMSBURG
Source(s): MOORE V.3.
Notes: GRAND-DAUGHTER OF PETER #3664.

HUBBARD, NOAH   ID: 2146
Date in Pee Dee: 1782
Source(s): GREGG P.409.
Revolutionary War service: SERVED AS PRIVATE IN MARION'S
BRIGADE.

HUBBARD, PETER   ID: 586
Date in Pee Dee: 1775
Location: CHERAW
Source(s): COOK.
Revolutionary War service: WISE'S COMPANY OF INFANTRY.

HUCCOBY, CHARLES   ID: 5626
Date in Pee Dee: 1759

Location: ST. DAVID'S PARISH
Source(s): MUSTER ROLL.
Notes: SERVED IN FRENCH AND INDIAN WAR AS PRIVATE IN
CAPTAIN GEORGE HICK'S COMPANY.

HUCKABY, ISHAM   ID: 2147
Date in Pee Dee: 1782
Source(s): GREGG P.409.
Revolutionary War service: SERVED AS SERGEANT IN
MARION'S BRIGADE.

HUCKABY, SAMUEL   ID: 2148
Date in Pee Dee: 1782
Source(s): GREGG P.409.
Revolutionary War service: SERVED AS SERGEANT IN
MARION'S BRIGADE.

HUCKABY, THOMAS   ID: 2149
Date in Pee Dee: 1759   Last Date: 1782
Location: ST. DAVID'S PARISH
Source(s): GREGG P.409, MUSTER ROLL.
Notes: SERVED IN FRENCH AND INDIAN WAR AS PRIVATE IN
CAPTAIN GEORGE HICK'S COMPANY.
Revolutionary War service: SERVED AS PRIVATE IN MARION'S
BRIGADE.

HUDSON, JAMES   ID: 2322
Spouse: JENNET GREGG
Children: JAMES WILSON, ELIZABETH HARRIET, JANNET
CAMPAIN, JOHN NELSON, MARY GREGG.
Date in Pee Dee: 1769   Last Date: 1811
Location: PRESENT BISHOPVILLE AREA
Source(s): MCCARTY.
Notes: FIRST MARRIED JANNET WILSON.

HUDSON, LODOWICK   ID: 3557
Spouse: ANNE [--?--]
Date in Pee Dee: 1736
Location: PRINCE FREDERICK PARISH

Source(s): BODDIE.

HUDSON, MARY   ID: 4624
Date in Pee Dee: 1779
Location: ST. DAVID'S PARISH
Source(s): RWNBC.
Notes: PROBABLY WIFE OF OBEDIAH.

HUGER, BENJAMIN   ID: 5196
Spouse: POLLY KINLOCH
Date in Pee Dee: 1772
Location: PRINCE GEORGE WINYAH PARISH
Source(s): CLEMENS.
Notes: MARRIED 1 DECEMBER 1772 AT KENSINGTON.

HUGER, DANIEL   ID: 587
Spouse: ELIZABETH CENDRON
Date in Pee Dee: 1708
Location: BLACK RIVER
Source(s): COOK, CLEMENS.
Notes: MARRIED 25 JANUARY 1710. MAY HAVE MARRIED MARY
CORDES 14 MAY 1741.

HUGER, MARGARET   ID: 2624
Spouse: ELIAS (I) HORRY
Children: DANIEL, ELIAS, JOHN, MARGARET, MAGDALENE.
Date in Pee Dee: 1704   Last Date: 1730
Location: SANTEE RIVER
Source(s): ROGERS, CLEMENS, BALDWIN.
Notes: MARRIED 17 AUGUST 1704.

HUGGINS, JOHN   ID: 2150
Date in Pee Dee: 1779
Location: PRINCE FREDERICK PARISH
Source(s): GREGG, BODDIE.
Revolutionary War service: CAPTAIN IN GILES' REGIMENT OF
MARION'S BRIGADE.

HUGGINS, JOHN   ID: 2485

Spouse: [--?--] CAMPBELL
Children: SOLOMON, HENRY, JOHN, THEOPHILUS, GEORGE,
ENOS, EBBEN.
Date in Pee Dee: 1740
Location: LITTLE PEE DEE
Source(s): SELLERS.

HUGGINS, MARK   ID: 4976
Date in Pee Dee: 1780
Location: WILLIAMSBURG
Source(s): BODDIE.
Revolutionary War service: CAPTAIN IN MARION'S BRIGADE.

HUGGINS, WILLIAM   ID: 4984
Date in Pee Dee: 1780
Location: WILLIAMSBURG
Source(s): BODDIE.
Revolutionary War service: SERVED AS LIEUTENANT IN
MARION'S BRIGADE.

HUGHES, HELEN   ID: 5391
Spouse: SAMUEL MILLER
Date in Pee Dee: 1743
Location: PRINCE FREDERICK PARISH
Source(s): RBPPFW.

HUGHES, HENRY   ID: 659
Children: HENRY.
Date in Pee Dee: 1735 DOB Last Date: 1754
Location: PRINCE FREDERICK PARISH
Source(s): MOORE, RBPPFW.
Notes: SON OF MERIDETH AND MARY HUGHES #648.

HUGHES, JOHN   ID: 4590
Spouse: ANNE [--?--]
Date in Pee Dee: 1759   Last Date: 1785 DIED
Location: ST. DAVID'S PARISH
Source(s): RWNBC, MUSTER ROLL.

Notes: SERVED IN FRENCH AND INDIAN WAR AS PRIVATE IN
LIDE'S COMPANY.

HUGHES, MEREDITH   ID: 589
Spouse: ELIZABETH [--?--]
Children: MEREDITH, HENRY, JOHN, ANN.
Date in Pee Dee: 1717   Last Date: 1739 DIED
Location: GEORGETOWN
Source(s): COOK, ROGERS, SMITH, H., RBPPFW.
Notes: APPEARS TO HAVE MARRIED MARY BEFORE BIRTH OF ANN.
ELIZABETH DIED 1729.

HUGHES, MEREDITH   ID: 4497
Spouse: ANN FORD
Date in Pee Dee: 1773
Location: PRINCE FREDERICK PARISH
Source(s): MOORE V.3, CLEMENS.
Notes: MARRIED AT SANTEE 9 JANUARY 1772.

HUGHES, SOLOMON   ID: 5244
Spouse: JUDITH (WIDOW) HAUGHTON
Children: ELIJAH, ANNE.
Date in Pee Dee: 1742   Last Date: 1745
Location: PRINCE FREDERICK PARISH
Source(s): RBPPFW.

HUGHES, THOMAS   ID: 3198
Spouse: CATHERINE NEANY
Date in Pee Dee: 1757   Last Date: 1757   DIED
Location: ST. MARK'S PARISH
Source(s): MOORE, RBPPFW.
Notes: MARRIED 1 AUGUST 1739. APPEARS TO HAVE MARRIED
ANNE HAWKINS 2 JUNE 1747.

HUGHES, WILLIAM   ID: 590
Spouse: SARAH POTTS
Date in Pee Dee: 1736   Last Date: 1764
Location: CEDAR CREEK (WILLIAMSBURG)
Source(s): COOK, RBPPFW, MOORE.

Notes: MARRIED 2 JUNE 1747 AT PARISH OF PRINCE FREDERICK WINYAW.

HUGHES, WILLIAM   ID: 5206
Spouse: ELEONORA [--?--]
Children: PETER.
Date in Pee Dee: 1737
Location: PRINCE FREDERICK PARISH
Source(s): RBPPFW.
Notes: BROTHER OF MERIDITH.

HULL, ELIZABETH   ID: 4468
Date in Pee Dee: 1773
Source(s): MOORE V.3.
Notes: NIECE OF WILLIAM #4462.

HULL, HANNAH   ID: 4465
Spouse: [--?--] BROWN
Date in Pee Dee: 1773
Location: PRINCE GEORGE WINYAH PARISH
Source(s): MOORE V.3.
Notes: DAUGHTER OF WILLIAM #4462.

HULL, JOSEPH   ID: 4466
Date in Pee Dee: 1773
Source(s): MOORE V.3.
Notes: NEPHEW OF WILLIAM #4462.

HULL, JUDITH   ID: 4463
Spouse: ROBERT BROWN
Date in Pee Dee: 1773
Location: PRINCE GEORGE WINYAH PARISH
Source(s): MOORE V.3.
Notes: DAUGHTER OF WILLIAM #4462.

HULL, MARTHA   ID: 4464
Spouse: JAMES CALHOUN
Date in Pee Dee: 1773
Location: PRINCE GEORGE WINYAH PARISH

Source(s): MOORE V.3.
Notes: DAUGHTER OF WILLIAM #4462.

HULL, WILLIAM   ID: 4462
Spouse: SARAH [--?--]
Children: JUDITH (BROWN), MARTHA (CALHOUN), HANNAH
(BROWN).
Date in Pee Dee: 1773   Last Date: 1773 DIED
Location: PRINCE GEORGE WINYAH PARISH
Source(s): MOORE V.3.

HULL, WILLIAM   ID: 4467
Date in Pee Dee: 1773
Source(s): MOORE V.3.
Notes: NEPHEW OF WILLIAM #4462.

HUME, ROBERT WILLIAM   ID: 594
Children: JOHN.
Date in Pee Dee: 1762   Last Date: 1780
Location: PRINCE GEORGE PARISH (ON SANTEE R.)
Source(s): COOK, MOORE V.3, ROGERS.

HUME, THOMAS   ID: 4956
Date in Pee Dee: 1759
Location: WILLIAMSBURG
Source(s): BODDIE.
Notes: SERVED AS SERGEANT IN FRENCH AND INDIAN WAR.

HUNT, ANN   ID: 3745
Spouse: JOHN HALL JR.
Children: JOHN HENRY, LEWEY CANNON.
Date in Pee Dee: 1766
Origin: AMELIA COUNTY VA.
Location: ST. DAVID'S PARISH
Source(s): MOORE V.3.

HUNT, CRISWELL   ID: 2151
Date in Pee Dee: 1779
Source(s): GREGG P.409.

Revolutionary War service: SERVED AS PRIVATE IN BENTON'S REGIMENT.

HUNT, JIM   ID: 5567
Date in Pee Dee: 1782
Location: ST. DAVID'S PARISH
Source(s): JVSDP.
Notes: AT 18 BOUND TO WILLIAM LANKFORD BY PARISH. LIKELY SIBLING OF LEWES AND SAUL.

HUNT, LEWES   ID: 5568
Date in Pee Dee: 1782
Location: ST. DAVID'S PARISH
Source(s): JVSDP.
Notes: AT 13 BOUND TO WILLIAM LANKFORD BY PARISH. LIKELY SIBLING OF JIM AND SAUL.

HUNT, NATHANIEL   ID: 2411
Date in Pee Dee: 1767   Last Date: 1777
Location: ST. DAVID'S PARISH
Source(s): RUDISILL, MOORE V.3, GREGG.
Notes: AN ORIGINAL SUBSCRIBER TO ST. DAVID'S SOCIETY.

HUNT, SAUL   ID: 5569
Date in Pee Dee: 1782
Location: ST. DAVID'S PARISH
Source(s): JVSDP.
Notes: AT 11 BOUND TO WILLIAM LANKFORD BY PARISH. LIKELY SIBLING OF JIM AND LEWES.

HUNTER, ROBERT   ID: 1389
Date in Pee Dee: 1735
Location: BRITTON'S NECK
Source(s): GREGG, SELLERS.
Notes: SAID TO HAVE COME FROM ENGLAND WITH BRITTON'S NECK COLONY.

HUNTER, SAMUEL   ID: 1735
Date in Pee Dee: 1744

Source(s): COOK.
Notes: MINISTER OF CIRCULAR CHURCH AT BLACK MINGO. THIS CHURCH LATER BECAME PRESBYTERIAN DUE TO LARGE NUMBERS OF THAT FAITH IN THE AREA.

HUNTER, WILLIAM   ID: 3582
Spouse: ANNE [--?--]
Children: NORSWORTHY, JOHN.
Date in Pee Dee: 1765   Last Date: 1765 DIED
Location: VICINITY OF CHERAW
Source(s): MOORE V.3.
Notes: AN UNBORN CHILD AT DEATH.

HURST, THOMAS   ID: 598
Spouse: ELIZABETH [--?--]
Date in Pee Dee: 1735
Location: BLACK MINGO CREEK
Source(s): COOK, SMITH, H..

HUSSELL, MARY   ID: 2739
Spouse: CHRISTOPHER GADSDEN
Date in Pee Dee: 1750
Location: PRINCE GEORGE WINYAW PARISH
Source(s): ROGERS.
Notes: SISTER OF THOMAS HUSSELL.

HUTSON, JOHN   ID: 5058
Date in Pee Dee: 1780
Location: WILLIAMSBURG
Source(s): BODDIE.
Revolutionary War service: SERVED AS PRIVATE IN MARION'S BRIGADE.

HUTSON, WILLIAM   ID: 5059
Date in Pee Dee: 1780
Location: WILLIAMSBURG
Source(s): BODDIE.
Revolutionary War service: PRIVATE

Early Pee Dee Settlers
--H--

HYRNE, ELIZABETH   ID: **5441**
Spouse: DANIEL BRITTON
Date in Pee Dee: 1747
Location: BRITTON'S NECK
Source(s): RBPPFW.

INMAN, PRISCILLA   ID: 5573
Date in Pee Dee: 1784
Location: ST. DAVID'S PARISH
Source(s): JVSDP.
Notes: AT AGE 8 BOUND BY PARISH TO ROBERT GEORGE WITH
CONSENT OF GRANDMOTHER.

IRBY, CHARLES   ID: 603
Spouse: MEHITABEL KOLB
Date in Pee Dee: 1740   Last Date: 1776
Location: CASHAWAY FERRY
Source(s): COOK, JVSDP, MOORE V.3.
Notes: SON OF EDMOND.
Revolutionary War service: PRIVATE IN MARION'S BRIGADE.

IRBY, EDMUND   ID: 1627
Date in Pee Dee: 1762   Last Date: 1780
Location: WELCH TRACT
Source(s): GREGG.
Notes: SON OF EDMUND #3457.
Revolutionary War service: LIEUTENANT IN MARION'S
BRIGADE.

IRBY, EDMUND   ID: 3457
Children: CHARLES, EDMOND, ROBERT, ELIZABETH, ROBERT.
Date in Pee Dee: 1762   Last Date: 1762 DIED
Location: ST. DAVID'S PARISH
Source(s): MOORE V.3.

Early Pee Dee Settlers

IRVIN, HUGH SR   ID: 5187
Children: HUGH.
Date in Pee Dee: 1780
Location: WILLIAMSBURG
Source(s): BODDIE.
Notes: SUPPLIED MARION.

ISABEL, PHILADELPHIA   ID: 5468
Spouse: JOHN TURBEVIL
Date in Pee Dee: 1747
Location: PRINCE FREDERICK PARISH
Source(s): RBPPFW.
Notes: MARRIED AT PARISH OF PRINCE FREDERICK WINYAW 19
NOVEMBER 1747.

ISBELL, HENRY   ID: 5298
Spouse: ELIZABETH [--?--]
Children: ANNE.
Date in Pee Dee: 1745
Location: PRINCE FREDERICK PARISH
Source(s): RBPPFW.

IZARD, RALPH   ID: 607
Date in Pee Dee: 1732
Location: NORTH SIDE OF SANTEE RIVER.
Source(s): COOK, GREGG.
Notes: GREGG SHOWS SAME NAME NEAR MARS BLUFF IN 1735.
MAY HAVE BEEN ABSENTEE OWNER.

IZARD, WALTER   ID: 1422
Spouse: ELIZABETH GIBBES
Children: DAVID.
Date in Pee Dee: 1735
Location: MARS BLUFF.
Source(s): GREGG, CLEMENS.
Notes: MARRIED 20 NOVEMBER 1739 AT BULL'S ISLAND.

JACKSON, EDWARD   ID: 1961
Spouse: [--?--] MANNING
Children: EDWARD, OWEN, WILLIAM, ERVIN, JOHN, REUBEN.
Date in Pee Dee: 1750
Origin: VIRGINIA
Location: CATFISH CREEK
Source(s): GREGG, SELLERS.

JACKSON, JOHN   ID: 1838
Date in Pee Dee: 1768
Location: ST. DAVID'S PARISH
Source(s): GREGG.
Revolutionary War service: LIEUTENANT IN MARION'S
BRIGADE.

JACKSON, RICHARD   ID: 3036
Date in Pee Dee: 1751
Location: CRAVEN COUNTY
Source(s): MOORE.
Notes: SEEMS TO HAVE BEEN A WARD OF WALLEXELSON #3033.

JACKSON, STEPHEN   ID: 2152
Date in Pee Dee: 1751   Last Date: 1780
Source(s): GREGG P.409, MOORE.
Revolutionary War service: CAPTAIN IN KOLB'S REGIMENT.

JACKSON, STEPHEN JR   ID: 2153
Date in Pee Dee: 1780
Source(s): GREGG P.409.

Revolutionary War service: PRIVATE IN MARION'S BRIGADE.

JACKSON, WILLIAM   ID: 2154
Date in Pee Dee: 1769   Last Date: 1782
Location: PRESENT MARION COUNTY
Source(s): GREGG, SELLERS.
Notes: SON OF EDWARD #1961.
Revolutionary War service: PRIVATE IN MARION'S BRIGADE.

JACOB, BENJAMIN   ID: 5644
Date in Pee Dee: 1759
Location: ST. DAVID'S PARISH
Source(s): MUSTER ROLL.
Notes: SERVED IN FRENCH AND INDIAN WAR AS PRIVATE WITH
LIDE'S COMPANY.

JAMES, ABEL   ID: 609
Date in Pee Dee: 1737   Last Date: 1759
Location: LONG BLUFF, ABOVE SEVERAL MILES.
Source(s): COOK, RWNBC, GREGG, MOORE.
Notes: ONE OF ORIGINAL WELCH TRACT SETTLERS. SON OF
JAMES #4751.

JAMES, ALEXANDER   ID: 2155
Date in Pee Dee: 1782
Location: WILLIAMSBURG
Source(s): GREGG, BODDIE.
Revolutionary War service: MILITIA LIEUTENANT WITH
MARION'S BRIGADE.

JAMES, ANN   ID: 1445
Spouse: PETER KOLB
Children: ABEL, ANN JAMES, HANNAH, BENJAMIN, SARAH.
Date in Pee Dee: 1760
Location: WELCH TRACT
Source(s): GREGG, SOMPAYRAC.
Notes: DAUGHTER OF PHILLIP #627.

JAMES, BENJAMIN   ID: 1866

Spouse: JANE [--?--]
Date in Pee Dee: 1759   Last Date: 1778
Location: ST. DAVID'S PARISH (CASHAWAY)
Source(s): GREGG, RWNBC, COOK.
Notes: SERVED IN FRENCH AND INDIAN WAR AS PRIVATE IN
KOLB'S COMPANY.

JAMES, CELIA   ID: 4031
Date in Pee Dee: 1764   Last Date: 1779
Location: ST. DAVID'S PARISH
Source(s): MOORE V.3, RWNBC.
Notes: DAUGHTER OF TABITHA COUNSELL #4029. PROBABLY WIFE
OF HOWEL JAMES.

JAMES, DANIEL   ID: 611
Date in Pee Dee: 1740
Location: LONG BLUFF, ABOVE SEVERAL MILES.
Source(s): COOK, RWNBC.
Notes: ONE OF ORIGINAL WELCH TRACT SETTLERS. SON OF
JAMES #4751.

JAMES, DAVID   ID: 612
Date in Pee Dee: 1740   Last Date: 1780
Location: LONG BLUFF, ABOVE SEVERAL MILES.
Source(s): COOK, BODDIE, GREGG.
Revolutionary War service: PRIVATE IN MARION'S BRIGADE.

JAMES, ELENOR   ID: 613
Spouse: WILLIAM SMITH
Date in Pee Dee: 1740   Last Date: 1772
Location: WELCH NECK
Source(s): COOK, RBPPFW, MOORE V.3.
Notes: MARRIED BY REV. FORDYCE. PROBABLY DAUGHTER OF
JAMES JAMES #617.

JAMES, ELISHA   ID: 4690
Date in Pee Dee: 1759   Last Date: 1761
Location: ST. DAVID'S PARISH
Source(s): RWNBC, MUSTER ROLL.

Notes: SERVED IN FRENCH AND INDIAN WAR AS ENSIGN WITH
CAPTAIN PLEDGER'S COMPANY.

JAMES, ELIZABETH   ID: 614
Spouse: SAMUEL WILDS
Date in Pee Dee: 1740   Last Date: 1761 DIED
Location: WELCH NECK
Source(s): COOK, MOORE V.3.
Notes: MARRIED BY REV. FORDYCE. PROBABLY DAUGHTER OF
JAMES JAMES #617.

JAMES, ELIZABETH JEAN   ID: 2933
Spouse: [--?--] HOLLINGSWORTH
Date in Pee Dee: 1750   Last Date: 1772 DIED
Location: WILLIAMSBURG, LATER ST. DAVID'S PARISH
Source(s): MOORE.
Notes: DAUGHTER OF WILLIAM #635.

JAMES, FRANCIS   ID: 3621
Date in Pee Dee: 1760
Source(s): MOORE V.3.
Notes: SON OF SHEARWOOD #3618. APPEARS TO HAVE DIED
BEFORE 1763.

JAMES, GAVIN   ID: 615
Date in Pee Dee: 1776   Last Date: 1781
Location: PRINCE FREDERICK'S PARISH
Source(s): COOK, BODDIE, MOORE V.3.
Revolutionary War service: CAPTAIN IN MARION'S BRIGADE.

JAMES, GEORGE   ID: 2156
Date in Pee Dee: 1782
Source(s): GREGG P.409.
Revolutionary War service: PRIVATE IN MARION'S BRIGADE.

JAMES, HOWELL   ID: 616
Spouse: PRISCILLA [--?--]
Children: JAMES, JESSE, ELIZABETH, MARY, SARAH.
Date in Pee Dee: 1755   Last Date: 1770 DIED

Location: WELCH NECK
Source(s): COOK, RWNBC, GREGG, JVSDP.
Notes: WIFE WAS PROBABLY CELIA JAMES #4031. SERVED IN
FRENCH AND INDIAN WAR WITH HICK'S COMPANY.

JAMES, JAMES   ID: 617
Children: PHILIP, RACHEL, ELEANOR, ELIZABETH, SARAH
(WILDS, DIED 1785).
Date in Pee Dee: 1737   Last Date: 1769 DIED
Location: LONG BLUFF, ABOVE SEVERAL MILES.
Source(s): COOK, GREGG, SOMPAYRAC, MOORE V.3.
Notes: ORIGINAL WELCH SETTLER. PHILIP WAS NOT MENTIONED
IN WILL. SIGNED NAME WITH MARK.

JAMES, JAMES   ID: 2931
Date in Pee Dee: 1750   Last Date: 1779
Location: WILLIAMSBURG
Source(s): MOORE, BODDIE.
Notes: SON OF WILLIAM #635. RAISED BY GAVIN WITHERSPOON.
Revolutionary War service: PRIVATE IN MARION'S BRIGADE.

JAMES, JAMES (I)   ID: 4751
Spouse: SARAH MILCHER
Children: ABEL, DANIEL, PHILIP.
Date in Pee Dee: 1735   Last Date: 1769 DIED
Location: ST. DAVID'S PARISH
Source(s): BARRINGER, GREGG.

JAMES, JANE   ID: 1585
Spouse: GAVIN WILSON
Date in Pee Dee: 1732
Origin: NORTHERN IRELAND
Location: WILLIAMSBURG
Source(s): WITHERSPOON.
Notes: DAUGHTER OF JOHN.

JAMES, JANE   ID: 1591
Spouse: WILLIAM COOPER
Children: JOHN, GEORGE.

Date in Pee Dee: 1751
Location: WILLIAMSBURG
Source(s): WITHERSPOON.

JAMES, JOHN   ID: 620
Spouse: JEAN MCCALLA
Children: JOHN, JANE, JAMES, MARY, ROBERT, GAVIN,
WILLIAM, JEAN, ELIZABETH.
Date in Pee Dee: 1734   Last Date: 1755
Origin: NORTHERN IRELAND
Location: WILLIAMSBURG (LYNCHES LAKE)
Source(s): COOK, BODDIE, MOORE.
Notes: ORIGINAL WILLIAMSBURG SETTLER. KNOWN AS "OX SWAMP
JOHN".

JAMES, JOHN   ID: 621
Spouse: JANE DOBEIN
Children: JOHN, SAMUEL, WILLIAM DOBIEN, ELIZABETH,
JANNET.
Date in Pee Dee: 1733   Last Date: 1791 DIED
Origin: NORTHERN IRELAND
Location: PRINCE FREDERICK'S PARISH
Source(s): COOK, BODDIE, WITHERSPOON.
Notes: REPRESENTATIVE TO SC LEGISLATURE. SON OF WILLIAM
#635.
Revolutionary War service: MAJOR IN MARION'S BRIGADE.

JAMES, JOHN   ID: 624
Spouse: MARY ERVIN
Children: JANE ERVIN, JOHN, JAMES ERVIN.
Date in Pee Dee: 1754 DOB Last Date: 1780
Location: WILLIAMSBURG (LYNCHES LAKE)
Source(s): COOK, BODDIE.
Notes: SON OF JOHN #621. SECOND MARRIED ELIZABETH WILSON
#5193.
Revolutionary War service: CAPTAIN IN MARION'S BRIGADE.

JAMES, JOHN   ID: 2556
Date in Pee Dee: 1740

Location: PRINCE FREDERICK'S PARISH
Source(s): ROGERS.
Notes: JOHN "OF THE LAKE".

JAMES, MARY   ID: 1507
Date in Pee Dee: 1732
Origin: NORTHERN IRELAND
Location: WILLIAMSBURG
Source(s): WITHERSPOON.
Notes: DAUGHTER OF WILLIAM #635. MAY HAVE MARRIED DAVID
HORRY.

JAMES, MARY   ID: 3623
Spouse: MATHEW SINGLETON
Children: JOHN.
Date in Pee Dee: 1763
Location: ST. MARK'S PARISH
Source(s): MOORE V.3.
Notes: DAUGHTER OF SHEARWOOD #3618.

JAMES, NATHANIEL   ID: 5060
Date in Pee Dee: 1780
Location: WILLIAMSBURG
Source(s): BODDIE.
Revolutionary War service: PRIVATE IN MARION'S BRIGADE.

JAMES, PHILLIP   ID: 627
Spouse: ELIZABETH THOMAS
Children: ANN, DANIEL, JAMES, PHILLIP.
Date in Pee Dee: 1735   Last Date: 1753 DIED
Occupation: MINISTER   Origin: PENNEPAC, PA
Location: WELCH NECK
Source(s): COOK, RWNBC, GREGG.
Notes: FIRST ORDAINED MINSTER OF WELCH NECK CHURCH. DIED
1753. SON OF JAMES JAMES.

JAMES, ROBERT   ID: 4030
Date in Pee Dee: 1764   Last Date: 1780
Location: ST. DAVID'S PARISH

Source(s): MOORE V.3, BODDIE.
Notes: SON OF TABITHA COUNSELL #4029.
Revolutionary War service: PRIVATE IN MARION'S BRIGADE.

JAMES, SARAH   ID: 631
Spouse: WILLIAM JAMES
Date in Pee Dee: 1755   Last Date: 1761 DIED
Location: WELCH NECK
Source(s): COOK, RWNBC.

JAMES, SARAH   ID: 2934
Date in Pee Dee: 1750   Last Date: 1759
Location: WILLIAMSBURG
Source(s): MOORE.
Notes: DAUGHTER OF WILLIAM #635. THERE WERE THREE OF
THIS NAME IN WELCH NECK IN 1759.

JAMES, SHEARWOOD   ID: 3618
Spouse: ANNE KING
Children: SHERWOOD, JOHN, MARY (SINGLETON), FRANCIS.
Date in Pee Dee: 1763   Last Date: 1764 DIED
Location: HIGH HILLS
Source(s): MOORE V.3.

JAMES, THOMAS   ID: 1756
Spouse: SARAH [--?--]
Date in Pee Dee: 1768   Last Date: 1778
Location: ST. DAVID'S PARISH
Source(s): GREGG, RWNBC, RUDISILL, JVSDP.
Notes: WIFE WAS PROBABLY SARAH DEWITT.

JAMES, WILLIAM   ID: 634
Spouse: ELIZABETH LUCAS
Date in Pee Dee: 1740   Last Date: 1784 DIED
Location: LONG BLUFF, ABOVE SEVERAL MILES.
Source(s): COOK, MOORE V.3, GREGG, RWNBC.

JAMES, WILLIAM   ID: 635
Spouse: ELIZABETH WITHERSPOON

Children: MARY, SAMUEL, MCCOLLUCK, JANET, ESTHER JEAN
(WITHERSPOON), JAMES, JOHN, ROBERT, ELIZABETH, WILLIAM,
SARAH, NATHANIEL.
Date in Pee Dee: 1732   Last Date: 1750 DIED
Origin: NORTHERN IRELAND
Location: WILLIAMSBURG
Source(s): COOK, BODDIE, MOORE.
Notes: BROTHER OF JOHN. ORIGINAL WILLIAMSBURG SETTLER.
SON OF JOHN OF NORTHERN IRELAND.

JAMES, WILLIAM   ID: 636
Spouse: SARAH [--?--]
Date in Pee Dee: 1755   Last Date: 1761 DIED
Location: WELCH NECK
Source(s): COOK, RWNBC.

JAMES, WILLIAM   ID: 1896
Spouse: JEAN [--?--]
Children: JOHN.
Date in Pee Dee: 1768   Last Date: 1773 DIED
Location: ST. DAVID'S PARISH (QUEENSBOROUGH)
Source(s): GREGG, JVSDP, MOORE V.3.

JAMES, WILLIAM DOBEIN   ID: 5061
Spouse: SARAH FORD
Children: WILLIAM HUGER, JOHN JUNIUS, FRANCIS MARION,
ELIZABETH, SARAH JANE (COWLING), HENRY M., CHARLOTTE
KEITH (ANDERSON), GEORGE FORD.
Date in Pee Dee: 1765 DOB Last Date: 1830 DIED
Location: WILLIAMSBURG
Source(s): BODDIE.
Notes: SON OF MAJ. JOHN #621.
Revolutionary War service: PRIVATE IN MARION'S BRIGADE.

JAMESON, WILLIAM   ID: 3750
Date in Pee Dee: 1766   Last Date: 1766 DIED
Location: NORTH OF SANTEE RIVER
Source(s): MOORE V.3, BODDIE.

Notes: SON OF WILLIAM AND MARGARET JAMESON. A SISTER
AGNES STILL LIVED IN IRELAND.

JAUDON, ELIAS   ID: 481
Spouse: ELIZABETH [--?--]
Date in Pee Dee: 1743   Last Date: 1745 DIED
Location: PRINCE GEORGE WINYAW PARISH
Source(s): MOORE.

JAUDON, ELIZABETH   ID: 2798
Children: PAUL, DAVID, ELISHA.
Date in Pee Dee: 1743   Last Date: 1743 DIED
Location: PRINCE GEORGE WINYAW PARISH
Source(s): MOORE, BODDIE.
Notes: MAY BE WIFE OF ELIAS JAUDON.

JAUDON, ESTHER   ID: 4311
Spouse: JAMES BERNARD
Children: PAUL, JAMES, WILLIAM, SAMUEL, ELISHA, ESTHER.
Date in Pee Dee: 1775
Location: PRINCE FREDERICK'S PARISH
Source(s): MOORE V.3.
Notes: DAUGHTER OF PAUL #480.

JAUDON, JUDITH   ID: 4477
Date in Pee Dee: 1774
Location: PRINCE FREDERICK'S PARISH
Source(s): MOORE V.3.
Notes: GRAND-DAUGHTER OF ELISHA JAUDON #4476. DAUGHTER
OF PAUL #480.

JAUDON, PAUL   ID: 480
Spouse: MARGARET LIEUBREY
Children: PAUL, SAMUEL, MARGARET, ESTHER, JUDITH, LYDIA,
HESTER.
Date in Pee Dee: 1736   Last Date: 1774 DIED
Location: PRINCE GEORGE WINYAW PARISH
Source(s): MOORE, RBPPFW, CLEMENS, BODDIE.

Notes: SON OF ELIZABETH JAUDON #2798. MARRIED 21
DECEMBER 1743 AT PRINCE FREDERICK'S PARISH.

JEANERET, JACOB   ID: 3262
Spouse: ELIZABETH [--?--]
Date in Pee Dee: 1726
Location: ON SANTEE RIVER.
Source(s): MOORE V.1.
Notes: WIFE WAS GRAND-DAUGHTER OF NOAH SERRE #3258. A
COUSIN OF JOHN JEANERET.

JEANERET, JOHN   ID: 4485
Spouse: SUSANNAH [--?--]
Children: ELIZABETH, SUSANNAH, CATHERINE.
Date in Pee Dee: 1774   Last Date: 1774 DIED
Location: PRINCE FREDERICK'S PARISH
Source(s): MOORE V.3.
Notes: COUSIN OF JACOB JEANERET.

JENKINS, CHARLES   ID: 638
Date in Pee Dee: 1767
Location: CASHAWAY
Source(s): COOK.
Notes: PROBABLY WELCH
Revolutionary War service: PRIVATE IN MARION'S BRIGADE.

JENKINS, JAMES   ID: 639
Date in Pee Dee: 1764   Last Date: 1783
Location: CHERAW DISTRICT (BRITTON'S NECK)
Source(s): COOK, SELLERS.
Notes: SON OF SAMUEL AND ELIZABETH JENKINS.
Revolutionary War service: LIEUTENANT IN MILITIA FOR 127
DAYS.

JENKINS, JOHN   ID: 640
Date in Pee Dee: 1768   Last Date: 1781
Location: BRITTON'S NECK
Source(s): COOK, JVSDP, GREGG.
Revolutionary War service: MARION'S BRIGADE

JENKINS, JOSEPH   ID: 1776
Date in Pee Dee:
Location: GEORGETOWN
Source(s): COOK.
Revolutionary War service: LIEUTENANT

JENKINS, REUBEN   ID: 2157
Date in Pee Dee: 1782
Source(s): GREGG P.409.
Revolutionary War service: LIEUTENANT IN MARION'S
BRIGADE.

JENKINS, SAMUEL   ID: 642
Spouse: ELIZABETH BRITTON
Children: JAMES, SAMUEL, JOHN.
Date in Pee Dee: 1735
Location: BRITTON'S NECK
Source(s): COOK, GREGG, BODDIE.
Notes: HER SECOND MARRIGAGE. ELIZABETH IS WIDOW JENKINS
OF WHOM GREGG TELLS.

JENKINS, SAMUEL   ID: 643
Date in Pee Dee: 1781
Source(s): COOK.
Revolutionary War service: IN MARION'S BRIGADE.

JENKINS, THOMAS   ID: 644
Spouse: MARY [--?--]
Children: SARAH, PATIENCE.
Date in Pee Dee: 1724   Last Date: 1731
Location: BLACK RIVER
Source(s): COOK, RBPPFW.
Notes: CLERK, SEXTON, AND REGISTER OF PARISH OF PRINCE
FREDERICK WINYAH IN 1731.

JENKINS, THOMAS   ID: 645
Spouse: DOROTHY [--?--]
Date in Pee Dee: 1736   Last Date: 1776
Location: BLACK RIVER IN VICINITY OF GEORGETOWN

Early Pee Dee Settlers
--J--

Source(s): COOK, BODDIE.
Revolutionary War service: CAPTAIN

JENNENS, EDWARD   ID: 3611
Date in Pee Dee: 1764   Last Date: 1765 DIED
Source(s): MOORE V.3.
Notes: BROTHER OF PETER AND JOHN.

JENNENS, JOHN   ID: 3613
Date in Pee Dee: 1764
Source(s): MOORE V.3.
Notes: BROTHER OF EDWARD AND PETER.

JENNENS, PETER   ID: 3612
Date in Pee Dee: 1764
Source(s): MOORE V.3.
Notes: BROTHER OF EDWARD AND JOHN.

JENNER, JAMES   ID: 5396
Spouse: FRANCES BROWN
Date in Pee Dee: 1736   Last Date: 1744
Location: PRINCE FREDERICK'S PARISH
Source(s): RBPPFW, BODDIE.
Notes: MARRIED 1 AUGUST 1744 AT PARISH OF PRINCE
FREDERICK WINYAW.

JENNER, MARTHA   ID: 5350
Spouse: JOHN WORTH
Date in Pee Dee: 1740
Location: PRINCE FREDERICK'S PARISH
Source(s): RBPPFW.

JENNERET, ABRAHAM   ID: 2639
Spouse: SUSANNAH FAVRE
Children: ABRAHAM, JOHN, STEPHEN, SUSANNAH.
Date in Pee Dee: 1744   Last Date: 1744 DIED
Location: PRINCE FREDERICK'S PARISH
Source(s): MOORE.

Early Pee Dee Settlers
--J--

JENNERETT, JOHN   ID: 2768
Date in Pee Dee: 1757
Location: ST. MARK'S PARISH
Source(s): ROGERS, MOORE V.3.
Notes: CAPTAIN NORTH SANTEE COMPANY OF MILITIA. SON OF ABRAHAM.

JERNIGAN, ALEXANDER   ID: 646
Date in Pee Dee: 1775
Location: CHERAW DISTRICT
Source(s): COOK.
Revolutionary War service: WISE'S COMPANY OF INFANTRY.

JERNIGAN, HENRY   ID: 3877
Spouse: ANN [--?--]
Children: NEEDHAM, HARDY RICE.
Date in Pee Dee: 1762   Last Date: 1762 DIED
Source(s): MOORE V.3.

JINKINS, JAMES   ID: 2158
Date in Pee Dee: 1782
Source(s): GREGG P.409.
Revolutionary War service: LIEUTENANT IN BENTON'S REGIMENT.

JOHN, ASAL   ID: 2005
Date in Pee Dee: 1780
Location: CHERAW DISTRICT
Source(s): GREGG.
Notes: TORY

JOHN, AZEL   ID: 2159
Date in Pee Dee: 1782
Source(s): GREGG P.409.
Revolutionary War service: PRIVATE IN BENTON'S REGIMENT.

JOHN, EMANUEL   ID: 5683
Date in Pee Dee: 1759
Location: ST. DAVID'S PARISH

Source(s): MUSTER ROLL.
Notes: SERVED IN FRENCH AND INDIAN WAR AS PRIVATE IN
PLEDGER'S COMPANY.

JOHN, GRIFFITH   ID: 649
Date in Pee Dee: 1740   Last Date: 1765 DIED
Location: WELCH NECK (ABOVE LONG BLUFF)
Source(s): COOK, RWNBC.
Notes: DIED AUGUST 1765. THIS POSSIBLY SHOULD BE JONES.

JOHN, JESSE   ID: 2160
Date in Pee Dee: 1783
Source(s): GREGG P.409.
Revolutionary War service: PRIVATE IN BENTON'S REGIMENT

JOHN, JONATHAN   ID: 2076
Date in Pee Dee: 1780
Location: CHERAW DISTRICT
Source(s): GREGG.
Notes: TORY

JOHN, THOMAS   ID: 2161
Date in Pee Dee: 1782
Source(s): GREGG P.409.
Revolutionary War service: PRIVATE IN BENTON'S REGIMENT

JOHN, TOM   ID: 2025
Date in Pee Dee: 1780
Location: CHERAW DISTRICT
Source(s): GREGG.
Notes: TORY

JOHNSON, ABEL   ID: 3211
Spouse: [--?--] COOPER
Children: THOMAS, ROBERT, SARAH, MARY.
Date in Pee Dee: 1758   Last Date: 1758 DIED
Location: ST. MARK'S PARISH
Source(s): MOORE.
Notes: WIFE WAS DAUGHTER OF SARAH COOPER #3505.

JOHNSON, CHARLES   ID: 5610
Date in Pee Dee: 1759
Location: ST. DAVID'S PARISH
Source(s): MUSTER ROLL.
Notes: SERVED IN FRENCH AND INDIAN WAR IN CAPTAIN JAMES
THOMSON'S COMPANY. LISTED AS DESERTER.

JOHNSON, DAVID   ID: 651
Date in Pee Dee: 1735
Origin: NORTHERN IRELAND
Location: WILLIAMSBURG
Source(s): COOK, BODDIE.
Notes: MAY HAVE BEEN ANOTHER OF THIS NAME WHO SERVED
WITH MARION. SERVED IN FRENCH AND INDIAN WAR.
Revolutionary War service: PRIVATE IN MARION'S BRIGADE.

JOHNSON, DEBORAH   ID: 2578
Spouse: ANTHONY WHITE SR.
Children: JOHN, ELIZABETH.
Date in Pee Dee: 1760
Location: LOWER BLACK RIVER
Source(s): STRAWN.
Notes: DAUGHTER OF PETER #655.

JOHNSON, GRESSETE   ID: 4592
Spouse: EDDY [--?--]
Date in Pee Dee: 1778
Location: ST. DAVID'S PARISH
Source(s): RWNBC.

JOHNSON, JACOB   ID: 1950
Date in Pee Dee: 1769
Location: ST. DAVID'S PARISH
Source(s): GREGG.
Notes: BROTHER OF RICHARD JOHNSON AND MARY HILL.

JOHNSON, JOHN   ID: 2162
Date in Pee Dee: 1781
Source(s): GREGG.

Revolutionary War service: PRIVATE IN BENTON'S REGIMENT

JOHNSON, JOSEPH   ID: 653
Date in Pee Dee: 1735   Last Date: 1773 DIED
Location: BLACK RIVER POTATO FERRY
Source(s): COOK, BOPDDIE, MOORE V.3.
Notes: COUSIN OF JOSIAH JUNE AND SAMUEL CLEGG.

JOHNSON, MAHITTABELL   ID: 3222
Spouse: SAMUEL CLAIG
Date in Pee Dee: 1731
Location: CRAVEN COUNTY
Source(s): MOORE V.1.
Notes: DAUGHTER OF PETER #3220.

JOHNSON, MARY   ID: 3223
Spouse: THOMAS BLACKWELL
Date in Pee Dee: 1731
Location: CRAVEN COUNTY
Source(s): MOORE V.1.
Notes: DAUGHTER OF PETER #3220.

JOHNSON, MARY   ID: 3807
Date in Pee Dee: 1755   Last Date: 1773
Location: WILLIAMSBURG
Source(s): MOORE V.3.
Notes: GRAND CHILD OF SARAH COOPER #3505. DAUGHTER OF
THOMAS JOHNSON #3695.

JOHNSON, MARY   ID: 4232
Spouse: [--?--] HILL
Date in Pee Dee: 1771
Location: PRINCE FREDERICK'S PARISH
Source(s): MOORE V.3.
Notes: SISTER OF RICHARD AND JACOB.

JOHNSON, MARY   ID: 4234
Spouse: JOHN FITZGERALL
Date in Pee Dee: 1771

Location: PRINCE FREDERICK'S PARISH
Source(s): MOORE V.3.
Notes: DAUGHTER OF JACOB.

JOHNSON, PETER   ID: 655
Spouse: DEBORAH [--?--]
Children: DEBORAH.
Date in Pee Dee: 1730
Location: BLACK RIVER AT POTATO FERRY
Source(s): COOK, STRAWN.
Notes: SON OF PETER #3220.

JOHNSON, PETER   ID: 3220
Spouse: MAHITTABELL [--?--]
Children: PETER, JOSEPH, JAMES, MAHITTABELL (CLAIG),
MARY (BLACKWELL).
Date in Pee Dee: 1731   Last Date: 1731 DIED
Location: CRAVEN COUNTY
Source(s): MOORE V.1.

JOHNSON, RACHEL   ID: 4233
Spouse: [--?--] KING
Date in Pee Dee: 1771
Location: PRINCE FREDERICK'S PARISH
Source(s): MOORE V.3.
Notes: SISTER OF MARY, RICHARD AND JACOB.

JOHNSON, RANDOLPH   ID: 5562
Date in Pee Dee: 1782
Location: ST. DAVID'S PARISH
Source(s): JVSDP.
Notes: BOUND TO JOHN WILSON BY PARISH.

JOHNSON, RICHARD   ID: 2626
Spouse: [--?--] HOWARD
Date in Pee Dee: 1755
Location: WILLIAMSBURG
Source(s): MOORE.
Notes: BROTHER OF JACOB JOHNSON AND MARY HILL.

JOHNSON, ROBERT   ID: 3809
Date in Pee Dee: 1755
Location: WILLIAMSBURG
Source(s): MOORE V.3.
Notes: GRAND CHILD OF SARAH COOPER #3505.

JOHNSON, SARAH   ID: 3214
Spouse: JOHN PURVIS
Date in Pee Dee: 1746   Last Date: 1758
Location: PRINCE FREDERICK'S PARISH
Source(s): MOORE, RBPPFW.
Notes: DAUGHTER OF ABEL #3211. MARRIED 2 APRIL 1746 AT
PARISH OF PRINCE FREDERICK WINYAW.

JOHNSON, SARAH   ID: 3806
Date in Pee Dee: 1755   Last Date: 1773
Location: WILLIAMSBURG
Source(s): MOORE V.3.
Notes: GRAND CHILD OF SARAH COOPER #3505. DAUGHTER OF
THOMAS #3695.

JOHNSON, THOMAS   ID: 3694
Spouse: MARY THOMSON
Children: SARAH, MARY.
Date in Pee Dee: 1757   Last Date: 1773 DIED
Location: BLACK RIVER
Source(s): MOORE V.3.
Notes: SON OF MARY POTTS #3691. UNDER 20 YEARS IN 1764.
SHE PREVIOUSLY MARRIED [--?--] FULTON.

JOHNSON, THOMAS   ID: 3808
Date in Pee Dee: 1755
Location: WILLIAMSBURG
Source(s): MOORE V.3.
Notes: GRAND CHILD OF SARAH COOPER #3505. APPEARS TO BE
SON OF JACOB.

JOHNSON, WILLIAM   ID: 2071
Date in Pee Dee: 1737   Last Date: 1775

Location: ST. DAVID'S PARISH
Source(s): GREGG, JVSDP, BODDIE.
Revolutionary War service: MILITIA

JOHNSTON, ARCHIBALD   ID: 2622
Children: ANDREW (#2731).
Date in Pee Dee: 1749   Last Date: 1763
Location: SANTEE RIVER
Source(s): ROGERS, MOORE.

JOHNSTON, HARMON   ID: 5292
Spouse: ELIS [--?--]
Children: THOMAS.
Date in Pee Dee: 1745
Location: PRINCE FREDERICK'S PARISH
Source(s): RBPPFW.

JOHNSTON, JOHN   ID: 2163
Date in Pee Dee: 1782
Location: ST. DAVID'S PARISH
Source(s): GREGG P.409, MOORE V.3.
Revolutionary War service: PRIVATE IN MILITIA.

JOHNSTON, MARTIN   ID: 5291
Spouse: SARAH [--?--]
Children: ISAAC, JACOB, WILLIAM, MARTHA.
Date in Pee Dee: 1745
Location: PRINCE FREDERICK'S PARISH
Source(s): RBPPFW.

JOHNSTON, TABITHA   ID: 4057
Spouse: PETER JUNE
Children: PETER.
Date in Pee Dee: 1767
Location: PRINCE FREDERICK'S PARISH
Source(s): MOORE V.3.

JOHNSTON, THOMAS   ID: 4770
Spouse: SARAH HOLDER

Children: JOSEPH.
Date in Pee Dee: 1776
Location: PRINCE FREDERICK'S PARISH (LOWER)
Source(s): MOORE V.3.

JOLANDS, ABSALOM   ID: 5663
Date in Pee Dee: 1759
Location: ST. DAVID'S PARISH
Source(s): MUSTER ROLL.
Notes: SERVED IN FRENCH AND INDIAN WAR AS PRIVATE WITH
MCINTOSH'S COMPANY.

JOLLY, HESTER   ID: 5356
Spouse: MOSES BRITTON
Date in Pee Dee: 1741
Location: PRINCE FREDERICK'S PARISH
Source(s): RBPPFW.

JOLLY, JAMES   ID: 5605
Date in Pee Dee: 1759   Last Date: 1759 DIED
Location: ST. DAVID'S PARISH
Source(s): MUSTER ROLL.
Notes: SERVED IN FRENCH AND INDIAN WAR AS PRIVATE IN
CAPTAIN JAMES THOMSON'S COMPANY.

JOLLY, JOSEPH   ID: 658
Children: JOSEPH, SARAH (O'BRIAN).
Date in Pee Dee: 1736   Last Date: 1758
Location: HURRICANE CREEK (N. OF CASHAWAY)
Source(s): COOK, MOORE.
Notes: DIED ABOUT 1760.

JOLLY, JOSHUA   ID: 4888
Spouse: MARY BROCKINTON
Date in Pee Dee: 1737   Last Date: 1750
Location: LOWER BLACK RIVER.
Source(s): BODDIE.

JOLLY, SARAH   ID: 3454

Spouse: PATRICK O'BRIAN
Date in Pee Dee: 1760
Location: WELCH TRACT
Source(s): MOORE V.3.
Notes: DAUGHTER OF JOSEPH #658.

JONES, [--?--]   ID: 661
Spouse: [--?--] MCINTOSH
Date in Pee Dee: 1755
Location: WELCH NECK
Source(s): COOK.
Notes: MARRIED MCINTOSH. DIED 12/30/64

JONES, ABRAHAM   ID: 5687
Date in Pee Dee: 1759
Location: ST. DAVID'S PARISH
Source(s): MUSTER ROLL.
Notes: SERVED IN FRENCH AND INDIAN WAR AS PRIVATE IN
PLEDGER'S COMPANY.

JONES, ANNE   ID: 662
Spouse: [--?--] DOUGLASS
Date in Pee Dee: 1755   Last Date: 1766 DIED
Location: WELCH NECK
Source(s): COOK, RWNBC.

JONES, DAVID   ID: 663
Date in Pee Dee: 1737
Location: LONG BLUFF, ABOVE SEVERAL MILES.
Source(s): COOK, RWNBC, GREGG.
Notes: ONE OF ORIGINAL SETTLERS OF WELCH NECK.

JONES, EDWARD   ID: 665
Spouse: MARY [--?--]
Date in Pee Dee: 1755   Last Date: 1784 DIED
Location: WELCH NECK
Source(s): COOK, MOORE V.3, GREGG, RWNBC.
Notes: SERVED IN FRENCH AND INDIAN WAR AS SERGEANT WITH
CAPTAIN PLEDGER'S COMPANY.

Early Pee Dee Settlers
--J--

JONES, FREDERICK   ID: 5658
Date in Pee Dee: 1759
Location: ST. DAVID'S PARISH
Source(s): MUSTER ROLL.
Notes: SERVED IN FRENCH AND INDIAN WAR AS CLERK WITH
MCINTOSH'S COMPANY.

JONES, JAMES   ID: 666
Spouse: ELIZABETH [--?--]
Children: DAVID.
Date in Pee Dee: 1740   Last Date: 1743
Location: CHERAW (PIDGEON CREEK (BUCKHOLDT'S))
Source(s): COOK, RBPPFW.

JONES, JAMES   ID: 2718
Date in Pee Dee: 1775
Location: UPPER PEE DEE
Source(s): SOMPAYRAC, COOK.
Notes: LEADER OF TORY PARTY THAT KILLED ABEL KOLB IN
1781. MAY HAVE SERVED F/I WAR.
Revolutionary War service: TORY CAPTAIN WITH GAINEY.

JONES, JOHN   ID: 668
Date in Pee Dee: 1775
Location: ST. DAVID'S PARISH
Source(s): COOK.
Revolutionary War service: LIDE'S COMPANY

JONES, JOHN   ID: 669
Date in Pee Dee: 1775
Location: CHERAW DISTRICT
Source(s): COOK.
Revolutionary War service: WISE'S COMPANY OF INFANTRY.

JONES, JOHN   ID: 1357
Date in Pee Dee: 1737   Last Date: 1759 DIED
Location: QUEENSBOROUGH TOWNSHIP
Source(s): GREGG, RWNBC.
Notes: ONE OF ORIGINAL WELCH NECK SETTLERS.

JONES, JOSEPH   ID: 1993
Date in Pee Dee: 1759   Last Date: 1780
Location: CHERAW DISTRICT
Source(s): GREGG, MUSTER ROLL.
Notes: A TORY. SERVED IN FRENCH AND INDIAN WAR AS
PRIVATE IN LIDE'S COMPANY.

JONES, LEVI   ID: 670
Date in Pee Dee: 1775
Location: ST. DAVID'S PARISH
Source(s): COOK.
Revolutionary War service: LIDE'S COMPANY

JONES, MARTHA   ID: 5420
Spouse: MOSES MARTIN
Date in Pee Dee: 1747
Location: PRINCE FREDERICK'S PARISH
Source(s): RBPPFW.

JONES, MARY   ID: 671
Date in Pee Dee: 1751   Last Date: 1751 DIED
Location: WELCH NECK
Source(s): COOK, RWNBC.
Notes: THIS IS PROBABLY WIFE OF EDWARD.

JONES, RICHARD   ID: 3535
Spouse: ELIZABETH [--?--]
Date in Pee Dee: 1736
Location: PRINCE FREDERICK'S PARISH
Source(s): BODDIE.

JONES, THOMAS   ID: 4310
Date in Pee Dee: 1759   Last Date: 1775
Location: PRINCE FREDERICK'S PARISH
Source(s): MOORE V.3, RWNBC.
Notes: SERVED IN FRENCH AND INDIAN WAR AS PRIVATE WITH
PLEDGER'S COMPANY.

JONES, WILLIAM   ID: 674

Date in Pee Dee: 1775   Last Date: 1779 DIED
Location: ST. DAVID'S PARISH
Source(s): COOK, JVSDP, RWNBC.
Revolutionary War service: LIDE'S COMPANY

JORDAN, CHRISTOPHER   ID: 3090
Children: CHRISTOPHER.
Date in Pee Dee: 1756
Location: PRINCE GEORGE WINYAW PARISH
Source(s): MOORE.

JORDAN, WILLIAM   ID: 2047
Date in Pee Dee: 1776
Location: ST. DAVID'S PARISH
Source(s): GREGG.
Revolutionary War service: MILITIA

JOSIAH, MANUEL   ID: 677
Date in Pee Dee: 1775
Location: ST. DAVID'S PARISH
Source(s): COOK.
Revolutionary War service: LIDE'S COMPANY

JUNE, CATHERINE   ID: 4175
Spouse: SAMUEL NEWMAN
Date in Pee Dee: 1766
Location: PRINCE FREDERICK'S PARISH
Source(s): MOORE V.3.
Notes: DAUGHTER OF JOHN #3763.

JUNE, JOHN   ID: 3763
Spouse: CHARLOTTE [--?--]
Children: JOHN, PETER, SOLOMON, FRANCES, LYDIA,
CATHERINE (NEWMAN).
Date in Pee Dee: 1765   Last Date: 1766 DIED
Location: PRINCE FREDRICK PARISH
Source(s): MOORE V.3.
Notes: WIFE WAS PROBABLY DAUGHTER OF THEODORE GOURDINE
#2268.

JUNE, JOHN   ID: 5216
Spouse: ANN [--?--]
Children: ELIZABETH.
Date in Pee Dee: 1744 DOB
Location: PRINCE FREDERICK'S PARISH
Source(s): RBPPFW.

JUNE, JOHN   ID: 5285
Spouse: LUCRETIA (LUCY) KENNEL
Children: JOHN, PETER.
Date in Pee Dee: 1743   Last Date: 1747
Location: PRINCE FREDERICK'S PARISH
Source(s): RBPPFW.
Notes: MARRIED 28 DECEMBER 1743 AT PARISH OF PRINCE
FREDERICK WINYAW.

JUNE, JOSIAH   ID: 4493
Date in Pee Dee: 1773
Location: PRINCE GEORGE WINYAH PARISH
Source(s): MOORE V.3.
Notes: COUSIN OF JOSEPH JOHNSON.

JUNE, PETER JR.   ID: 3764
Spouse: TABITHA JOHNSTON
Children: PETER, OTHERS.
Date in Pee Dee: 1765   Last Date: 1767 DIED
Location: PRINCE FREDRICK PARISH
Source(s): MOORE V.3.
Notes: GRAND-SON OF SOLOMON. SON OF STANLEY. COUSIN OF
WILLIAM MICHAU.

JUNE, SOLOMON   ID: 3882
Children: STANLEY, PETER.
Date in Pee Dee: 1762   Last Date: 1762 DIED
Location: PRINCE FREDRICK PARISH
Source(s): MOORE V.3.

JUNE, STANLEY   ID: 3888
Spouse: SARAH [--?--]

Children: WILLIAM, PETER, SARAH.
Date in Pee Dee: 1766   Last Date: 1766 DIED
Location: PRINCE FREDRICK PARISH
Source(s): MOORE V.3.
Notes: SON OF SOLOMON #3882.

JUNE, WILLIAM   ID: 3885
Date in Pee Dee: 1762   Last Date: 1762 DIED
Location: PRINCE FREDRICK PARISH
Source(s): MOORE V.3.
Notes: GRAND-SON OF SOLOMON #3882.

KARWON, CRAFTON   ID: 678
Date in Pee Dee: 1740
Location: PRINCE FREDERICK PARISH
Source(s): COOK, RBPPFW.
Notes: CHURCH WARDEN AND SEXTON OF PARISH OF PRINCE
FREDERICK WINYAW IN 1740.

KAVANAGH, HUGH   ID: 4498
Date in Pee Dee: 1773   Last Date: 1773 DIED
Origin: NORTHERN IRELAND
Location: GEORGETOWN
Source(s): MOORE V.3.
Notes: HIS FATHER JAMES WAS IN IRELAND. SIGNED WITH
MARK.

KEATLY, JOHN   ID: 5439
Spouse: JANE TROUBLEFIELD
Date in Pee Dee: 1746
Location: PRINCE FREDERICK PARISH
Source(s): RBPPFW.
Notes: MARRIED 16 DECEMBER 1746 AT PARISH OF PRINCE
FREDERICK WINYAW.

KEBLE, ELIZABETH   ID: 5390
Spouse: EDMUND CARTLIDGE
Date in Pee Dee: 1743
Location: PRINCE FREDERICK PARISH
Source(s): RBPPFW.

KEEBLE, KARY   ID: 5454
Spouse: MARY KELLY
Date in Pee Dee: 1747
Location: PRINCE FREDERICK PARISH
Source(s): RBPPFW.
Notes: MARRIED AT PARISH OF PRINCE FREDERICK WINYAW 21
DECEMBER 1747.

KEELS, ABRAHAM   ID: 5062
Date in Pee Dee: 1780
Location: WILLIAMSBURG
Source(s): BODDIE.
Revolutionary War service: PRIVATE IN MARION'S BRIGADE.

KEELS, ISAAC   ID: 5063
Date in Pee Dee: 1780
Location: WILLIAMSBURG
Source(s): BODDIE.
Revolutionary War service: PRIVATE IN MARION'S BRIGADE.

KEELS, JOHN   ID: 5064
Date in Pee Dee: 1780
Location: WILLIAMSBURG
Source(s): BODDIE.
Revolutionary War service: PRIVATE IN MARION'S BRIGADE.

KEEN, ANN   ID: 5195
Spouse: JOHN GARNIER
Date in Pee Dee: 1786
Location: GEORGETOWN
Source(s): CLEMENS.
Notes: MARRIED JULY 1786.

KEEN, JOHN   ID: 5215
Spouse: ELIZABETH PELLEO
Children: ANDREW.
Date in Pee Dee: 1738   Last Date: 1739
Location: PRINCE FREDERICK PARISH
Source(s): RBPPFW.

Notes: MARRIED 2 JULY 1738 AT PARISH OF PRINCE FREDERICK WINYAW. SEXTON OF PARISH OF PRINCE FREDERICK WINYAW IN 1739.

KEEN, THOMAS   ID: 5281
Spouse: MARY [--?--]
Children: ELIZABETH.
Date in Pee Dee:
Location: PRINCE FREDERICK PARISH
Source(s): RBPPFW.

KEENE, BUCKINGHAM   ID: 2509
Spouse: [--?--] HORRY
Date in Pee Dee: 1750
Location: PRESENT MARION COUNTY
Source(s): SELLERS.
Notes: WIFE WAS SISTER OF COL. PETER HORRY.

KEIL, WILLIAM   ID: 2164
Date in Pee Dee: 1782
Source(s): GREGG P.410.
Revolutionary War service: PRIVATE IN MARION'S BRIGADE.

KEITH, CORNELIUS   ID: 681
Date in Pee Dee: 1767   Last Date: 1782
Location: CASHAWAY
Source(s): COOK, GREGG P. 410.
Notes: PROBABLY WELCH
Revolutionary War service: PRIVATE IN MARION'S BRIGADE.

KELLY, AGNES   ID: 5235
Children: JOHN.
Date in Pee Dee: 1742
Location: PRINCE FREDERICK PARISH
Source(s): RBPPFW.
Notes: JOHN WAS SON OF GEORGE SAUNDERS #5234.

KELLY, JAMES   ID: 1968
Date in Pee Dee: 1770   Last Date: 1780

Location: WILLIAMSBURG
Source(s): GREGG, JVSDP, BODDIE.
Revolutionary War service: PRIVATE IN MARION'S BRIGADE.

KELLY, JOHN   ID: 5066
Spouse: ELIZABETH [--?--]
Date in Pee Dee: 1780
Location: WILLIAMSBURG
Source(s): BODDIE.
Revolutionary War service: PRIVATE IN MARION'S BRIGADE.

KELLY, MARY   ID: 5455
Spouse: KARY KEEBLE
Date in Pee Dee: 1747
Location: PRINCE FREDERICK PARISH
Source(s): RBPPFW.

KELLY, SAMUEL   ID: 5067
Date in Pee Dee: 1780
Location: WILLIAMSBURG
Source(s): BODDIE.
Revolutionary War service: PRIVATE IN MARION'S BRIGADE.

KEMP, WILLIAM   ID: 1223
Spouse: ELIZABETH [--?--]
Children: SARAH, STEPHEN.
Date in Pee Dee: 1737   Last Date: 1741
Location: PRINCE FREDERICK PARISH
Source(s): RBPPFW.

KENNEDY, ALEXANDER   ID: 5068
Date in Pee Dee: 1780
Location: WILLIAMSBURG
Source(s): BODDIE.
Revolutionary War service: PRIVATE IN MARION'S BRIGADE.

KENNEDY, BRYAN   ID: 5304
Spouse: MARY [--?--]
Children: RICHARD, MARY, JAMES.

Early Pee Dee Settlers
--K--

Date in Pee Dee: 1736   Last Date: 1745
Location: PRINCE FREDERICK PARISH
Source(s): RBPPFW, BODDIE.

KENNEDY, JAMES   ID: 5069
Date in Pee Dee: 1775   Last Date: 1780
Location: WILLIAMSBURG
Source(s): BODDIE, CLEMENS.
Notes: MAY HAVE MARRIED NANCY CHALMERS.
Revolutionary War service: PRIVATE IN MARION'S BRIGADE.

KENNEDY, JOHN   ID: 4960
Date in Pee Dee: 1759
Location: WILLIAMSBURG
Source(s): BODDIE.
Notes: SERVED IN FRENCH AND INDIAN WAR.

KENNEDY, JOSEPH   ID: 5070
Date in Pee Dee: 1780
Location: WILLIAMSBURG
Source(s): BODDIE.
Revolutionary War service: PRIVATE IN MARION'S BRIGADE.

KENNEDY, STEPHEN   ID: 2166
Date in Pee Dee: 1782
Location: WILLIAMSBURG
Source(s): GREGG, BODDIE.
Revolutionary War service: PRIVATE IN MARION'S BRIGADE.

KENNEDY, THOMAS   ID: 687
Date in Pee Dee: 1767   Last Date: 1780
Location: WILLIAMSBURG
Source(s): COOK, BODDIE.
Notes: PASTOR OF FIRST PRESBYTERIAN CHURCH IN
WILLIAMSBURG.
Revolutionary War service: PRIVATE IN MARION'S BRIGADE.

KENNEL, LUCRETIA (LUCY)   ID: 5392
Spouse: JOHN JUNE

Date in Pee Dee: 1743
Location: PRINCE FREDERICK PARISH
Source(s): RBPPFW.

KERR, ISAAC   ID: 5367
Spouse: ABIGAIL HAWKINS
Date in Pee Dee: 1741
Location: PRINCE FREDERICK PARISH
Source(s): RBPPFW.
Notes: MARRIED 31 DECEMBER 1741 AT PARISH OF PRINCE
FREDERICK WINYAW.

KERR, JOHN   ID: 4263
Date in Pee Dee: 1771   Last Date: 1771 DIED
Origin: NORTHERN IRELAND
Location: ST. MARK'S PARISH (LOWER)
Source(s): MOORE V.3.
Notes: SON OF WILLIAM, SISTERS PURCHASE, MAHITIBEL
(GIBSON), MARGARET (MCCORKLE).

KERSHAW, ELI   ID: 1726
Spouse: MARY CANTEY
Date in Pee Dee: 1755   Last Date: 1766
Origin: YORKSHIRE, ENGLAND
Location: CHERAW DISTRICT
Source(s): GREGG, BURGESS, CLEMENS.
Notes: BROTHER OF JOSEPH. ALSO SPELLED ELY. LATER MOVED
TO CAMDEN. MARRIED NOVEMBER 1769.
Revolutionary War service: CAPTAIN IN MARION'S BRIGADE.

KERSHAW, JOSEPH   ID: 1727
Spouse: SOPHIA MATHIS
Children: MARY, JOHN, JAMES, SARAH.
Date in Pee Dee: 1755   Last Date: 1766
Occupation: MERCHANT   Origin: YORKSHIRE, ENGLAND
Location: CHERAW, LATER CAMDEN
Source(s): GREGG, BURGESS, MOORE V.3.
Notes: BROTHER OF ELI AND WILLIAM. SON OF JOSEPH.
Revolutionary War service: COLONEL IN MARION'S BRIGADE.

KERSHAW, WILLIAM   ID: 5479
Date in Pee Dee: 1755
Origin: ENGLAND
Location: CAMDEN
Source(s): BURGESS.
Notes: BROTHER OF ELY AND JOSEPH.

KERWIN, CRAFTON   ID: 4903
Spouse: MARY HALL
Children: THOMAS.
Date in Pee Dee: 1737   Last Date: 1747 DIED
Location: PRINCE FREDERICK PARISH
Source(s): BODDIE, RBPPFW.
Notes: MARRIED 16 MAY 1737 AT PARISH OF PRINCE FREDERICK
WINYAW.

KERWIN, THOMAS   ID: 4981
Date in Pee Dee: 1780
Location: WILLIAMSBURG
Source(s): BODDIE.
Revolutionary War service: LIEUTENANT IN MARION'S
BRIGADE.

KILGORE, HENRY   ID: 2167
Date in Pee Dee: 1782
Source(s): GREGG P.410.
Revolutionary War service: PRIVATE IN MARION'S BRIGADE.

KILLINGSWORTH, JOHN   ID: 5689
Date in Pee Dee: 1759
Location: ST. DAVID'S PARISH
Source(s): MUSTER ROLL.
Notes: SERVED IN FRENCH AND INDIAN WAR AS PRIVATE IN
PLEDGER'S COMPANY.

KILLINGSWORTH, SARAH   ID: 4685
Date in Pee Dee: 1760   Last Date: 1760 DIED
Location: ST. DAVID'S PARISH
Source(s): RWNBC.

Notes: PROBABLY WIFE OF WILLIAM (I).

KIMBROUGH, ELIZABETH   ID: 1486
Spouse: LEMUEL BENTON
Date in Pee Dee: 1765
Location: CHERAW DISTRICT
Source(s): GREGG.
Notes: DAUGHTER OF JOHN #693.

KIMBROUGH, JOHN   ID: 693
Spouse: HANNAH KOLB
Children: ELIZABETH.
Date in Pee Dee: 1756   Last Date: 1782
Origin: WAKE COUNTY NC
Location: CHERAW DISTRICT
Source(s): COOK, JVSDP, GREGG.
Notes: DIED 1796.

KING, ANN   ID: 633
Spouse: SHEARWOOD JAMES
Date in Pee Dee: 1750
Location: PRINCE GEORGE WINYAH PARISH
Notes: DAUGHTER OF RICHARD #342.

KING, CHARLES   ID: 1206
Spouse: MARY [--?--]
Children: RICHARD, MARY ANNA, MARY, SARAH (BERISFORD).
Date in Pee Dee: 1734   Last Date: 1734 DIED
Location: PRINCE GEORGE WINYAW PARISH
Source(s): MOORE.

KING, CHARLES   ID: 5245
Spouse: MARY [--?--]
Children: PRISCILLA, SARAH BERRISFORD.
Date in Pee Dee: 1742
Location: PRINCE FREDERICK PARISH
Source(s): RBPPFW.
Notes: APPEARS TO BE SON OF CHARLES #1206.

Early Pee Dee Settlers

--K--

KING, ELIZABETH   ID: 5467
Spouse: THOMAS HANDLEN
Date in Pee Dee: 1749
Location: PRINCE FREDERICK PARISH
Source(s): RBPPFW.

KING, GEORGE   ID: 694
Spouse: MINNIE HILL
Date in Pee Dee: 1759   Last Date: 1775
Location: GEORGETOWN
Source(s): COOK, GREGG, STEPHENSON, JVSDP.
Notes: SECOND MARRIED MARY HANNAH. LIEUTENANT IN
HITCHCOCK'S COMPANY DURING FRENCH AND INDIAN WAR. LATER
COMMANDER.

KING, JAMES   ID: 2840
Spouse: ELIZABETH THOMPSON
Date in Pee Dee: 1736   Last Date: 1752 DIED
Location: PRINCE FREDERICK PARISH
Source(s): MOORE, BODDIE, RBPPFW.
Notes: MARRIED 19 OCTOBER 1745 AT PARISH OF PRINCE
FREDERICK WINYAW.

KING, JANET   ID: 4518
Spouse: JOHN FRIERSON
Date in Pee Dee: 1771   Last Date: 1774 DIED
Location: PRINCE FREDERICK PARISH
Source(s): MOORE V.3.
Notes: LATER MARRIED TO A NEILSON.

KING, JASPER   ID: 2819
Spouse: DINAH [--?--]
Children: ELIZABETH.
Date in Pee Dee: 1734   Last Date: 1749 DIED
Location: PRINCE GEORGE WINYAW PARISH
Source(s): MOORE, RBPPFW.
Notes: VESTRY MAN OF PARISH OF PRINCE FREDERICK WINYAW
IN 1743.

KING, JOHN   ID: 695
Date in Pee Dee: 1740   Last Date: 1751
Location: PRINCE FREDERICK PARISH
Source(s): COOK, RBPPFW.
Notes: VESTRY MAN OF PARISH OF PRINCE FREDERICK WINYAW
IN 1751.

KING, JOSEPH   ID: 696
Date in Pee Dee: 1740   Last Date: 1759
Location: ST. DAVID'S PARISH
Source(s): COOK, MUSTER ROLL.
Notes: SERVED IN FRENCH AND INDIAN WAR AS PRIVATE IN
CAPTAIN GEORGE HICK'S COMPANY.

KING, MARY ANNA   ID: 2811
Spouse: JOSEPH WHITE
Date in Pee Dee: 1734   Last Date: 1750
Location: PRINCE GEORGE WINYAW PARISH
Source(s): MOORE, RBPPFW.
Notes: DAUGHTER OF CHARLES KING #1206.

KING, RICHARD   ID: 342
Children: ANN.
Date in Pee Dee: 1734
Location: PRINCE GEORGE WINYAW PARISH
Source(s): MOORE.
Notes: SON OF CHARLES KING #1206.

KING, SARAH   ID: 2814
Spouse: [--?--] BERISFORD
Date in Pee Dee: 1734
Location: PRINCE GEORGE WINYAW PARISH
Source(s): MOORE.
Notes: DAUGHTER OF CHARLES KING #1206.

KING, WILLIAM   ID: 2955
Spouse: JANET [--?--]
Children: WILLIAM, ESTHER, JANET, MARGARET.
Date in Pee Dee: 1750   Last Date: 1764 DIED

Location: WILLIAMSBURG
Source(s): MOORE.
Notes: SIGNED WITH MARK.

KINLOCH, CLELAND   ID: 698
Spouse: HARRIET SIMMONDS
Date in Pee Dee: 1780   Last Date: 1786
Location: KENSINGTON (GEORGETOWN VICINITY)
Source(s): COOK, CLEMENS.
Notes: MARRIED APRIL 1786 AT CHARLESTON. SON OF FRANCIS
KINLOCH.

KINLOCH, FRANCIS   ID: 1720
Spouse: ANNE CLELAND
Children: FRANCIS, CLELAND, MARIE ESTHER, HARRIOT.
Date in Pee Dee: 1737   Last Date: 1767
Location: GEORGETOWN
Source(s): COOK, SMITH, H..
Notes: RICE HOPE PLANTATION ON SANTEE. SON OF JAMES.

KINLOCH, FRANCIS   ID: 700
Spouse: NANCY CLELAND
Date in Pee Dee: 1751   Last Date: 1780
Location: NEAR SANTEE
Source(s): COOK, CLEMENS.
Notes: MARRIED 7 FEBRUARY 1751 AT CHARLESTON.

KINLOCH, JAMES   ID: 701
Children: FRANCIS.
Date in Pee Dee: 1720   Last Date: 1757 DIED
Origin: SCOTLAND
Location: SANTEE RIVER
Source(s): COOK, ROGERS.

KINLOCH, POLLY   ID: 5197
Spouse: BENJAMIN HUGER
Date in Pee Dee: 1772
Location: PRINCE GEORGE WINYAH PARISH
Source(s): CLEMENS.

Notes: MARRIED 1 DECEMBER 1772 AT KENSINGTON.

KIRBY, CHARLES   ID: 5697
Date in Pee Dee: 1759
Location: ST. DAVID'S PARISH
Source(s): MUSTER ROLL.
Notes: SERVED IN FRENCH AND INDIAN WAR AS PRIVATE WITH
KOLB'S COMPANY.

KIRBY, JAMES   ID: 2168
Date in Pee Dee: 1782
Source(s): GREGG P.410.
Revolutionary War service: PRIVATE IN MARION'S BRIGADE.

KIRBY, RICHARD   ID: 5698
Date in Pee Dee: 1759
Location: ST. DAVID'S PARISH
Source(s): MUSTER ROLL.
Notes: SERVED IN FRENCH AND INDIAN WAR AS PRIVATE WITH
KOLB'S COMPANY.

KIRTON, WILLIAM   ID: 2510
Spouse: [--?--] AVANT
Children: JOHN, WILLIAM.
Date in Pee Dee: 1770
Origin: NORTHERN IRELAND
Location: PRESENT MARION COUNTY
Source(s): SELLERS.

KITE, EDMUND   ID: 5565
Date in Pee Dee: 1782
Location: ST. DAVID'S PARISH
Source(s): JVSDP.
Notes: AT AGE 6 BOUND BY PARISH TO AMBROSE SINGLETON
UNTIL 21 YEARS OF AGE. SIBLING OF SALLEY?

KITE, SALLEY   ID: 5566
Date in Pee Dee: 1782
Location: ST. DAVID'S PARISH

Source(s): JVSDP.
Notes: AT AGE 5 BOUND BY PARISH TO AMBROSE SINGLETON
UNTIL 21 YEARS OF AGE. SIBLING OF EDMUND?

KNIGHT, JAMES   ID: 1804
Date in Pee Dee: 1768   Last Date: 1775
Location: ST. DAVID'S PARISH
Source(s): GREGG, JVSDP.
Revolutionary War service: CAPTAIN IN MARION'S BRIGADE.

KNIGHT, NIGLET   ID: 2169
Date in Pee Dee: 1782
Source(s): GREGG P.410.
Revolutionary War service: PRIVATE IN MARION'S BRIGADE.

KNOCKS, MARY   ID: 4869
Date in Pee Dee: 1780
Location: PRINCE FREDERICK PARISH
Source(s): MOORE V.3.
Notes: COUSIN OF GEORGE SNOW.

KNOWLES, THOMAS   ID: 5688
Date in Pee Dee: 1759
Location: ST. DAVID'S PARISH
Source(s): MUSTER ROLL.
Notes: SERVED IN FRENCH AND INDIAN WAR AS PRIVATE IN
PLEDGER'S COMPANY.

KNOX, ARCHIBALD   ID: 5071
Date in Pee Dee: 1780
Location: WILLIAMSBURG
Source(s): BODDIE.
Revolutionary War service: PRIVATE IN MARION'S BRIGADE.

KNOX, HUGH   ID: 704
Date in Pee Dee: 1760   Last Date: 1780
Location: WILLIAMSBURG
Source(s): COOK, BODDIE.
Revolutionary War service: CAPTAIN IN MARION'S BRIGADE.

Early Pee Dee Settlers
--K--

KNOX, JENET   ID: 5358
Spouse: WILLIAM RUTLEDGE
Date in Pee Dee: 1741
Location: PRINCE FREDERICK PARISH
Source(s): RBPPFW.

KNOX, ROBERT   ID: 5072
Date in Pee Dee: 1780
Location: WILLIAMSBURG
Source(s): BODDIE, CLEMENS.
Notes: MAY HAVE MARRIED CHRISTINA FREDERICK.
Revolutionary War service: PRIVATE IN MARION'S BRIGADE.

KNOX, WILLIAM   ID: 705
Date in Pee Dee: 1760   Last Date: 1800
Source(s): COOK.
Notes: MINISTER OF CIRCULAR CHURCH AT BLACK MINGO.

KOLB, SEE CULP, KOLP

KOLB, ABEL   ID: 706
Spouse: SARAH JAMES
Children: ANN, SARAH, JAMES.
Date in Pee Dee: 1759   Last Date: 1776
Location: WELCH TRACT
Source(s): COOK, GREGG.
Notes: SON OF PETER #712. CAPTAIN OF MILITIA IN FRENCH
AND INDIAN WAR.

KOLB, ANN   ID: 986
Spouse: JAMES POUNCEY
Children: WILLIAM, JAMES, JOHN A., PETER A. K..
Date in Pee Dee: 1781
Location: CHERAW DISTRICT
Source(s): COOK.

KOLB, BENJAMIN   ID: 707
Spouse: ELIZABETH MURPHY
Children: NANCY, HARRIET, ABEL, SARAH, BETSY, MARY.

Date in Pee Dee: 1767
Location: CASHAWAY
Source(s): COOK.
Notes: SON OF PETER #712.

KOLB, HANNAH   ID: 692
Spouse: JOHN KIMBBROUGH
Children: ELIZABETH.
Date in Pee Dee: 1767   Last Date: 1767
Location: CASHAWAY
Source(s): COOK, GREGG.

KOLB, HENRY   ID: 708
Spouse: SARAH (ELLISON) [--?--]
Date in Pee Dee: 1751   Last Date: 1759 DIED
Location: CASHAWAY
Source(s): COOK, MOORE.
Notes: THREE ELLISON STEP CHILDREN.

KOLB, JACOB   ID: 709
Spouse: ELIZABETH SAUNDERS
Date in Pee Dee: 1740   Last Date: 1759 DIED
Origin: PENNSYLVANIA
Location: CHERAW DISTRICT
Source(s): COOK, SMITH.
Notes: SERVED IN FRENCH AND INDIAN WAR AS PRIVATE IN
KOLB'S COMPANY. DIED IN SERVICE.

KOLB, JOHANNES   ID: 710
Children: TILLMAN, SARAH, MEHITABEL, PETER.
Date in Pee Dee: 1736
Origin: HOLLAND
Location: CAUSEWAY NECK
Source(s): COOK.

KOLB, JOHN   ID: 2170
Date in Pee Dee: 1759   Last Date: 1780
Location: ST. DAVID'S PARISH
Source(s): GREGG P.410, MOORE.

Notes: SON OF PETER. SERVED IN FRENCH AND INDIAN WAR IN
CAPTAIN JAMES THOMSON'S COMPANY.

KOLB, MARTIN   ID: 711
Children: RACHEL.
Date in Pee Dee: 1759   Last Date: 1768
Location: CASHAWAY
Source(s): COOK, MOORE, GREGG, JVSDP.

KOLB, PETER   ID: 712
Spouse: ANN JAMES
Children: SARAH, ABEL, ANN, BENJAMIN, HANNAH.
Date in Pee Dee: 1751   Last Date: 1784
Origin: PENNSYLVANIA
Location: CASHAWAY
Source(s): COOK, RWNBC, GREGG, SOMPAYRAC.
Notes: SERVED IN FRENCH AND INDIAN WAR AS LIEUTENANT IN
KOLB'S COMPANY.

KOLB, SARAH   ID: 713
Spouse: EVANDER MCIVER
Children: CATHERINE, JOHN KOLB, ABEL, PETER KOLB, ELIZA,
THOMAS A., MARY ANN (WILLIAMS).
Date in Pee Dee: 1767   Last Date: 1781
Location: CASHAWAY
Source(s): COOK.
Notes: SISTER OF ABEL KOLB #706. DAUGHTER OF PETER #712.

KOLB, TILMAN   ID: 715
Spouse: BEERSHEBA WATKINS (WIDOW)
Date in Pee Dee: 1738   Last Date: 1740
Location: WELCH NECK
Source(s): COOK, RBPPFW.
Notes: MARRIED BY REV. FORDYCE 19 DECEMBER 1738. GIVES
NAME AS TINMAN ONE PLACE.

Early Pee Dee Settlers
--K--

KOLBAN, JONATHAN   ID: 1776
Date in Pee Dee: 1776
Location: GEORGETOWN
Source(s): COOK.
Revolutionary War service: LIEUTENANT

KOLP, SEE CULP, KOLB